Facing The DARK

Pamela Elaine Telford

Library of Congress Control Number: 2026905608

ISBN: 979-8-89228-896-5   (Paperback)
ISBN: 979-8-89228-897-2   (Hardcover)
ISBN: 979-8-89228-898-9   (eBook)

Book Ordering Information:
Atticus Publishing
548 Market St PMB 70756
San Francisco, CA 94104
(888) 208-9296
info@atticuspublishing.com
www.atticuspublishing.com

Printed in the United States of America

CONTENTS

DEDICATION

For those who stood beside me and said,
Keep going.

For the ones who listened without needing to fix,
who believed this story mattered,
and who trusted me to tell it in my own time.

For every person who encouraged me to write,
in conversations, in quiet messages,
and in moments when I wasn't sure I could.

For the woman I am becoming,
because she did not stop when it would have been easier
to be silent.

And to my most Dearest, my most Handsome Man,
a beautiful gift from the Universe,
who is not only my rock
but also the other half of me
that makes me whole.

PROLOGUE

When *The Big Dark* ended, I believed I had told the story.

I had spoken the truth that once felt impossible to name. I had walked away from what nearly destroyed me. I had stepped into the light with the certainty that survival, once achieved, would be enough to carry me forward.

But life does not move that cleanly.

What I did not understand then was that telling the truth is not the same as being free. Leaving does not undo what has been learned in fear. And safety, when it finally arrives, can feel strangely unfamiliar, almost threatening, after years of living on alert.

I was no longer trapped, but my body didn't know it. I startled easily. I hesitated where I once would have spoken. I measured rooms, people, silences. The vigilance that kept me alive had not yet learned how to stand down. Even in freedom, I was bracing.

There is a moment after prolonged trauma when the noise finally quiets enough for everything else to surface. The grief that had been postponed. The anger that had nowhere to go. The questions that had been buried beneath survival. That was where I found myself, not in the darkness anymore, but not yet whole.

This book begins there.

Not at the breaking, but in the aftermath. In the space where the danger has passed, yet its imprint remains.

Where the world expects resolution, but the work has only just begun.

I was learning who I was without fear organizing my life. Learning how to trust my own instincts again. Learning how much of myself had gone missing, and how slowly she would return.

What follows is not a continuation of the story you already know, but the living of it. The long, uneven process of rebuilding a self after it has been dismantled. The quiet reckonings that happen when no one is watching. The choices that don't look heroic from the outside, but require more courage than staying ever did.

I did not write this because I had answers.

I wrote it because I was still listening.

CH. 1 — The In-between

Here I am, a free woman who just escaped an abusive life, with all my worldly goods packed tightly into a small U-Haul truck, finally returning "home" after thirty-three years of hell. I knew that I was going to have to start over at the age of 53, and even though that may seem scary for many, I was not daunted by the prospect at all.

When you finally reach the bottom and you understand that your mental health can't take anymore, then ascending anywhere in the opposite direction from where you came from will be, at that time, the most glorious day of your life. And that is exactly what it was for me when I finally reached the end of my exodus and arrived in Yakima.

I didn't care that I was starting over with very little. I didn't care that I was doing this alone. I didn't care what life had waiting for me. I only knew that I was finally free to create whatever life I wanted going forward.

Up to now, the entire ride from North Carolina to Washington State was a nerve-wracking ordeal. I held on to that steering wheel of the U-Haul so tight, hunched forward with my shoulders tense and my foot pushed as far down on the gas pedal that it could go. Even though I was now almost three thousand miles away from my abusive old life, I still felt the urgency to return to Yakima as soon as I could where I knew I would be safe.

I had left one world behind; a world that had been so dark and suffocating. And now I was approaching my new world – one that held all the promises of my deepest dreams and desires. I felt like I couldn't truly feel safe until I got out of that truck and hugged my dad, who was waiting for me at the U-Haul place in Union Gap.

I had been pushing forward every day on the road with such urgency, afraid to slow down in case some dark entity from my past would catch up to me, that I could feel my entire being vibrating. Logically, I knew I was safe, but my nervous system was still in total "flight" mode. I could feel the tingling sensation from both the excited anticipation of coming home, and the anxious fear-filled state of making my escape, surge through every cell.

I had no idea what this new life was going to look like, but I knew it would be better than where I came from. So, I just set my electrically – buzzed brain to focus forward as I allowed myself to believe that I was finally going to be safe and happy.

At that time, I had no idea that I still had a long way to go before I could finally let go of the pain – filled past I was running from.

When I wrote **The Big Dark,** I was writing it from a perspective of pain, guilt, shame, and confusion. I was in the midst of living a nightmare where the one person who was supposed to love and protect me became the one person I feared the most in this life. I wrote to reveal the manipulative emotional trappings that kept me from seeing my worth so hopefully others could avoid the same fate.

When I finally understood that he was never going to change, I then convinced myself that I couldn't leave until the kids were old enough not to be traumatized by the truths that had been hidden all those years. That decision cost me another sixteen years of hell and it almost destroyed me.

How devastating to look back now and to see how many years were lost, how many tears were shed in secret because I believed that I didn't have the right to shake the family foundation that my kids believed was solid. I was living a hollow existence – a shell of myself – and couldn't see a way out any sooner.

Many will think, after reading my first book, that the healing started when I had escaped. But it didn't. Think about it like this: when you pull yourself out of the fire, the first thing that you do is get as far away from it as possible so you can't get burned again. That's what I did.

But, unfortunately, the blisters and the scars from that fire are still forming long after you have pulled yourself out. The healing doesn't come until much later, when your body – your subconscious – tells you that it is time to finally face all the damage that was done while you were stuck in the middle of the flames.

So, I am writing this now, after coming out of the other side of this darkness, and I will tell you that the healing comes in stages and, *only* when your subconscious is finally ready for you to face it.

When I first got back to Yakima, you couldn't make my face stop smiling for a long time. I was deliriously happy to be free of that prison I was in. I was floating above the entire world, seeing only the beauty that I had missed out on for all those years. I had no idea at that time what depth of darkness I would still have to face in order to earn the life I deserved to live.

I can look back now and see that there were distinct phases of my new life: one where everything was new and exciting, another where I fell into the beautiful rhythm of life, the reckoning – where I was finally forced to face the darkness, and then, the end – when I was able to finally reconcile the deep pain that had held me hostage all these years.

For now, at this moment, driving into Yakima, I had no idea what was coming for me. I only knew that I was finally out of the fire that had consumed me and was now heading toward a beautiful unknown with a promise of the life I had always deserved to live.

I was beyond happy to finally be at the end of my harried exodus and to finally arrive at the U-Haul parking lot where my dad, my Norma and my friends were waiting for me after all these years.

At this moment, there wasn't any room for anything other than pure joy. And since it was an emotion that I had rarely experienced, I was going to just let it wash over me for as long as I could before I even dared to consider that any rocky roads lay ahead.

They say ignorance is bliss. I was okay with being ignorant of what was yet to come. After all the years of living in darkness, I deserved whatever light shined on me in that moment.

For now, let me float in the clouds. I earned it.

****

This chapter of my life is called

"Smile Again"

doodles

CH. 2 — Back in Yakima

It felt incredible to be back in Yakima, a happiness so intense that it bordered on delirium. My high school friends, Ray and Matt, met me at the U-Haul place to help unload my truck into the storage unit I had rented. My dad and my Norma (which is what I called my stepmom) were there too, and I kept stopping just to take it all in. It was hard to believe that this long-awaited homecoming was real. I must have hugged everyone a dozen times just to make sure they knew how much their presence meant to me.

Ray and Matt played football for my dad in high school. Watching them swap old stories and laughter felt like stepping into a gentler time. I silently thanked my friend, Lisa, for recruiting them to help.

After we finished unloading all that I brought with me from North Carolina, my dad, my Norma, and I met Lisa for dinner at Bob's Burgers and Brews on the northeast side of town. Lisa had been a bridesmaid at my wedding, and when I told her back in late March that I was leaving Mike and moving back, she didn't hesitate to support me. Not only did she round up Ray and Matt, but she was also letting me stay with her until I was ready to move into my apartment on the first of July. I was so grateful that she helped me make a soft landing and an easy transition when I returned to Yakima.

Dinner was wonderful and it wasn't because of the food. I honestly don't remember what I ate. What I do remember is how great it felt to finally get to see a true friend. Someone who didn't hesitate when I finally reached out for help.

I remember being so excited that my voice pitched higher than usual, almost a squeal. It reminded me of how dogs react after being reunited with their people; when they wiggle, squirm, jump, squeal and bark all at once. For the first time, I understood that kind of happiness. That was exactly how it felt for me to be back in Yakima and to see Lisa again.

The meal may have filled my stomach, but the company filled my heart. Reuniting with my dad, my Norma, and Lisa made me feel like the past thirty years was only a bad dream and that this beautiful group of souls was a part of my long-awaited new reality.

Dad and my Norma had invited me to stay with them in Goldendale, but it was too far from Yakima. My heart had always belonged here. So, after dinner, I hugged them goodbye and followed Lisa to her house in Selah, just outside of town.

Lisa's place was a cozy little home near the town center, and I was deeply grateful to have a bed waiting for me those first two weeks. She told me she worked only three or four days a week. Not as much as she could, but enough to live comfortably and to keep her life balanced. I was impressed that she was prioritizing her quality of life. She seemed genuinely happy and grounded in her independence, surrounded by friends and content in her own rhythm.

I was a bit jealous. She had a network of family and friends close by that helped her navigate her divorce and her new life as a single mother. Her kids were now older, but they were still close by for frequent check-ins. I would have loved to have had family and friends around when I was going through the dark times.

I don't know if she realized how fortunate she was to have such a wide support group around her. I was taking mental notes of what my new life could look like and at that moment I was loving every part of it.

Lisa had promised to gather some of our high school friends for a little party in my honor. When I asked about it, she said she would make it happen by the end of the week. The idea thrilled me. I wanted to soak up everything Yakima again, and seeing old friends felt like reclaiming another piece of myself.

We stayed up a bit longer, talking and catching up, but she had work in the morning, and I had plans of my own to get ready for the next day. Eventually, we said goodnight. Even though my body and nerves had been running on edge for the past week, I was still fortunate to be able to find the sleep that my body needed.

It was summertime, near the solstice and the longest day of the year. I have always loved this season in Yakima. The sun rose close to five in the morning and lingered until nearly ten at night. My body was still tuned to Eastern time, so I was up early. But that Tuesday, June 17th, 2014, I let myself stay in bed a while longer.

Lisa was working through Thursday at the insurance office, leaving me free to fill in my days. Lying in bed gave me an opportunity to think through and plan the many options that I had.

I thought about running around Franklin Park or through my old neighborhood, but I decided to wait. I'd been running, literally and emotionally, for weeks since escaping Mike in North Carolina. Now, I wanted to just be. So, I gave myself permission to just lie there and revel in the new reality that I was creating.

Once Lisa left for work, I got myself up and got ready for the day ahead of me. I had to go to the Yakima School District office to sign my teaching contract and then get a required drug test. If time allowed, I wanted to stop by Davis High School to finally meet the assistant principal who had hired me.

Driving into the district office to get my new life started reminded me how good it felt to be back in Yakima again. It felt surreal. After all this time living in darkness, I felt like I was floating outside of myself and watching the wheels of my new life starting to turn in a positive direction.

The school district was located on 3rd Avenue, and it seemed as if I had floated the whole way there. Somehow, with my head in the clouds, I didn't get lost and I was able to quickly sign my contract. What brought me back to the present was how the staff at the district office commented about my southern accent. After twenty-eight years in the South, I hadn't realized how much of it had stuck. I'd always thought I'd preserved my Washington dialect. To me, the accent was light. To others, it was very noticeable.

I tried to hear it myself. There was a softness now, a faint drawl that gave me away. It made me a little self-conscious, but I decided to take it in stride. If that was the worst of my transition back to the Pacific Northwest, I could live with it.

After signing my contract, the staff at the YSD office directed me to the lab where I would need to do the required drug test. It happened to be conveniently located close to Davis High School where I would meet with the assistant principal, so I set off directly to get it done.

I think back to that day, and I just remembered how every mundane task I completed seemed so delightful. Here I was, off to give a urine sample, definitely not high on anyone's list of "good times", and I couldn't hide the smile on my face. After living such an emotionally contracted life, every experience seemed to be a gift from the Universe.

It was there, while waiting to give my sample, I got a call from Jack. What a glorious surprise. It immediately put a bigger smile on my face.

The last time I had chatted with him was the Thursday before when I was driving towards Arkansas. His voice was still cheery, as usual. He always had a way with it so that you could feel his beautiful smile behind it.

He wanted to know if I had made it to Yakima yet. I told him not only did I make it to Yakima, but I was at the LabCorp, just a couple of blocks away from him.

Since Jack's work was conveniently close by, he suggested that I stop by for a visit as soon as I was done. It would be thirty-one years since we last saw each other.

I was beyond excited. I couldn't hide the giant smile on my face. I was now going to meet this beautiful soul of a man that I had recklessly let go when I was just twenty years old.

His mom told me before I left North Carolina that he had a girlfriend. What I didn't know was how serious it was. I had made the biggest mistake of my life when I broke up with Jack "temporarily" when I was in college. I can still hear my mom berating me for it and saying, "he'll never take you back." I was so rocked with shame at the time with what I had done that I "assumed" that he wouldn't forgive me, so I slid into a life of darkness that I thought I could change.

That was the biggest single regret of my life and it will be forever tied with my marriage to Mike. For over thirty years I had lived in a silent hell and darkness.

The price I paid for that single decision was too high.

If I could go back in time, the least I would do is face Jack with my biggest and most sincere apology and let him decide my fate. I would bravely face him and wait for the worst.

It would have been devastating if he rebuked me. It would have hurt me to my core, but then, isn't that what I did to him when I broke up with him out of the blue? I can only imagine the deep pain that I caused that man, and the shame that I still carried for that decision was keeping me from being whole.

What I didn't allow myself to see at the time was the possibility that he would have forgiven me and would have taken me back. I may have gone through moments of shame and guilt and there would have been many tears shed in relief that he had forgiven me. But I also know that we would have still been together today.

Not that our life wouldn't have had challenges and hard times, but this man would never ever have treated me with the cruelty and disdain that I experienced with Mike. I would have been with someone who would've loved me for everything that I was.

But I would never know what Jack would have done if I had humbled myself to him because I lacked the self-worth to ask for his forgiveness or risk his rejection those thirty plus years ago.

Now, after all these years, I was finally going to get to see him.

Even though he had a girlfriend, I was done "assuming" anyone's intentions. I had already assumed he wouldn't take me back all those years ago and look at what happened to my life. I didn't know how serious his relationship was with his girlfriend, so I was going to let him tell me. I was done with regrets. I had given myself the opportunity to start over after I had spent more than thirty years of my life in hell, and I wasn't going to waste any more time or opportunities.

I knew that I was still deeply emotionally connected to Jack. I wanted him to know that he didn't do anything wrong. I wanted to explain as best as I could how it all happened. Whatever he decided to do with my confessions would be up to him.

Either way, I was now going to face Jack for the first time since I had left Yakima back in 1983. I was finally going to have a chance to confess and take full responsibility for everything, just what I should have done all those years before.

When I finished with my lab sample, I quickly texted Jack that I was on my way over. It was a quick drive, and I found a parking spot somewhere out in front of his work under the shade of a tree. I looked towards the entrance and there he was, standing out front, looking in my direction and waiting for me.

I was unprepared for the competing emotions of nerves and excitement. My stomach had tightened but the smile on my face widened. It was close to noon, and the sun was generously coming down. I had my sunglasses on as I got out of the car to make my way towards Jack.

I could feel my body shaking a bit but the smile on my face hadn't eased up. I kept my gaze on him as I started walking across the wide lawn that separated the parking area from his work entrance. I was so focused on Jack that I didn't see the gentleman sitting on the bench in the shade of the tree.

"You look absolutely stunning." The voice startled me, and I turned my head to see who had said it.

It was an older gentleman who seemed content to just enjoy the beauty of the late morning under the shade of a tree. I wasn't used to having a powerful compliment coming from anyone, let alone a stranger.

It caught me so off guard that I stopped and briefly thought, *what a nice thing to say. I needed that.*

I had to admit that I was nervous about how Jack would react to seeing me after so much time had lapsed. I had taken back my life, one step at a time, and that included making time for my health. I had been consistently working out for six days a week since January, and here it was, mid-June, almost six months into my personal rehab and a stranger noticed the results.

I felt good about my physical transformation but no one, not Mike or anyone in North Carolina, had mentioned anything about my progress. This was the first time that anyone reaffirmed what I had perceived.

It was such a beautiful gift from a stranger.

I stopped and turned to the gentleman and told him thank you. Actually, I said something more like this, "Wow, what a nice thing for you to say. I really appreciate it. Nobody has ever said anything like that to me that I can remember. Thank you, I really needed that right now."

He said a few more sweet words to reaffirm his initial comment, and I thanked that beautiful stranger for the lovely gift of self-confidence that he gave me right when I needed it the most.

Never underestimate the power of your words. It doesn't cost anything to be kind and to say kind things to people. It is a beautiful gift you give to someone who's not expecting it.

I turned back and continued my approach to Jack. Now I was walking with more confidence.

He was just as tall as I remembered. His hair was getting grayer, but he still wore it the same way and he wasn't wearing a mustache like he was when I last saw him. As I got closer, I found it impossible to reign in my smile. It just kept getting bigger.

Finally, I found myself wrapping both my arms around his beautiful shoulders and giving him the biggest hug. He gave me a hug back and it felt so good to see him again. I told him how good he looked, and he just smiled. Jack was never one to waste his words and I could sense that he was nervous about this reunion. We found a table outside in the sun and sat down to get caught up.

I could see how nervous he was to see me. He kept his eyes diverted away and he only looked in my direction just a few times. I realized this wasn't the place to talk about why I left him so many years ago, so I kept it light. I pulled out my phone and showed him pictures of the kids, and we chatted about a few major milestones in our lives.

He told me he had been married twice before and each marriage produced children: two girls and a boy, just like me. I could hear in his voice that he hadn't wanted any of his marriages to fail. He was sharing his personal recollections with a tinge of melancholy.

As I sat and listened to his stories, I thought about how different both our lives would have been if I hadn't left him. It seemed that both of us had experienced extreme heartache – me with Mike and his darkness and Jack with the sting of having both his wives leave him.

I can imagine how his self-worth had been challenged, first by me and then his other two wives. He had to have been deeply and personally wounded – left to sort it out himself and to find something within himself that made him feel worthy of anyone else's affection.

We had both lived a huge part of our lives in a personal struggle of self-worth and we both left a trail of emotional damage behind us. It seemed that both he and I were still carrying this emotional wound and it was weighing us down.

I said to Jack, "I'm so sorry. If we had been married, we would have still been together." Jack kept looking straight ahead and replied in a low voice, "We probably would have gotten a divorce."

I noted the cynicism in his statement. I didn't blame him. He had such a beautiful heart, and I know he deserved to have the kind of marriage and life that he had always dreamed of. He hadn't planned on going through two divorces.

His own parents had divorced when he was in his early teens and, being the oldest, he took on the emotional responsibilities for his mom and his three younger sisters at an early age.

He was their rock, and he never shied away from that burden. He embraced it and found honor in being the cornerstone for the family. Now he had gone through two failed marriages after I had left him and his statement of, "we probably would have gotten a divorce" was his way of saying that he didn't believe he was worthy of a lasting marriage or relationship.

I told Jack, "No. We still would have been married. If I could live in hell for over thirty years, then there is no way we would have gotten a divorce."

That statement caused him to briefly look at me. He didn't offer a response. I'm sure he was caught up in the "what ifs" and was trying to digest what I just revealed.

We didn't talk much more after that. He had to get back to work, and I was still going to try to meet with the assistant principal at Davis High School.

Jack wanted to walk me back to my car. I was happy to have some extra time with him, and he seemed to lighten up on the walk. He made some lively comments about my new car and how the trunk could open and close with the push of a button.

I took advantage of his lighter mood and decided to give him the birthday gift that I had tucked away in the car. His birthday wasn't for a couple more weeks, but I wasn't sure when I would see him again.

The gift was wrapped in simple brown paper with jute string. I liked that I kept the wrapping neutral. It was symbolic. Since I didn't know what Jack's intentions were for me or us, I chose to stay neutral, just like the paper.

It was a CD of the 70's-80's rock band, STYX. Jack had taken me to see them back in 1980 and 1981. They were the first and only concerts up to this point that I had ever seen. I remembered how he liked their music, and I was hoping that he would appreciate the sentiment. He was genuinely surprised by the gift and thanked me.

We gave each other a big hug and said goodbye. There was no promise to keep in touch or get together again and I had no idea when I would see him next.

I drove away with a bit of my own sadness.

I had this momentary thought flash through my head that I had no right to interfere in his life. But then I reminded myself that it was he who called me and it was he who invited me to connect with him at his work.

I had been so grateful when he decided to reach out to me when I was still in North Carolina when he didn't have to. He had called me several times to check to see how I was doing before the day came when I was able to escape. And it was he who advised me on where to find an apartment in Yakima where he thought I would be safe. I felt and appreciated the kindness and compassion he had shown me when he didn't have to.

I still wasn't sure of his intentions with me, but with every phone call that he initiated, I felt some hope.

Today wasn't the time or place to talk to him about what happened all those years ago. If we ever did meet up again, I might get the opportunity. This wasn't a topic that could be forced. It had to flow naturally or not at all. I just had to be grateful for anything and everything that was coming my way and, so far, I was.

Here I was – in Yakima, for less than twenty-four hours and my soul was already filled with so much joy. I knew whatever lay ahead of me would be better than what I had left in North Carolina.

I was in charge now and I soaked in all the possibilities with confidence that this would be the best part of my life. This time, there would be no regrets.

****

The truth is

You've always been good enough

You just forgot who you were

Welcome home.

-spiritdaughter

CH. 3 — Who to Trust

Trust is earned, respect is given, and loyalty is
demonstrated.
Betrayal of any one of those is to lose all three
Ziad K Abdeinour

I was floating on feel-good energy. In less than twenty-four hours back in Yakima, I had reunited with my dad, my Norma, with a couple of old high-school friends, and, most importantly, with Jack. I couldn't stop smiling. My cheeks were already sore, but it was the kind of ache I didn't mind.

Earlier that day I met Heather Hastie, the assistant principal who'd hired me to teach science at Davis High School. She walked me through my new classroom where I would be teaching this coming school year. I felt so connected with her energy as we stood there looking over my new classroom. She was genuinely excited to have me teaching at Davis High School and right then, I knew that this was going to be a good fit.

Later that afternoon when Lisa got off work, we met up with Ray to continue catching up. I appreciated how Lisa folded me into her established social circle. They may have also been old classmates of mine as well, but I hadn't seen most of them since graduating in 1979. We were still getting reacquainted; piecing together who we were back then and who we had become.

Ray played football and basketball for my dad at Carroll High School. Now he was an accountant, working for his sister's step-nephew at a newly opened restaurant in Yakima. One of his sons was about to join the Navy. The other was heading into his junior year of high school. I remembered that his family was quite musical and he was part of a band with his dad on accordion and he on drums.

Ray had been very generous with his time by showing up yesterday to help me unload my U-Haul the moment I rolled into town. Now the three of us sat in a small burger café off Yakima Avenue, catching up on all the years we'd missed.

This was the part I would struggle with for a while – trying to find "my story" to tell anyone who would ask what brought me back to Yakima. Everyone wanted the short answer. I was still learning how to tell the true one.

Leaving Mike was still raw. I knew the marriage had become toxic and dangerous, but I hadn't begun to process the toll it had taken on me. I hadn't even been able to talk it through with Lisa yet, so when I tried to summarize it for Ray, it came out in fragments.

I found myself pulling out pieces from the past almost at random: *how Mike wouldn't let me watch sports* or *let me dance, how he threatened suicide, how I'd wrestled a gun away from him more than once.*

I saw the shock in both Ray and Lisa's faces, so I backed off a bit and shifted the conversation to how I left Jack all those years ago and how he'd recently helped me transition back to Yakima.

Ray was curious about Jack and asked more questions. I made sure I answered carefully. Jack had lived in Yakima his entire life, and it was quite possible that I would come across people who would know him. I wanted to protect him, so I kept things vague.

Unfortunately, Lisa took it upon herself to blurt out, "His name is Jack Elliott."

I quickly turned my head towards her and showed both surprise and disappointment that she betrayed my confidence so quickly.

Ray's reaction came just as fast: "I know Jack Elliott. His son and my son are best friends!"

Perfect. Exactly what I didn't want.

I had just escaped from a small town where I'd managed to hide Mike's abuse for nearly thirty years, and here, within a single day, someone from my past already knew more than I was ready to share. I felt exposed and betrayed.

When I reconnected with Lisa back in March before leaving Mike, I thought I'd found a confidant; someone I could trust with the darker pieces of my life, someone who might help me move towards a healthier future. But now ... I could feel this nudge in my intuition that told me I had to be careful with this "friend".

Now, instead of settling in, I found myself scrambling to patch the hole Lisa had torn open.

I insisted that Ray keep this to himself. It wouldn't be fair for Jack to be blindsided by gossip that could undermine his current relationship with his girlfriend or whatever future might exist between us. Ray promised he wouldn't say anything, and I had no choice but to trust he'd honor that.

As for Lisa, the lesson learned was instant. I realized I'd have to be careful about what I shared with her, especially anything I wasn't ready to have repeated. I offered her some grace, but the boundary was clear: I needed to tread carefully from now on.

Not even a day back in Yakima, and I had just learned a big lesson: even though I may have had a mutually respectful relationship with Lisa in the past, it didn't guarantee that she would have my best interest in mind in the present.

That moment also reinforced my decision not to tell my close friends in North Carolina about my plan to escape. If something as small as Jack's name could slip out so quickly, then the truth of my escape from Mike wouldn't have stood a chance.

It was a hard but necessary lesson; one I needed if I was going to protect my healing and the people who didn't deserve to be pulled into the fallout. For that, I thanked Lisa for the betrayal.

Later that evening, Lisa tried to repair what she sensed she had damaged. She admitted she had a huge crush on Ray and hoped it might turn into something more. I assumed that her blurting out Jack's name was her attempt to gain more of Ray's approval; an attempt by her to seem important – to impress him somehow. What she didn't realize was, in doing so, she cracked the inherent trust I had given to her.

As for her wish that Ray would move forward into something more intimate, I knew it wasn't going to happen. Thirty years of living on high alert around Mike had sharpened my ability to read body language; it had been a survival skill. Watching them together, it was obvious that Ray felt only a friendly, almost sibling-like energy towards Lisa – nothing deeper.

I didn't tell her that. I let her continue with her stories about how they hang out and share the love of food. The fantasy of the two of them someday getting together made her happy, and I knew she would eventually find out for herself in her own time.

In the meantime, the reunions kept coming. Those first three weeks in Yakima were a blur of dinners, walks, lunches, and coffee dates with people I hadn't seen in decades. Lisa made good on her promise to gather a group at Jackson's East in Terrace Heights, and it was there I reconnected with so many familiar faces, including Scott St. Mary, one of my old high-school boyfriends.

It felt good to hug everyone, exchange numbers, and slip back into an easy familiarity. Scott was especially sweet, greeting me with the biggest hug. We'd dated almost our entire freshman year. It was one of those young relationships that rarely lasts but still leaves its mark. It was a real joy to see him happy and healthy.

Later that night, Lisa and I were lying in our separate rooms, chatting back and forth to each other, sharing the texts rolling in from our friends. I loved the attention, the banter, and the sense of belonging. Something I rarely experienced in North Carolina.

Scott's messages were playful and funny. At first, Lisa laughed along with me, but then her tone shifted. "Wow," she said after a pause, "he's sending you a lot of texts."

I could feel the edge in her voice. Jealousy? Annoyance? I wasn't sure. She had just admitted her crush on Ray, so I didn't understand why Scott's text messages to me seemed to disturb her. But the discomfort was clear, so I let my text conversation with Scott trail off and went to sleep.

The next day, Lisa launched into stories about her past relationships, how she'd gotten close to this person or that one after her two divorces. I listened with a mix of admiration and curiosity. Part of me thought, *good for her.* She was exploring, living, and trying. But another part of me sensed she was searching for a connection to patch a loneliness she hadn't yet faced.

I began to see Lisa as more vulnerable than she let on, and I realized she felt a bit threatened by the attention I was getting after returning to Yakima. I resolved to be sensitive to how my reappearance stirred her insecurities. But I also had a need to connect with friends; people I could talk to, people who could help me to start releasing the trauma that had settled so deeply inside me.

Both Ray and Scott continued to reach out, inviting me to hang out and continue catching up. I loved the feeling of having somebody who wanted to spend time with me. With Mike, time together had always been transactional; if it didn't benefit him, he wasn't interested. Now I have people who genuinely wanted to spend time with me. It felt really good to finally be wanted.

Ray called a few times during the day, and since it was summer and school wouldn't start until late August, I had the freedom to join him. We ran errands, had lunch at Olive Garden downtown, and met up at Holy Family Church on 56th so his dog could run around the wide-open grounds.

I appreciated his company. Sometimes our conversations drifted toward Jack. Because Ray knew both of us, he had a unique insight into the history I was trying to untangle. I needed someone I could talk to, and Lisa was proving not to be that person. By now, I had already moved out of her house and into my Lake Aspen apartment, and the conversations between us were becoming less frequent. She visited sometimes, and we texted, but I had stopped counting on her as a confidant.

Sometime after the Fourth of July, where she and I spent the evening in Selah watching fireworks, she told me she didn't like me hanging out with Ray. She explained how much she liked him and said she felt I was getting in the way of whatever she hoped might develop between them.

I was surprised. She knew I was still hoping for something with Jack, so her fear of me getting in between her and Ray didn't make sense to me. I reassured her gently: I didn't see Ray that way. He was simply a friend helping me sift through all my confusing emotions.

I thought everything was resolved between us until...

One Sunday morning in early July, I set out on my bike for an adventure. I loved how bikeable Yakima felt. There weren't any dedicated bike lanes in the city, but compared to North Carolina, with its humidity that swallowed you whole the moment you stepped outside, Yakima felt like freedom.

I headed toward the Yakima River and picked up the long pedestrian-bike path that ran for miles along the water. I rode until the trail finally tapered out, then turned to head home. It was on the return that things went wrong.

When I reached Sarge Hubbard Park in Terrace Heights, I stopped for a quick drink of water. In that brief pause, something happened. When I got back on the bike, the pedals wouldn't move. Neither would the wheels.

I hopped off and inspected it the best I could, but nothing looked jammed or broken. Still, the bike was frozen. I was four or five miles from my apartment with no way to roll it home. So, I tried calling a few friends - Lisa, Matt, and Ray, but no one answered. It was a Sunday in the summer, and I figured everyone was busy, so I didn't even bother leaving messages.

A cab wasn't even a thought. I'd never taken one before, so my instincts defaulted to handling things myself. So that's what I did: I picked up the bike and started walking.

It was awkward and heavy. I had to lift it high enough to clear my stride, and the weight pulled me off balance. I had to continually shift it from side to side to keep my arms from burning. In moments like this, I was grateful I had kept up with my workouts, but my muscles were still getting more of a workout than I had planned.

The walk was slow. I crossed the interstate, made my way down into the center of the city, and by the time I reached Yakima Avenue I was exhausted and overheated. I ducked into the McDonald's on the corner of Yakima and 1st Street to rest.

Without a bike lock, I had to haul the whole thing inside with me while I used the restroom and bought a cold bottle of water. I must have looked ridiculous, but at that point, survival outweighed my pride.

When I was getting ready to resume my trek home, I realized the wheels and pedals were suddenly working again. Just like that. With no explanation and no clue as to why they froze in the first place or why they decided to cooperate now. But I wasn't about to question it. I hopped on and started pedaling my way home.

My route took me up Yakima Avenue and then onto Summitview. I was just approaching the small park near 10th Avenue when I saw it happen.

A car blew straight through the stop sign at 11ᵗʰ and Summitview and into the path of an oncoming vehicle.

The impact was violent and immediate. The car heading into town T-boned the other, sending one spinning across the opposite lane and the other skidding into the front yard of a house.

The sound was sharp and short-lived: screeching brakes, crushing metal, then sudden stillness. When I took a good look, the driver of the car that ran the stop sign was slumped halfway out of the driver's seat with his head hanging between the open driver door and the curb.

I grabbed my phone and called 911. Yakima Regional was only a few blocks away, so the ambulance and police arrived almost instantly. I stayed to comfort the shaken passenger from one car and to help calm the furious driver from the other. After giving my statement to the police, they released me, and I continued home, grateful that my bike was still cooperating. At that point, carrying it the rest of the way would have broken me.

I don't remember what time I finally walked through my door; I only know that I had been gone far longer than planned. I was hot, sweaty, hungry, and worn out. I decided to swing by the grocery store and grab something from the deli.

That's where I ran into Ray.

I practically burst with everything that had happened: the frozen bike, the long walk, the accident. It felt good to finally unload the chaos of the day onto someone who would listen. Ray was amused at how much I'd managed to cram into a single morning. After catching up, he headed to the checkout while I wandered back to finish my shopping.

It was later that day when Lisa finally called back. She said she'd seen my missed calls but had been at church. I told her about the frozen bike, the walk, the accident, my whole wild morning, and then ended with how I'd run into Ray at the grocery store. She went quiet. I noticed the shift, but I didn't realize at the time that it would be the last conversation we would have.

I had no idea that simply crossing paths with Ray would push her over the edge. I only understood something was wrong when, a couple of days later, she didn't reply to my texts. I waited, tried again, waited some more. Nothing. I might have sent a third message before it finally clicked: she was ghosting me.

I was furious. I wasn't about to start compromising myself again just to make someone else feel comfortable. I had just left an abusive marriage where silence was used as a weapon – one of Mike's favorite tools. I had broken free of that kind of emotional manipulation, and I wasn't going back to it. If Lisa chose silence, then I chose to be done.

The irony was she had been so important in my transition back to Yakima. She was the one who had arranged for Ray and Matt to help unload my U-Haul. She had also graciously allowed me to stay with her until I moved into my apartment. I really believed that I had reconnected with a true friend who would help take me past my healing journey and into the rest of my life.

But our friendship wasn't meant to last. She had already betrayed my confidence early on by revealing Jack's identity to Ray, and I was forced to be cautious with her ever since.

Even though I was deeply hurt that she had turned her back on me that day, I eventually realized that Lisa was only meant to be in my life for a specific reason and not for the whole journey. She played the part of helping me get back to Yakima; for that brief purpose, I thank her, I forgive her, and I wish her well on her own path.

This was an early lesson in becoming a healthier version of myself: not everyone is meant to continue the journey with you. As you heal, as you grow into gratitude and strength, new people will appear to guide you to the next step. And some will gently, or abruptly, fall away.

What matters is remembering that their departure is not a reflection of your worth. Growth changes us. It reshapes what we need, what we tolerate, and whom we resonate with. Some people simply won't evolve with you, and that's okay. Everyone has their own lessons to learn, their own struggles to face.

So, when someone's chapter in your life ends, let them go with a blessing. Make space for the next blessing waiting up ahead. If you lead with love, compassion, empathy, and grace towards yourself and others, you will grow stronger. And little by little, you will shed the version of your past that once held you down.

Now, on to my next lesson.

****

Note to self:

Sometimes as an adult, I have to decide,

'This is the last time these people are going to make me feel this way,' and stand by it.

@motivationapp

CH. 4 — Jack

I always loved Yakima's summer mornings. Daylight slipped in a little after five, and the air was always cool and still. When my family first moved here in 1974, I started getting up around 5:30 to go for a run around Franklin Park. It was only a couple of blocks from our house with its mix of gentle slopes, steep inclines, and shaded pathways.

What I loved most was the solitude. The sun was up, but the world wasn't awake yet: no cars, no people, just the birds. It seemed like I owned the place. I could go for a run and be in the silence of the world around me. Even at 13, I found the beauty and the quiet of the morning nurturing and meditative.

When I moved back to Yakima in the summer of 2014, returning to those early runs was one of the first things I wanted to do. I wasn't working yet, so the mornings were mine to claim. And being fresh off East Coast time made waking up early in the morning easy for me. I would slip into my running shorts, grab my iPod, and head to my old neighborhood area of Summitview, Barge-Chestnut, and Franklin Park.

I would park behind Fiddlesticks on 16th and Summitview, made sure my I-Pod was on a good station, took a last sip of water, and then started up Summitview to take in my old neighborhood again.

What a wonderful feeling it was to run those familiar streets. It was such a contrast to North Carolina, where even at sunrise the humidity clung to you, and my routes there were limited to the uneven pavement of Ferry Road and the small housing development where I lived.

In Yakima, the mornings were light and crisp. It was filled with so much energy that it helped me to tackle the inclines that would sneak in and challenge my heart and lungs.

Sometimes I'd turn off Summitview and onto Gilbert Drive then continue west on Barge. The old trees had been standing there for decades, creating a leafy canopy that shaded the homes and offered a safe refuge for birds. Running beneath them filled me with a kind of bright nostalgia where I got to bathe myself in the beautiful memories of my past.

Most mornings I found myself parking behind Fiddlesticks and heading up Summitview. There were endless routes to choose from, each one familiar and comforting. I could loop through Franklin Park, run the terraces or the perimeter, or weave through the shaded streets of the Barge–Chestnut neighborhood before heading back down Summitview to my car.

On one of those runs heading back down Summitview, I stopped to look at a real-estate flyer tucked inside a box. I was renting an apartment for the moment, but once the divorce was finalized, I intended to buy a house. The place on the flyer was a small, single-story home not far from where I used to live. I stood there on the sidewalk with my back to the street and my radio blasting in my ear when a car pulled into the driveway beside me and stopped.

I looked up, and there was Jack.

I was completely surprised to see him there. He rolled his window down and had that electric smile on his face when he said hi.

I was happy to see him but completely surprised. He had told me he worked from seven to three, but here it was almost 7:15 in the morning when he stopped to say hi. I had purposely timed my run so he'd already be at work. Not because I didn't want to see him, but because these early-morning loops were my therapy...my time alone. I didn't want him driving past every day thinking I was staging my runs to get his attention.

And there I was sweaty, hair plastered to my head, my face bright red from the run, and I was facing a smiling Jack. I said something like, "I must look terrible" to which Jack responded with a big smile, "I think you look great!"

We chatted a bit. I told him I'd just stopped to look at a listing, trying to get a feel for the market. As we talked, I noticed the car he was driving, a white station wagon that looked very much like the one I used to own before it ended upside down in a ditch. I walked around it, comparing details. They were different models but they were both white and the same model year.

I had been taking mental notes for the past few months on the parallels between Jack's life and mine. We both had ended up in dead end, toxic marriages that produced two girls and one boy with one girl having a major health event and both boys becoming pilots. We had the same last four digits of our phone number, and both bought our first home, on a cul-de-sac, at the same time.

I would go on to uncover even more parallels between us, but in that moment, I was simply struck by how his white station wagon looked so much like the one I'd flipped upside down into a ditch.

It was a complete surprise to have Jack stop by and say hello that morning while I was out for a run. It put a smile on my face, but it also made me feel like I had to adjust my running routes so it wouldn't happen again. Not because I didn't want to see him, far from it, but because those mornings were my private sanctuary. Still, it didn't matter. It seemed that we were destined to run into each other anyway.

The next time it happened was a Saturday morning. I had parked farther up Summitview at 45th and decided to run west on Chestnut to 56th, then up toward Englewood. My old high-school track sat off 56th and Chestnut and one of our routes for training was to run up 56th then continue west on Englewood. I was never good at running that long, continuous incline up 56th, but I loved the challenge.

This time, my heart couldn't take the familiar route, so I turned around at Englewood and took advantage of the long downhill that let my legs stretch out in front of me as it lengthened my stride. It was a quicker trip down the hill and I got back to Summitview in what seemed like a few seconds. I was finally able to take a moment to catch my breath in front of the Safeway when, there he was: Jack.

I hadn't expected to see him on a Saturday, especially that early. He rolled down the passenger window to say hello. I heard the CD I'd given him for his birthday playing softly in the background. We chatted for a moment, just the normal pleasantries.

I was a bit burned out from my run, and since he was headed in the direction where my car was parked, I asked if he could drop me off on his way. I climbed in and got to spend a beautiful one minute with him until he dropped me off. It was yet another pleasant, but unexpected run-in with him.

I still didn't know exactly where Jack stood with his girlfriend or with me. I tried to stay neutral, waiting for him to either tell me or give a clear signal that there was no future between us. I wasn't going to push anything. I would let Jack set the tone. In the meantime, my random run-ins with him were a welcome gift that I accepted, and I tucked them away in my heart in case they were the last.

It wasn't long after moving back to Yakima, I reached out to Jack's mom, Barbara. She had been so kind to pass along the letter I wrote to him while I was still in North Carolina. She sounded genuinely delighted to hear from me, and it wasn't long before I ended up at her house catching up on all the years we'd missed.

It was so good to see her again. Her eyes were still bright, and she had a radiant smile. I knew exactly where Jack got his. She told me her health had slowed her down and that she'd recently stopped driving. I could see how navigating her spacious home was becoming difficult, so we settled out on the deck with cold drinks and let the conversation flow.

Talking with Barbara was effortless. I filled her in on my final weeks in NC and how I'd escaped Mike. She listened intently, asking thoughtful questions—some of them difficult, but all of them kind. What I appreciated most was her willingness to go deep. She didn't judge; she simply nudged me toward a clearer understanding of my own story.

It was exactly what I'd been missing. Since coming back, I didn't have anyone who could help me explore the hard questions or help me sift through the emotional toxicity of my marriage. I had hoped Lisa would be that person, but it turned out to be Barbara who took on that task.

When victims leave their abusers, they are still in a mental fog—still unsure of what happened, why it happened, or how the abuse slowly tightened around them. It takes time to see the walls that were built to survive and then to be able to peel back the layers of trauma and finally name them. Having someone safe and steady to talk to is one of the first steps toward healing but not everyone can hold that kind of emotional load for the victim.

I was fortunate and grateful that Barbara was willing to help me unpack that dark chapter of my life.

Because she no longer drove, Barbara relied on others to take her shopping or stop by for company. I visited her several times that summer and even took her out to lunch at the Apple Tree Golf Course. I could see how much our visits lifted her spirits. She held space for my painful reflections with such gentleness. I appreciated her kindness more than I could express.

We talked a bit about Jack, but I kept it light. I didn't want her to share anything he hadn't already told me, and I certainly didn't want Barbara thinking I was using our friendship to get information. The truth was this: Barbara was a living thread to a time in my life that had been full of light. After I left Jack and was with Mike, that light went out. Apart from the moments I had with my kids, I didn't have any good memories to look back on. It was all pain and darkness. Being welcomed into Barbara's home gave me an opportunity to touch the past that I once had and to remember that it was beautiful and it was real.

On one of our visits, she confided that Jack's girlfriend, Celina, had found out about my spending time with her and had chastised her for it. Barbara looked visibly shaken as she described how Celina made her feel as though she was betraying both she and Jack.

I felt bad for her. I hadn't imagined my visits would put her in a difficult position. From Celina's limited point of view, I could understand the curiosity or even insecurity. But I would never have spoken to someone as selfless as Barbara to make her feel bad about being a friend to someone.

Celina's insecurities weren't Barbara's burden to carry. If Celina had concerns, that conversation belonged between her and Jack. Why hadn't he reached out to me if my visits were causing tension? Why hadn't he reassured Celina enough that she wouldn't feel threatened by my presence at all?

When I asked Barbara what she wanted to do, she didn't hesitate. She said she wanted to continue our visits. "We never talk about Jack and Celina," she said firmly. "I know I haven't done anything wrong." She understood how important it was for me to have someone trustworthy to talk to.

I assured her I would never put her in a situation that compromised her relationship with her son.

Still, the whole incident made me wonder even more about what Jack's intentions were. I didn't know how serious things were between him and Celina, and neither he nor Barbara had offered any clarity. The silence itself became its own kind of message—one I wasn't sure how to interpret yet.

I wasn't sure what to make of Celina's reaction. Was her insecurity brought on because Jack wasn't as committed as she wanted? Was their relationship already strained, and my reappearance only highlighted the imbalance? I didn't know. But her behavior made me doubt the strength of their relationship and, if I'm honest, it gave me a flicker of hope that my presence was making Jack question it too.

And then there was Jack himself, still calling and texting. Just little check-ins and friendly hellos. A week after I'd moved into my apartment, I drove over to Renton to pick up shelves I'd bought at IKEA. I was just hitting Snoqualmie Pass on my way home when Jack called on his lunch break. I smiled the moment I heard his voice and I could hear his smile on the other end.

I told him where I was and what I'd bought. The shelves were heavy, and I knew I'd need help getting them inside. He immediately offered to come by after work to carry them in. I felt a wave of gratitude. I asked if he could also help me hook up my grill to the propane tank, and he said it would be no problem.

I had barely been home when he showed up. I let him in and gave him a quick tour. He had lived in these apartments for several years after his last divorce, and he was curious how my unit compared to his, so he poked his head around every corner with a kind of nostalgic amusement.

When he circled back to the entryway where I was standing, he looked at me and said, very sincerely, "What are we going to do?"

I thought he was talking about the shelves. I started to answer, pointing to where I imagined placing them. "Well, I thought we could pull the sofa back and put the shelves over there—"

He shook his head. "No. I mean… about us."

It stopped me quick. Until that moment, I didn't know there was an "us." I had no clear sense of what he felt about my return to Yakima. Yes, he had been keeping in touch, finding reasons to stay connected, but I didn't know what any of it meant. And suddenly he acknowledged that maybe there was something bigger.

All I knew to do was to step forward and give him a hug and a kiss on the cheek. He didn't respond and didn't pull away, but he also didn't say anything more. I waited for him to continue, to explain what "us" meant to him.

But he said nothing.

I quickly changed the subject and began shifting furniture to make space for the shelves. They were heavier than they looked; the frame was lightweight aluminum, but each shelf was thick glass. We carried them up the flight of stairs in two trips, both of us slightly winded by the end.

Then I brought Jack out to the deck where the grill was.

I had never hooked up a propane tank before, and the thought of doing it wrong, of blowing something up, always intimidated me. I confessed my fears while he crouched beside the grill, tightening the connections and explaining each step so I'd feel confident doing it myself next time. When he was almost finished, he shot me a mischievous look and whispered, "Boom."

We both burst out laughing. I appreciated the way he eased my nerves with something so simple as a lighthearted jab at my expense.

I wasn't ready for Jack to leave yet. We still hadn't talked about what happened between us in 1981. And every time I saw him, I wondered if it might be the last.

We sat beside each other on the sofa while I showed him pictures of the kids and shared pieces of my fractured past. He noted that my son and his son had the same motorcycle when he saw a picture of Craig riding around our large property. It was another similarity between us that I added to my already growing list.

Eventually, I was able to tell him the best I could of what happened when I "temporarily" broke up with him all those years ago. I'd turned the story over in my mind countless times, trying to understand it, trying to make sense of the version of myself who made that choice. I'd sorted out most of it, but there were still holes I couldn't fill.

What had been missing in me back then?
What belief about myself led me to think a fling with
Mike would make me whole?
Why did I sabotage something so pure, so safe, so real?

I was still trying to figure that out.

Jack sat quietly as I tried to explain what had happened back then. Telling him was harder than I expected, but he made it easy. It was always easy with him. It was important to me that he knew that he'd never done anything wrong. He needed to hear that I had spiraled into guilt and shame after betraying him, and that my lack of courage, my lack of self-worth, had kept me from ever asking for his forgiveness.

When I finished, a silence settled between us. Then Jack stunned me when he softly said, "I would have taken you back."

Imagine that.

If I hadn't allowed myself to drown in shame and if I had simply humbled myself and apologized, he would have forgiven me. He would have taken me back.

Shame and guilt, when allowed to persist, kept me from living the life I was meant to live.

I told him that hurting him was the single greatest regret of my life. At the time, I thought breaking up with him was an honorable choice; that it was better than cheating. But each step after that only compounded the mistake. The biggest one was assuming he wouldn't take me back.

"It was supposed to be you, Jack," I said quietly. "It was always supposed to be you."

He looked at me with a gentleness that felt familiar and far away. "I'm in a pretty committed relationship right now," he said.

There it was. The clarity I had waited for. He was committed to Celina.

I asked why he hadn't told me earlier. Why had he kept calling and texting if he was already deeply involved with someone else. He didn't answer.

I told him that if he had been clear from the beginning, not calling or texting me, I would have backed away immediately. But because he didn't, he left the door open, just enough for hope to slip through. I had already made a big mistake may years ago by "assuming" he wouldn't take me back. I wasn't going to do it again by "assuming" he was all in with Celina until I heard it from him.

Still, I couldn't understand why he kept reaching out to me if he was committed to her.

I asked again. He looked at me, eyes heavy with remorse and shame.

So, I answered for him. "It was because you were curious," I said softly. "You just wanted to see me again."

Jack didn't deny it. He just held my gaze, sorrowful and silent.

I could see where things were heading with Jack. It was coming to an end.

For more than thirty years I had carried him in my heart. I held on to the guilt, the shame, and the blame for all that happened. Through all the years with Mike, when my life narrowed and darkened, I had kept my beautiful memories of Jack as my touchstone to keep me sane and to remind myself that I was worthy of that kind of love.

A part of me had always hoped we would somehow find our way back to each other. But now, it had come to an end. I was beginning to feel the weight of my regret from all those years ago starting to crush me once again.

I could never hate Jack. I never have, and I never will. I just knew our time had passed. The goodbye between us was quiet and sorrowful. We gave each other a hug, knowing it might be the last time. He said a few things to me that I will always keep private. And then I watched him drive away.

Those memories I'd carried for decades had been a beautiful gift from him. Jack had shown up in so many of my dreams during my darkest moments, reminding me to keep going.

His message in that dream back in March had given me the courage to finally leave Mike. But now I understood that my path forward would be without him.

I slipped into another state of mourning. I let it wash over me and let it soak into every part of my body. I needed to feel it, to name it, so I could eventually move through it.

I knew I would most likely never see Jack again and that hurt. But I still held my memories of us and his parting words deep in my heart. I looked for a way to process these emotions all the while trying to navigate my way out of the abusive fog I had just escaped.

There were so many layers of emotions that I had to peel away and work through. And, except for Barbara, I had no one who was capable and willing to help me through it.

So, I started running again.

I was deliberately more careful now when I went running so I could avoid crossing Jack's route to work. The quiet mornings, empty streets, and the steady rhythm of my breath gave me some emotional control and helped me to center my tormented thoughts.

It was on one of those runs, when I felt tucked away and invisible in the early morning light, that I saw Jack again.

I had just finished an early run and returned to my car at the Safeway off 56th. I was organizing a few groceries in the trunk when I saw Jack drive by in his white station wagon.

I watched his brake lights flash hard, and then his car disappeared toward the intersection. A moment later, he reappeared, pulling around the side of a small building across the street. He stopped there, in a spot that gave him a perfect view of the Safeway parking lot and of me.

That was all the confirmation I needed. He had seen me. Why else would he hit the brakes, turn around and just sit there? I thought he must have wanted to see me, so I waited for him to come over. But he never did. After a brief moment, he drove off again.

He had to have been looking for me. There was no other logical explanation. I wasn't anywhere near the street; he wouldn't have spotted me by accident. And that confused me. He had told me he was in a committed relationship with Celina. So why linger? Why watch me? Why act as if there was still something unspoken between us?

Whatever it was, I could feel the old connection tugging at both of us. What we had shared, however brief and however young we were, had been powerful. That connection between us had been resurrected when we reconnected and perhaps, he was having a difficult time letting me go again.

On the next visit I had with Barbara, I filled her in on Jack and me and how he made it clear he was committed to Celina. I also told her how I had seen Jack watching me from across the street.

This information surprised Barbara and the next time I saw her, she had her own surprise for me. She said she'd mentioned the incident to Jack, and he'd given her a different version: he had pulled into that lot to use the mailbox, nothing more.

But I knew better. The mailbox wasn't anywhere near where he had stopped.

I didn't argue with Barbara. If that was the story Jack wanted her to believe, I let it be.

I was deeply disappointed that Jack lied. He had been caught, and I'm sure he felt embarrassed about how it might look to his mom, so he protected himself the only way he knew how by distorting the truth. I let it stand, but the realization settled in hard: I was going to have to change my entire routine to be sure I didn't run into him again.

His behavior had been confusing: seeking me out, then telling me he was committed to someone else, then secretly watching me from a distance. Which version was real? Instead of trying to untangle it, I made the decision for both of us.

If I ever saw him out in public again, I would turn and walk away. And I would no longer run the old familiar routes that meant so much to me. That choice hurt. Those paths held decades of healing memories, but they also crossed too closely with his daily routes. So, I let them go.

I realized that another part of my past was coming to an end and that shedding my past was going to be necessary to heal. I had to let go of Lisa and now I had to let go of the one person I held dearest to my heart.

This wouldn't be the last time that I had to shut a door to my past, but this was a big one.

I had been emotionally alone for the thirty-three years I was with Mike, and now I found myself alone again and without trusted friends who could help me sift through the abuse I had survived. Barbara had been a godsend. Her questions pushed me to dig deep, and her steadiness helped me face the truth. But now my pain included Jack, and I refused to lean on her in a way that would burden her emotionally or jeopardize her relationship with him.

It was time to look elsewhere for the connection and support I needed. Thankfully, I still had family in the area. So, I leaned into that precious resource as I moved forward to discovering my new self and trying to find a path forward that was meant for me.

****

Even though you didn't make it to the end of my story,

I will always have the corner folded down
on your page...

Because it was one of my favorites.

@stardust_poetry1

CH. 5 — FAMILY

It's true. You rarely appreciate what you have until it's gone. You don't cherish the rain until you've had weeks of sun, and you don't long for the sun until gray days stack up like they'll never end. Life needs contrast. The soft and the harsh, the stillness and the upheaval. Without them, we can't recognize what truly brings us joy.

I had lived away from family for more than thirty years. Sometimes five years would pass before I saw my parents. Returning to Yakima felt like stepping into a forgotten part of myself, one that was suddenly full again. I soaked it in.

On my first Sunday back, I wandered through the Farmer's Market in front of the old Capitol Theatre. It was a perfect June morning; blue skies, crisp air, the kind that made me grateful just to be alive. As I strolled along, taking in the familiar rhythm of home, I suddenly found myself face-to-face with my Uncle Harold.

What a gift. After decades of distance, here I was, less than a week into my return, simply *bumping* into family. This was something that I had envied my friends for back in NC for years. He pulled me into a big hug. He hadn't heard I'd moved back, which didn't surprise me. Only a handful of people knew about my escape, and I had only told my mom a few days earlier when I was just crossing into Washington with my U-Haul behind me.

We walked through the market together, chatting about familiar things, and then promised to meet up again soon. It reminded me of childhood weekends when family gathered without effort or planning. I had lost that for such a long time. Now it was finding its way back to me.

A few days later, I met my mom, now remarried and living in Zillah, at Miner's, the iconic burger spot in Union Gap. Over lunch, I told her what I could emotionally manage about the toxic, abusive marriage I'd finally escaped. My mind was still fogged with the residue of that life, but I shared the pieces I could. It was a start. It was something like coming home.

She listened with such empathy. Then she gently shared the impressions she'd gathered about Mike over the years. She admitted she'd never felt at ease around him, and she pointed out how he made no effort to connect with her or with anyone in my family. She remembered visiting us in North Carolina and watching him retreat to the garage instead of joining in; even skipping our family trip to Washington, D.C. altogether.

She wasn't wrong. Mike always kept my family at arm's length. He'd say, "They're your family, not mine," as if that excused his distance. Yet he expected me to warmly embrace his family whenever they visited, and I always did. I could never imagine dismissing them the way he dismissed mine. His coldness toward my family was just another way of telling me I didn't matter.

Because in his mind, what was in it for him?

I apologized to my mom for the many times he made her feel small. It stunned me how subtle and yet how widespread his passive-aggressive, narcissistic habits had become.

They hadn't been aimed only at me; they'd quietly seeped into the way he treated my family too.

When I visited my dad and my Norma, in Goldendale, they echoed with the same observations. Dad recalled how Mike always seemed to be hiding in the garage during their visits, rarely making time to interact with anyone.

Yes. Mike was an a**hole. My parents had felt his disregard firsthand. For years, I had assumed I was the only one he treated that way. We lived so far from family, and visits were so rare, I didn't think they'd seen enough to notice the selfishness I lived with daily.

I remembered feeling that sting when he refused to join us for outings during their visits, but I never realized my parents had sensed it too.

I had been isolated from my family for my entire marriage, East Coast versus West Coast. That distance created the perfect conditions for trauma bonding, the perfect cover for his emotional manipulation. With no family consistently around to witness how he treated me, he could shape my reality however he wanted.

There had been no one close enough to witness the subtle control Mike held over me. No one saw the way he chipped at my confidence, or how carefully he twisted reality. With no trusted person nearby, I had nowhere to voice the confusion that lived inside me.

But now, freshly returned to Yakima after finally escaping him, I discovered that even in the few brief encounters my parents had with Mike, they'd sensed his toxic nature. It made me wonder, if we had lived closer, how long would it have taken before they stepped in? Would I have seen the truth sooner?

Maybe. At the very least, I wouldn't have felt so alone. When I discovered Mike's cross-dressing in January of 1987, I was pregnant with my second child and terrified. If I had regular, close contact with my parents, I might have had the courage to speak up then. They would have helped me find a way out.

Isolation is a crucial part of domestic abuse. Abusers cut their victims off from family and friends so that the victim becomes dependent on them emotionally. They erode trust by insulting the victim's loved ones, creating physical distance, sabotaging visits, and guilting the victim for wanting time with anyone but them.

This is why maintaining strong connections to family and friends matters. If you notice your own world shrinking or if someone you care about is quietly drifting into isolation, you must take it seriously. Step back and assess where your relationship is heading. And if it's a loved one who's withdrawing, be intentional about staying connected. Your presence might be their lifeline.

I had missed that lifeline for my entire marriage. Mike and I moved five times in the first three years, and every time, I had to start over. There was never enough time to build lasting friendships, so eventually, all I had was him. And we all know how that turned out.

Reconnecting with my mom opened the door to her side of the family as well. Before long, I joined their regular get-togethers, sometimes meeting at Miner's with a whole group of relatives, other times gathering at my Uncle RC and Aunt Betty's house off Washington Avenue.

The women in my mom's family loved getting together for lunch or dinner, and I soaked it all in. After more than thirty years away, these simple moments felt almost sacred. Being surrounded by people who loved me, people I had missed for so long, was deeply healing. I hadn't realized how starved I'd been for that sense of community.

When I started teaching at the end of summer, my free time evaporated, but my mom and I made a promise: we'd have dinner together every Thursday. We rotated restaurants, catching up on our week and talking about whatever weighed on our minds. Those evenings became an anchor for both of us.

One night, after finishing dinner at the Golden Wheel on 1st Street, we went to pay our bill and learned that another diner had already taken care of it. The cashier explained that they'd overheard us talking about our Thursday tradition and were touched by our commitment to each other and they wanted to honor it.

How beautiful is that? I've picked up the tab for strangers before, but no one had ever done it for me. I want to thank that kind soul, whoever they were. Their generosity has been paid forward many times since.

I continued leaning into family as the weeks passed. My Uncle Harold became a constant touchstone. He was an avid tennis player and a member of the Yakima Tennis Club, and he was also a solid golfer. One day, he offered to meet me at Westwood West Golf Course and teach me how to swing a club.

I've always been athletic and happiest when I found ways to play. But during my marriage to Mike, that part of me had withered. I stopped giving myself permission to pursue anything just for joy. Now, I was free again. Having my uncle to teach me golf wasn't just an outing, it felt like reclaiming a piece of myself.

I found a cheap set of clubs on Craigslist and joined my uncle at the driving range whenever we could. Yakima summers heat up fast, so we always met before 9 a.m. It was such a joy connecting with him. He helped me with my swing, then walked me over to the putting green to practice chipping from different distances.

I bought a bag of wiffle golf balls and took them to Franklin Park, where I practiced my chipping and driving on quiet summer mornings. School would start soon, and I wanted to give something back to myself while I still had the time. Those solitary practices were surprisingly healing; the simplicity of the moment quieted my thoughts in a way I hadn't experienced in years.

I appreciated Uncle Harold not just for teaching me golf, but for giving me his time and attention. Mike had withheld that kind of connection throughout our marriage. He only engaged when something benefitted him, and I hadn't realized how starved I was for genuine companionship until I felt it again.

Contrast reveals everything. Having lived so long without intimate connection, I might not have recognized how meaningful my uncle's kindness truly was. He was a beautiful soul sent, it seemed, by the Universe to help guide me back toward wholeness. Thank you, Universe. And thank you, Uncle Harold.

The summer brought even more chances to reconnect. We had a mini reunion at Uncle RC and Aunt Betty's when family flew in from Oklahoma, and later a surprise birthday celebration for my Uncle Chuck in Walla Walla.

Both gatherings filled me with gratitude. I saw familiar, loving faces from my past, and we all had the chance to acknowledge how much we meant to one another.

These family connections grounded me throughout my return to Yakima. But even surrounded by their love, I still had an ache inside me. I missed having someone special to share life with, someone I could point out something beautiful in nature to, someone to laugh with during a silly moment on TV or to sit beside at a summer concert in the park.

I had been married for over thirty years, yet emotionally alone for most of it. I was tired of that loneliness. I longed for intimacy, for someone I could trust with my desires, my dreams, my regrets. Reconnecting with family filled part of that void, but not all of it.

Even though I had just escaped Mike only a month earlier, I allowed myself to begin searching for the intimate connection my soul had been craving for so long.

****

Today,

Be a blessing.   Be a friend.   Encourage someone.
Take time to Care.

Let your words heal and not wound.

Count your blessings and be grateful
that you are in a position to help others.

@proactiveyellowworld

CH. 6 — Searching

There had been a dull ache in my soul for almost my entire marriage. Mike's abusive behavior slowly stripped me of the intimate connection every human being needs. At the heart of it was the absence of safety.

His explosive temper, the emotional blackmail, the way he dismissed my pain—it all eroded the basic emotional security that allows a person to grow into their full self. Every one of us has a responsibility to make the space around us safe for others to be authentic. Mike pretended he could do that before we married. I truly believed he would love, respect, and support me. I believed he'd always have my back. But that promise never materialized.

The first deep crack in that trust was his hidden cross-dressing. He kept it from me before we married. He took away my right to decide whether it was something I could accept or support. That secrecy wasn't love; it was manipulation meant only to serve him. How could trust survive that?

Trust is the foundation of intimacy. Without it, there is no emotional safety, no place to be vulnerable or honest. And in my marriage, trust didn't just erode, it shattered.

Then came the betrayal I still feel in my bones: Mike's refusal to confront his friend after he sexually assaulted me. Part of intimacy is knowing your partner will protect you and that they will always have your back. That event was one of the lowest in my marriage and it came at a time when I was the most vulnerable; three small children under the age of four with no access to my own income and living three thousand miles away from family. I was dependent on him financially, which meant I felt trapped.

And where was the man who had promised to protect me? He was right there, watching it happen and doing nothing about it.

That betrayal cut deep because he was supposed to be *the* one person in the whole world who was supposed to protect me. After that, I knew that I was going to be emotionally alone in my marriage. And, so I was.

Intimacy isn't just sexual. It is all things that touch our deepest core that helps us to figure out ourselves and our place and purpose in the world around us. Intimacy is having someone so attuned to you, your heart, your spirit that they willingly witness your journey through life. They understand their responsibility in helping you navigate that journey with love instead of judgment. And true intimacy can never be one-sided. It only thrives when it is fully reciprocated and supported by both partners.

We all crave intimacy to feel whole.

There is intellectual intimacy where you have the freedom to share your opinions, questions, and curiosities without fear. It might be discussing your views on social matters in your city or discussing a movie or news article. This kind of connection helps us understand who we are and how we fit into the shared world around us.

Mike never created that kind of space. Any differing opinion from me was met with anger or verbal abuse. He treated my perspective as a personal attack instead of an invitation to exchange ideas. His voice was the only one allowed. I learned early to surrender all the oxygen in the room, because expressing myself simply wasn't safe.

There is also social intimacy when you recognize the importance of spending quality time with your partner. It can be as simple as making the bed or cooking a meal together, taking dance lessons, walking around the neighborhood, or exploring a new place side by side. These moments say: "Your company matters to me. Your interests matter because you matter."

I tried so many times to connect with Mike in that way. I asked him to walk with me, to take short trips, to explore nearby towns. I even dreamed of going on a cruise together. His response? "Why would I want to go on a boat when I spend six months on deployment?" How about because it mattered to me?

That was always the pattern. Walk with me? No. Bike ride? No. Explore somewhere new? No. Go visit Jillian in Wilmington? Yes, but only because he could then hijack the visit to shop for tools. Time together only counted if it benefitted him.

Weekends should have been an easy opportunity for Mike to connect with me and the kids. Instead, he routinely made plans on his own by helping friends with projects, heading out on his motorcycle for a day's ride, shopping for more tools, and going hunting. And always, this was done without discussing any of it with me. I probably would have been fine with most of those plans, but there was never space left for *us*. Never any thought to how the kids or I might fit into his weekend.

I eventually stopped asking, "What should *we* do this weekend?" and switched to, "What are *your* plans for the weekend?" There was even a time when I had to literally write "family time" on the calendar just to keep him from scheduling himself elsewhere. How sad is that? And yet, if the roles were reversed, he never would have tolerated it from me.

He was incapable of seeing anyone else's needs. He did what he wanted, and it rarely included the family. I was so starved for connection that I grasped at whatever scraps I could.

I would simply go into the garage while he was working on something and offer to help, then just sit on the steps hoping for conversation. But that never happened. He just dismissed me, calling me "weird" for wanting to be near him.

That was the story of my marriage; denial of the intimacy my soul craved. His discard of me and his indifference when I was emotionally at my lowest cut the deepest where there was no validation that I and my heart mattered.

I understood why people thought that searching for an intimate partner so soon after leaving Mike wasn't wise. But they didn't understand the decades I had spent emotionally alone. There was emptiness so intense that I knew that I couldn't move forward and make my life whole again without it.

Well-meaning friends and family kept insisting that I should wait a year before dating again.

Really? Who decided that rule?

If I needed a year, I would have taken a year. If I needed two years, I would have taken two. But what if what I needed was three months, five days, and six hours? Healing isn't one-size-fits-all. We move through hell and back at our own pace, with our own needs.

I have already spent over thirty years ALONE.

I was tired of being ALONE.

I didn't want to be ALONE anymore.

So, I moved forward with the intention of finding that intimate connection knowing that family and friends would not understand.

I joined a local "friends" group and went to a couple of their activities, but nothing clicked. Everyone was friendly enough, but I didn't feel any genuine connection. I also went to a few Thursday night concerts downtown with a cousin and met some of her friends. A couple of guys showed aggressive interest, but it wasn't authentic, so I shut that down immediately.

My high school friend, Cory, set me up with someone she knew, and I agreed to my first and only blind date. He seemed pleasant at first, but the evening unraveled almost immediately. We were making small talk when he asked me a question. As soon as I began answering, he turned his head away and stared at the wall to his right. I kept talking for a few moments, then stopped since it was clear he wasn't listening to me.

When he finally turned to look back at me all I did was just smile at him. He seemed embarrassed because he had no idea what I had just said and for how long I had quit talking. Maybe he was scrambling inside, wondering if he'd missed a question he was supposed to answer.

I left shortly after. My smile never wavered, but it had shifted into something else: *I see you, and you're free to move along.* He asked for my phone number, and I simply said, "If you really want it, you can get it from Cory," then walked away.

I had no intention of investing my time or heart in anything that felt like a dead end. After everything I had endured with Mike, I owed myself better. And it became clear that finding a meaningful, intimate partner wasn't going to happen through casual social groups or random introductions.

So, I did something I never imagined I would: I joined a dating site.

At the time, the only one I knew of was Match.com thanks to the commercials. So, I went online, took a deep breath, and began the process.

This was all completely new to me. I remembered when the internet first arrived and people started meeting strangers online. I thought it sounded wild and dangerous. And yet here I was, years later, dipping my toes into that very world, cautiously testing whether this unfamiliar medium might actually lead me to the connection I'd been missing.

The first step was creating a profile. The basics were easy: age, email, marital history, kids, smoking or drinking habits, education level. But then came the questions I wasn't prepared for. Questions that required me to look inward: *What's your idea of a perfect date? What activities do you enjoy? Are you open to someone with different political views?*

After so many years with Mike, I had slowly lost touch with myself. I no longer knew who I was. I had given up so much of my own identity just to keep his ego soothed and to protect myself from his unpredictable anger.

It was a stunning realization that one of the casualties from the long-term abuse was for me to lose the deep connection I had to myself.

I had to pause and really dig deep about what I wanted in a relationship. I certainly knew what I didn't want; I had decades of examples of behaviors I would never tolerate again. So, I used that as my starting point and simply looked for the opposite of everything Mike had been.

I wanted someone who valued family and friends. Someone who communicated well, who could handle difficult conversations without becoming defensive. Someone emotionally mature. Someone who loved sports and was active, who wouldn't feel threatened by my own sports knowledge. Someone who appreciated quiet time together and who would prioritize me. And I wanted someone who was fiscally responsible; I didn't want to build a future with anyone who didn't know how to manage money responsibly.

I also had my deal breakers. It was a hard NO to smokers because of my allergies. It was another hard NO to men with young children since I had already raised mine. And it was an absolute NO to anyone in the military. I'd lived that life, and I had no desire to return to it.

What I loved about the dating site was that everyone knew why they had joined. We were all looking for a long-term partner, so there were no mixed signals about intent. I could scroll through profiles and immediately rule out those that didn't align with where I was in my life. Of course, you are counting on each participant to be honest. When you are looking for a life partner, you're wasting your time pretending to be someone you're not.

The dating site used algorithms to match me with profiles it thought would be a good fit. I sifted through countless matches and selected the ones that interested me. Then I waited to see who would reciprocate.

A few responses came in almost immediately, which was unexpectedly fun. The platform felt surprisingly safe as it allowed me to talk to people without exposing my phone number or email.

Reading profiles, choosing whether to reach out, and seeing how someone responded saved me weeks of dead-end dates. There were no hard feelings if someone backed away; if you're serious about finding "the one," you appreciate people who don't waste your time.

And how do you know which profile to pursue more deeply? Intuition. A gut feeling. Either there's a spark or there isn't. At first, I lingered longer than I should have on a few profiles, but eventually, their mismatches surfaced.

There was one man who lived in Texas and had two small children. This was clearly a stretch from the algorithm. Another lived near Seattle. A tad far for me, but we chatted for a bit. Then he became possessive, insisting I call him every morning before work and again when I got off.

Absolutely not.

I had just left a controlling marriage; I wasn't about to tolerate even a hint of that again.

Then, on Tuesday, just two days after my profile went live, I got a ping from another man in Seattle. Again, the distance wasn't ideal, but his picture caught my attention. He was sitting next to a bright-eyed teenage girl at a Seattle Sounders game, smiling like someone who had joy in his life. We exchanged messages for a bit, and he suggested we talk by phone the next day.

I hustled around to rearrange my day so I'd be ready when he called. It was a gorgeous mid-August afternoon, so I positioned myself on my deck overlooking Lake Aspen with a glass of iced tea when he called.

We hit it off immediately.

We must have talked for more than two hours, and I'm certain we were both smiling the entire time.

He had been divorced for a couple of years and was experienced with dating sites, so he understood this early phase when two profiles suddenly collide with possibility. He asked meaningful and reflective questions that revealed values, not trivia. I loved that. After so many years without true intellectual connection, I was stunned by how naturally it came to him. In just two hours, I learned a great deal about him and about myself.

This is what intellectual intimacy looks like. When two people dive into conversations about values, dreams, and goals, you learn how the other person approaches life, how they handle complexity and how they think. I had been starved of that for years, and now here was this man on the other end of the line engaging with me so openly and so easily.

He made me feel heard and he made me feel valued. Aside from my dad and Jack, no man had ever treated my thoughts and insights with such genuine respect. This guy made it easy to talk about any subject - nothing felt off-limits and the conversation simply flowed.

He suggested we meet in person right away. He told me that too much online messaging and phone calls can only take you so far before the initial energy fades. He was a veteran of online dating, so I trusted his judgment.

We planned to meet that upcoming Saturday, August 16th. He would drive over from Seattle, and we'd spend the day together in downtown Yakima for lunch, dinner, and whatever conversations unfolded in between.

Let me cut to the highlights:

I joined Match on Sunday.

His profile went live on Monday.

We chatted online on Tuesday.

We spoke on the phone on Wednesday.

We met on Saturday.

And after that, it was every day.

Bam! Just like that, our souls found each other.

It all felt too good to be true, and it unfolded faster than I had expected. The connection caught me completely off guard with its energy. But before I allowed myself to fully commit my heart, I needed to be certain he wasn't simply "performing" the role of the man I hoped he was, the way Mike had all those years ago.

I was determined never to fall into another toxic, controlling relationship. So even though everything felt incredible from the start, I held back a part of myself until I truly knew that he was real.

I was going to start work on Monday and I had a lot to do to get my classroom set up and lesson plans ready before students returned the following week. I was adding a lot to my emotional and mental plate with this new relationship, and I was determined to take it slowly.

What I didn't realize was that my body was undergoing its own transformation. For years, I had lived in a constant flood of cortisol and adrenaline – always braced for the next emotional blow.

When you are a victim of long-term abuse, it takes your body a while to catch up to the reality that you are finally in a safe place. That chemical shift that takes place in your body is real and will manifest itself when you least expect it.

For the first time in decades, I was shifting towards a healthier hormonal balance, and the physical effects of that shift were so powerful that it nearly caused me to crash my car while driving over Manastash Ridge.

****

Think for yourself.   Trust your Intuition.   No one else is walking your path.

OWN YOUR JOURNEY

mae

CH. 7 — No Wife of Mine

When someone truly loves you, their biggest fear is to hurt you.
But, when someone is in love with how you make them feel, their biggest fear is to lose you.
Your job is to know the difference.
@nsg

I had lived for more than three decades in a constant state of stress. My body had been pumping out cortisol and adrenaline for so long that it finally had enough. I suffered from hair loss, impetigo, weight gain, twitching eyes, and an ER visit for abdominal pain that no one could explain.

The day I escaped, I stayed on high alert, terrified that Mike would come home and find me loading the U-Haul. He had shown me more than once how volatile he could be, and he had used the threat of a gun as leverage before. I had driven from North Carolina to Washington State with my foot pressed to the floor and adrenaline carrying me across every mile. I didn't allow myself to breathe until I reached Yakima.

Back home, finally surrounded by familiar faces and places, I could feel the tension finally beginning to loosen. I settled into the promise of a new life without fear and trauma. I knew rebuilding wouldn't be easy, but every day I caught myself smiling because I was finally safe and figuring out my own path.

But Mike wasn't done. His dark energy kept reaching out to me. He didn't dare call, but he texted constantly, trying to keep me off balance. At first, the messages were desperate pleas for me to return laced with the same promises to change that he had dangled for years. I had believed those promises before; believed them enough to allow countless do-overs. But he always slid back into manipulation. It was the one pattern of his that I could count on.

After one text message insisting he was in therapy and had changed, I texted back, "Good. I hope for your sake you have. I hope you can figure out how to be happy." He didn't like that. I hadn't taken the bait and fallen for his "woe is me" tactic. He was starting to realize that his manipulative tactics were losing their hold.

Then the gifts started showing up: a Fitbit watch, and a gold heart pendant. A note explained that he had melted down his wedding band and reshaped it into a heart for me to wear around my neck.

Was he delusional? Did he really expect me to keep him close to me in the form of a gold heart? How sick was his mind? After all the hell he put me through, did he honestly think I would wear that pendant? What was I supposed to tell people who asked about it? "Oh, this lovely gold heart? My abusive husband, the one I finally escaped from after thirty-plus years of abuse, gave me this lovely gift so that I could always remember how much he tormented me."

I took the pendant to Ron's Coin and Collectibles on Third Street, where the owner, my old classmate Joe Mann, looked it over. He warned me gold prices were down, so I wouldn't get much. I told him I didn't care. When he heard the story behind it, he gave me a disgusting look of his own, handed me a few dollars, and that was that.

The Fitbit went too. Did he really think I'd wear something from him against my skin, something I'd have to look at multiple times a day and be reminded of him? Absolutely not. These gifts were nothing but attempts to exert control from across the country, and I refused to let a single object tether me to him.

He kept pushing his "peace offerings," each one more tone-deaf than the last. All those years we were married, I was never a priority. He spent money on himself while I managed our bills with whatever scraps were left. Now suddenly I was worth expensive gifts? Did he think I'd swoon over his newfound generosity and crawl back?

Then came the motorcycle offer. A motorcycle!

Years earlier I had gotten my motorcycle endorsement just to try to spend more time with him, one of my last desperate attempts to bridge the distance between us. Now, after I had left, he wanted to buy me one.

Apparently, he had inherited some money after his father passed and seemed eager to burn through it. He even called a Yakima dealer to check inventory before texting me the details.

I responded with the only answer he deserved: "No. I don't want it."

When I told my family about the motorcycle offer, several of them said, "Let him buy it and then sell it." But for me, it was still a hard no.

They suggested he was acting out of guilt. That was another hard no.

Guilt requires self-reflection, and he had never once acknowledged doing anything wrong. He understood that his behavior wouldn't look acceptable to others, that's why he saved it for me, but true accountability was never part of his vocabulary. The motorcycle wasn't remorse; it was an attempt to manufacture goodwill. He wanted people to say, "Wow, what a great guy, *buying her* that." I refused to give him that narrative.

When he found out I was eating on an old card table, he shifted to offering to buy me a fancy dining set. Again, I said no. That's when his tone changed. His texts grew snarky, edged with frustration, and he tried to pull rank by reminding me, "You are still my wife, and no wife of mine will be eating off a card table."

Cue the eye roll.

Suddenly I "deserved the best" from him because I was still legally tied to him? This from a man who never prioritized me a single day of our marriage. His concern wasn't about my living conditions; it was about power. It was one more attempt to flex authority he no longer had.

And the way he phrased it, reducing me to something he owned, infuriated me.

Hey, Mike. If you haven't noticed, I'm gone. Legally married or not, I am not your wife anymore, and you don't get to dictate my life.

Once he realized his influence was gone, he switched tactics again. He started trying to intimidate me with "legalese."

"You'd better not start dating anyone. You're still legally my wife, and that would be considered infidelity."

Another eye roll.

His threats held no weight anymore. I was on the opposite side of the country, far from anyone who could report back to him. He was grasping at the frayed end of his rope, tossing out anything that might rattle me. He knew he'd lost control, so he tried to shake my emotions from afar.

Then he asked if I had seen Jack. He had weaponized Jack throughout our marriage, tossing his name out whenever he wanted pity or reassurance. He would even say, "You should have married Jack instead of me," hoping I'd rush to defend my loyalty towards him. The truth? He was right, I should have married Jack. But his intent was always manipulation, never honesty.

Now, here he was again, wanting to know if I'd reconnected with Jack. It was none of his business. Jack was my precious memory, and I refused to let Mike contaminate it.

I once read that victims of narcissistic abuse sometimes will start to reminisce about the "good times" they had with their abuser after they escape. Some of these victims may even start to long for their abuser as their memory alters their abusive past. That was never me.

I had emotionally detached from Mike nearly sixteen years before I escaped. I stayed only until the kids were old enough to handle the truth of why I left. I had no good times to miss, just scattered "moments" when he acted decent, and even those were calculated. Every kindness was a lure, an attempt to reel me back in after he'd crossed a line.

That's the cruel architecture of trauma bonding: tiny breadcrumbs of kindness dropped just often enough to keep a victim hoping the abuser might return to the person they pretended to be in the beginning. Hope becomes the trap.

Please remember this: they were never truly wonderful at the beginning. That version of them was a fabrication. The real person is the one revealed through repeated behavior, not the charm they used to hook you. When you hang on to hope, you keep the door open. That's all an abuser needs to regain control – your hope.

Stop giving them that power. Let the hope go. They will not change.

I had long given up any hope that Mike would change, and I recognized his attempts for exactly what they were: efforts to regain emotional control. I had no authentic good memories to look back on, so there was zero chance I would ever miss him.

And let me add this, if you are a victim of narcissistic abuse and you've managed to get away, do not let those manufactured "good times" manipulate you. Leaving was the hardest part; you already climbed that mountain. The last thing you want is to go back. Astonishingly, 75% of domestic violence victims are killed by their abuser *after* leaving the relationship. If you are one of the lucky 25% who got out alive, do not test your luck by returning. An abuser will make sure you don't leave a second time.

I had escaped Mike's abuse, returned safely to Yakima, and was deflecting every attempt he made to manipulate me through texts. I was like Teflon, nothing stuck anymore. My nervous system was settling into something like equilibrium for the first time in decades. And on top of that, I had just met this fabulous guy on Match.com.

After he spent a wonderful weekend visiting me in Yakima, he had to return to Seattle for a planned event with close friends he considered family. He invited me to follow him over the mountains so I could meet them. It would only be for a couple of hours before I had to turn around and start back. I had to work the next day, and I was mentally calculating the timing. It seemed like an aggressive schedule for the day, but it was also do-able.

I really wanted to meet his friends. I was cautious about the intensity of our-immediate connection, and I believed spending time with the people closest to him would help me understand whether he truly was who he seemed to be. There's a saying: You are known by the company you keep. If these friends were like family to him, I would learn a lot by being around them.

We took off toward Ellensburg, me following behind him in my car. We hadn't gone far over Manastash Ridge when a wave of exhaustion slammed into me – so sudden and overwhelming it felt like I had been drugged...like the blood had drained straight out of my head.

I felt a sensation of complete internal collapse. I had never experienced anything like that crushing darkness, and it terrified me. My head kept dropping forward, and I had to jerk it back up again and again. I tightened my grip on the steering wheel and tried to shake it off, but the waves kept coming: heavy, suffocating, almost physical in their force.

I flashed my headlights, turned on my hazards, and tried calling my date, but nothing caught his attention. He kept driving ahead of me unaware. Somehow, I made it to Ellensburg and finally got him to pull over at a fast-food place. One look at me and he knew something was wrong. We went inside, and he got me a drink while I sat at a table with my head in my hands. I must have looked awful, because a stranger approached him to ask if I was okay.

(To that stranger: thank you for noticing me and caring enough to ask.)

We both realized there was no way I could continue to Seattle. I turned around for the thirty-minute drive home, gripping the steering wheel and forcing my eyes to stay open.

What just happened to me? Where had that sudden, crushing darkness come from?

I barely made it back to my apartment, stumbled into bed, and passed out instantly. It was just twelve o'clock.

I woke up around six that evening, hungry and groggy. There were a couple of missed calls and several texts waiting, but they would have to wait longer. I picked up a simple dinner nearby and went straight back to bed after I had eaten.

The next morning was my first day of work, and my head was still foggy. I dragged myself up, dressed, and headed out, hoping whatever this was would pass. Calling in sick during my first week wasn't an option.

After that first day at Davis High School, the exhaustion hit again. I returned a few calls, then talked with the wonderful man I'd met on Match.com. I told him more about the strange episode on Manastash Ridge, and he sounded genuinely concerned.

I ate a light dinner, took a warm bath, and crawled into bed before seven. It was still bright outside with the late-summer light lingering, so I put on a sleep mask. Once again, I fell asleep immediately and didn't wake up until my alarm the next morning.

It wasn't until I started writing my first book, **The Big Dark**, that I discovered the reason for my excessive exhaustion.

Apparently, when a person who has lived with trauma for an extended period finally becomes safe, the stress hormones, cortisol and adrenaline, drop back to normal. That reset can send the body into deep exhaustion, sometimes for weeks as it tries to repair the damage. The nervous system, after years of running on high alert, finally gets permission to rest.

I was shocked to learn this. I had survived years of emotional, psychological, mental, financial, sexual, physical, and verbal abuse. I used to congratulate myself for making it through each moment. Each moment then turned into one day and then each day turned into another. I may have believed I was "dealing" with the trauma, but my body had been keeping score the entire time.

When you are inside the abuse, you don't realize how heavy the weight is. You're too busy surviving it. It's only when you step out of it and your nervous system believes you're truly safe that your body finally tallies up the total cost. That's when your body collapses into the rest it has been denied for so long.

Do not be surprised if you find this physical phenomenon happens to you when you finally escape your abuser. Honor it. Your body is trying to heal. Rest as often and as deeply as it tells you to.

It had been two months since I escaped Mike, and my body was finally resetting. I had just met an incredible man, but I was still cautious. I needed to be. I would never allow myself or my body to walk back into that kind of abuse again.

I needed to meet his friends. I needed to meet his family. I needed to see how he handled my independence. Would he respect it? Or would he try to manipulate me like Mike had? He seemed too good to be true, and it was all happening quickly. I reminded myself to keep my eyes open before letting my heart take over.

I would have my first chance to meet some of his closest friends the following Saturday when he invited me to join him at Teatro ZinZanni, the dinner circus theater near the Seattle Center.

I had my fingers crossed that I would be able to take a step closer to finding out if this guy was as wonderful as he seemed. He had to be. After going through that scary hormonal detox, there was no way I was ever going to be caught up in another destructive relationship again.

****

I forgive myself for making myself smaller to protect their fragile ego, when I was always meant to take up space unapologetically.

@yourcourageouscom

CH. 8 — MKD

I met Mike when I was twenty and finally escaped at fifty-three. More than half my life was spent tethered to a narcissistic abuser. In those years, I let go of my own dreams and sat back while he went full speed ahead with whatever he wanted to do.

He wanted model rockets and a dirt bike, so he got them and made sure that he carved time out of his week to use them. I got the pleasure of "watching" him have fun.

He wanted to go hunting, so he got the guns and the equipment, even a reloader so he could reuse the ammunition. Skeet shooting? You bet. And lucky me got to sit and watch him.

Then came scuba diving. He took the class, bought all the equipment, and headed out on trips while I stayed home with the kids. When I pushed back, he said I could always come along and "sit on the boat while he's in the water."

Doesn't that sound like a grand time?

It boosted his ego to have "his woman" watching and cheering him on. Yes, can't you see it now...the dashing fighter pilot hero flexing his testosterone by showing off to *his* woman, who is proudly watching *her* man do mighty feats of daring and dangerous activities.

He enjoyed having the world *and me* revolve around him.

There was never room for my dreams or passions. He made sure of it by refusing to watch the kid or just keeping our bank account so low that I couldn't justify doing anything for myself anyway. If I dared to shine too brightly, he found ways to snuff it out. When I pushed back, I learned that his wrath and his intimidations were real. My ambitions shrank until all that was left was being a wife to him and a mother to the kids.

I lost decades of my life by just surviving. I spent more than thirty years in a fog of fear, confusion, and constant emotional management. But now I was free of him and his manipulative control, and I wanted to make up for lost time.

I felt a quivering urgency inside me, as if I were living on borrowed time. I felt like I needed to move quickly to make up for all the years spent being "less than." I didn't feel I had a moment to waste. I became impatient with life; hungry to experience every ounce of freedom, joy, and self-love I had been denied.

That included finding a true partner; someone to finish my life's journey with. If this man I met on Match wasn't it, I needed to know right away so I could keep moving forward. Meeting his friends that Saturday felt like a pivotal step in finding out who he really was.

Before Saturday arrived, I still had to finish my first week at Davis High School. It was mostly meetings, lesson planning, and getting my classroom ready before the students arrived the following week. I was busy getting my professional life moving forward.

But my thoughts kept drifting between preparing for the first day of school and this upcoming weekend. I had been talking with this new guy every night, and the energy between us remained so positive. But I needed proof that he wasn't another Mike wearing a mask. I was hoping that meeting his friends would give me clues about his character. I was counting on that insight.

We were going to spend the evening with one of his close friends, Oakley Carlson, and Oakley's girlfriend, Lori. Another friend, Cal, would be there with his parents. It was Cal who got the tickets and had given us two of them. We all sat front-row center of the stage. I thought it was lovely that my date's friend was treating his parents to a special night and including his friends as well. Those were the kinds of people I wanted in my life, people who valued their friends and family.

I needed a dress and shoes for the evening, but couldn't find anything in Yakima, so I headed to Seattle early on Saturday and browsed the Northgate Mall. I finally found a perfect dress at JCPenney. I had been texting with my date, and since he didn't live far from the mall, he surprised me by showing up at the store.

It felt strange, in a good way, to have a man show interest in what I was going to wear. I had spent decades with someone who barely noticed me, so this kind of personal attention was new and disarming. He explained that he wanted to see my dress so he could choose a shirt to complement it – he wanted us to match.

Wow. This was a level of consideration I had never experienced. He cared enough about the evening and about us, even in this early stage, to choose an outfit that complemented mine. The only times I had ever dressed up before were for the Marine Corps Birthday Ball and Mike wore his Dress Blues. Outside of that, he never took me anywhere special or even cared enough to compliment me on what I was wearing.

This new man made me feel seen and feel special. I could feel a glow rising in me, and at the same time I kept gently tamping it down, determined not to let excitement cloud my judgment. I wanted to stay present, keep my eyes open, and make sure his character matched his charm.

The evening was fabulous. His friends were gracious and lovely. My date was attentive and genuine. I watched the way he chatted with Cal's parents, how he treated me in their presence, and how he moved through the night without any hint of pretense. He seemed authentic in everything he did. So far, so good but I still needed more evidence.

Another piece of the puzzle fell into place the next day when he drove me around Ballard, showing me "his town." At one point he asked me to keep an eye out for a street where we needed to turn. I kept my eyes on the road looking for the street but somehow, I had missed it. As soon as I told him that we had missed the turn, I shrank into the corner of my seat, pressing toward the window, bracing for his anger.

It hit me immediately: PTSD. After years of Mike exploding over missed turns or small mistakes, my body went straight into protection mode.

But this man just said, "No biggie. Let's turn around." That was it. No irritation, no edge, no lecture.

I uncurled myself and sat there stunned, not just by his gentleness, but by how quickly my nervous system had defaulted to fear. In that moment, the contrast between the two men was blinding. If I were keeping a scorecard, this new man was way ahead in the "plus" column.

The first day of class with my students was later that week. I was summoned to the front office to find a bouquet of flowers waiting for me. This wonderful guy had sent them with a beautiful note of encouragement. I gave him another check in the box.

After I texted him a thank you for the flowers he promptly sent me a link to a song on YouTube with lyrics that made my heart smile. Check again.

He was doing an amazing job of making my heart feel special but so did Mike in the beginning, and he turned out to be a monster. I recognized these gestures as signs of "love bombing" and I intended to keep my full emotional commitment at bay.

The next weekend I went back to Ballard to spend time with him. He took me out both Friday and Saturday night, wandering up and down Main Street, slipping in and out of shops and restaurants. I was surprised by how many people he knew just walking around town.

Men and women alike lit up when they saw him, rushing in with huge hugs. I watched, amused, as he greeted his male friends with a hug and a kiss on the cheek. I'd never seen that before. What struck me even more was how naturally everyone received it, no awkwardness and no hesitation. You could tell this was simply how he moved through his community, and people genuinely liked him.

And what spoke volumes was what happened *after* each encounter. When we walked away and out of earshot of his friends. He never criticized them, never gossiped, never undercut them the way Mike always did. He only had gracious words to share about them. How beautiful it was to be with someone who shared the same soul to soul connection with others the way I did.

Every restaurant we entered, the bartender or owner, or both, came out to give him the biggest hugs and then offer us free food and drinks. I kept thinking, *Who is this guy? The mayor of Ballard?* He was being received like a beloved local celebrity. *Could he really be as wonderful as he seemed?*

We alternated weekends between Yakima and Ballard, and at every potential moment when a manipulative streak might show itself, it didn't. When I introduced him to my friends, he was genuinely interested in who they were. I watched him connect easily and authentically with everyone he met.

And what about the unfortunate – the ones that are easily overlooked? There were never any harsh words of criticism or judgement, only empathy for their situation and gratitude for his own blessings. Later, I learned he had a tradition of preparing meals and delivering them to the homeless during the holidays.

How about family? Mike used to declare how important family was, and then his actions proved the opposite. I wondered: what were this guy's true feelings toward family?

I paid close attention when we visited his sister's house. I watched him interact with her, her wife, and their friends and I watched how they interacted with him. It was obvious he wasn't a stranger to anyone there. Every person at that backyard gathering greeted him with a huge smile and a big hug, and he responded the same. There was an ease of familiarity that couldn't be faked.

He shared with me that after divorcing his daughter's mom, he chose to stay in the same neighborhood so his daughter's life wouldn't be disrupted. He and his ex lived only a few blocks apart so their daughter could move between houses easily and still stay close to her school and friends.

That showed real sensitivity towards his daughter's predicament of being caught up in the middle of a divorce. "It's not her fault her mom and I divorced," he said. "She shouldn't lose her friends or her school on top of everything else."

A few more checks in the "plus" column.

When he met my mom and stepdad, it was like he'd known them for years. His genuine smile lit up the evening. I admired how effortlessly it was for him to engage in any topic that interested my mom and stepdad. He especially bonded with my mom when they learned they both came from large families. He had an innate gift to make everyone feel better about themselves.

But when he met my dad... that was a different experience.

I had been hesitant to tell my dad I was seeing someone. He has always had my best interests at heart and wanted to protect me from connecting with another Mike. I knew dad would be concerned about me dating someone so soon. Even at fifty-three, I still felt like a little girl looking for her father's approval.

We invited my dad and my Norma over for an early September barbecue, and this beautiful man insisted on doing the cooking. He had a salmon recipe he wanted to make in honor of meeting them for the first time. I became his sous chef, peeling and chopping whatever he asked for.

I loved that simple intimacy of preparing dinner together. It might seem small, but working side by side said, *I enjoy spending time with you, and I want to share this moment with you.* I felt considered and valued and not viewed as how I could-"serve" him. We were partners.

The four of us sat on the deck enjoying the meal he had made and navigating the questions my dad had clearly prepared. My dearest took it all in stride and was so calm, gracious, and respectful of my dad because he understood the real meaning behind my dad's questions.

When Norma and I got up to clear the dishes, my dad and my dearest were left alone. I stood next to the open sliding door listening to the conversation. My dad faced me while I stood behind my dearest's back, not letting him know I was there.

My dad spoke first: "I want you to know, you seem like a nice guy and all. But the jury is still out." My dearest answered in a slow, thoughtful tone: "I want you to know that I think your daughter is pretty special." My dad leaned forward, arms on his thighs, hands clasped, looking my dearest straight in the eyes with serious intent and said very solemnly, "So do I".

Later that evening, my dearest laughed at the spectacle of it.

"Here I am, fifty-five years old, and I'm getting the talk from your dad!" he said. He thought it was beautiful, my father's fierce protection of me. Instead of being offended or defensive, he saw it for what it was: a dad guarding his daughter's heart.

I loved that he understood. He saw the love behind my dad's caution and respected him for it. From then on, he joked that my dad had tried to intimidate him and started calling him the *Don of the Yakima Mafia.*

I was further amused when we drove down to Goldendale to visit my dad and my Norma. My dearest walked right up to my dad and gave him a huge hug and a kiss on the cheek. My dad was so startled he just chuckled, unsure what to do with that level of affection. It didn't take long, though, for him to realize that my dearest truly was who he appeared to be. The two of them eventually grew to love each other deeply.

This man I found on Match.com was unlike anyone I had ever known. Every day revealed something new: another layer of kindness, depth, or sincerity. But what made me sink fully into his heart was the way he created space for my vulnerability. He let me share the darkest parts of my marriage without flinching.

There was no judgment about why I hadn't left earlier. There was no rush to try to solve my problems. He simply listened—fully, quietly—as I carefully revisited some of the worst moments of my past. And when I finished, he offered me reassurance that my days would get better and that the darkness I had endured would help me to become stronger. All that as he held me gently, stroking my arms.

I needed that. I needed him. He filled a part of me I didn't even realize I needed – that deep little affirmation bucket I had carried empty for years. With him, I finally felt safe and seen. He surprised me even more when he said, "There's a reason the Universe brought us together."

I had been feeling that too—that sense of something larger at work, a kind of perfect timing, like our lives had aligned exactly when they were meant to. But he was the one who said it out loud in a way that resonated.

Yes. The Universe brought us together. It knew that we both needed each other at this time. Everything seemed to be perfectly aligned for us.

Then he gave me a gift that only someone sensitive and reflective could offer.

He noticed that I struggled to even say Mike's name. Every time I did, it made me physically sick. I tried using "my soon-to-be-ex," but that still tied me to him in a way I didn't want. My dearest gently pointed out that I was giving too much energy to the past and suggested I refer to him simply as "My Kids' Dad"—MKD.

I liked it. When I would talk about MKD, there was no hint of marital status attached to it. I didn't have to say I was still married, or refer to him as an ex or soon-to-be-ex. He was simply *My Kids' Dad*. Neutral. Clean. Done.

And with that shift, I realized I was done with the mental scorecard I'd been keeping on this new man—measuring, tallying, checking for warning signs. I could finally wad that list up in my mind and toss it away.

My heart and soul resonated with his in a way that felt deep and undeniable. It seemed as if we had been brought together to help each other through the final, richest chapters of our lives. We were each other's reward—proof that we had survived the hard years and still had beauty left to experience.

His name may have been Saul, but I found myself calling him by something more endearing that better suited what my heart felt: *My Handsome and My Dearest.*

****

I know I sought intimate companionship quickly after escaping MKD. I also know the risks. Many survivors end up in another abusive relationship, which is why the people around you will urge you to take your time. And they're right, you should take your time. However much or however little you need.

There is no universal waiting period before dating again. That choice is as individual as the person making it.

Don't feel obligated to follow anyone's expectations. People with good intentions will offer advice, and sometimes it becomes a lot of noise. But the only voice you truly need to listen to is the one inside you. You'll know when you're ready.

When you do start looking for an intimate partner, be careful not to let their "potential" blur your judgment. Move slowly. Protect your right to a relationship built on safety and trust.

If something feels off, take it seriously. Address it directly. How a person responds to your honesty and vulnerability will tell you everything you need to know.

If they dismiss your feelings or tell you you're "making too big a deal" over something, walk away. You've already lived in a relationship where your feelings were minimized. It is not your job to teach someone how to be a partner. You tried that. It didn't work.

If they acknowledge your feelings but never change their behavior, walk away. Words are easy. Behavior is the truth.

Don't expect that you can change someone. You tried that with the abusive relationship you just left, and all it did was shrink you into someone you barely recognized.

After everything you've survived, you never again need to beg, hope, or wish for someone to become who you need. Let them **be** who they are. *Watch* who they **show** you they are. And from there, you get to decide whether their truth aligns with what you deserve.

The habit of changing yourself to make someone else more comfortable ends now.

Once you rediscover the best in yourself, once that beautiful inner flame reignites and whispers, "I love who I am" your whole aura begins to glow. And when it does, you will naturally attract people who can truly *see* and respect your gifts.

The ones who deserve you will find their way toward your light. The ones who feel threatened by your strength, the ones who try to dim you, will fall away, because you'll *refuse* to be anything other than your authentic, brilliant self.

So, take the time you need to find your light again. Let it shine brightly before you look for an intimate partner. If that takes a couple of years, then that's what it takes. If, like me, it takes only a few months, that's okay too. It's your timeline, no one else's.

Just remember: your only job is to live as authentically as you can, in ways that allow you to shine without apology. Never again let anyone make you feel like you are not enough.

You have always been enough.

****

You don't have to explain why you want what you want, do what you do, love what you love.

You are allowed to live a life some people don't understand.

Laura McKnowen

CH. 9 — Being Seen

It amazed me how quickly the world around me changed once I made it back to Yakima. The differences were immediate—the light, the air, the land itself. Yakima's dry heat and endless sunshine stretched across rolling hills, with Mt. Adams and Mt. Rainier rising like guardians through the clear blue sky. Eastern North Carolina, by contrast, was flat and heavy with humidity, the air thick with mosquitoes and sudden sheets of rain that could flood a neighborhood in minutes. Even still, its beaches and coastal towns had their own quiet beauty.

The shift wasn't only in the landscape. The voices around me lacked the soft Southern drawl I'd grown used to. License plates read "Washington" instead of "North Carolina." After racing across the country, desperate to leave my tormented life behind as quickly as I could, I hadn't paused to notice the gradual transition of terrain or time zones. Only when I arrived did the contrast hit me, how thoroughly one world had given way to another.

Being back felt like stepping into a different timeline. The sharpness of the change forced me to look up, to take in where I'd landed, and to marvel at how far I had come.

But the most unexpected shift wasn't the weather or the scenery. It was people. Strangers looked at me. Some offered compliments, struck up conversations, or simply watched me with open curiosity. That had never happened in North Carolina.

Why now?

I knew I'd changed physically. Since January, I made my health a priority. I had carved out time each day for myself and it had paid off—I'd lost twenty pounds, gained strength and tone, and felt more grounded in my own body than I had in years. But back in North Carolina, no one seemed to notice. Not even my daughter, Jillian or MKD. No one seemed to notice my change.

Their silence reminded me how unseen I had been in that life. No one saw the abuse I endured for thirty plus years. I wore a mask everywhere I went, hiding the sadness and trauma that I couldn't escape. It was rare to "see" the real me because even I didn't know who the real me was anymore.

In Yakima, the mask was gone. People saw me, really saw me—and it startled me every time. After years of invisibility, the simple act of being noticed felt like stepping into the sun again.

My dad was the first to notice something I hadn't. He squinted at me and asked, "What's that bump on your forehead?"

I had no idea what he meant until I went to the mirror. And there it was—right above my right eyebrow, a small, unmistakable bump. How had I missed it? How could I be looking at myself in the mirror every day and not see the bump above my right eye?

It wasn't long after that I scheduled a physical with Cory Slobig, an old high school friend who was now a nurse practitioner. The moment she saw me, she zeroed in on the same bump. Then she studied my face more closely and asked about my right cheek. It sat slightly fuller than the left, and when she palpated it, she felt a denser mass beneath the skin. She ordered an MRI to have both checked out.

Two people—within weeks—had seen what no one in North Carolina ever had. Not doctors, not family, not friends, and certainly not me. I thought back to all the appointments I'd sat through, all the physicals I had endured, and wondered how everyone had missed it. How invisible had I been?

And once people started noticing, it felt like everyone noticed. My Handsome Man. My mom. Even some of my students pointed it out. Suddenly the bump loomed larger in my mind than it did on my forehead.

By October 2014, I found myself at Yakima Regional Hospital for the MRI. My dad and my Norma insisted on coming with me. I didn't think it was necessary. I was used to doing everything alone. The thought of having anyone come with me was non-existent. But they came anyway – their presence was their quiet way of saying, "We've got your back." And I realized how long it had been since anyone wanted to be there for me.

When I returned to Cory to go over the MRI results, she explained that the mass in my cheek was a cavernous hemangioma and the bump above my eye was a lipoma. She referred me to a specialist at Children's Hospital in Seattle for the hemangioma and to an ENT in Yakima, Dr. Gross, for the lipoma.

I won't deny it—I was spooked. I had been running and working out for months without a second thought, and now I seem to be hyper aware of the increased blood flow under my cheek after I worked out. It was as if my heartbeat announced itself through my cheek, reminding me I needed to be cautious.

Maybe it was all in my head, but it freaked me out enough that I eased up on my workouts until I could see the specialist in Seattle.

At Children's Hospital, I felt a bit out of place. Hemangiomas are usually discovered at birth, most of them external, so the waiting room was filled with children and their parents. I was the lone adult patient that day, an odd fixture among bright colors and tiny chairs.

The specialist reviewed my MRI and pointed to the mass beneath my right cheek. On the screen, it was unmistakable, a tangled cluster of blood vessels. He explained that I'd been born with it. Because it was buried under tissue, it had gone unnoticed for decades. His recommendation was simple: no surgery. The risk of damaging facial nerves—and causing permanent paralysis—was too great. The only precaution I needed was to alert dentists before any tooth extraction on that side since the blood flow could make things complicated.

Noted.

I snapped pictures of the MRI images, knowing I would need them on hand for any future medical inquiries.

After Seattle, I met with Dr. Gross in Yakima to evaluate the lipoma over my eyebrow. He recommended removal, and in a quick outpatient procedure, he excised the fatty mass. I was so fascinated by its size that I took a picture next to a penny for scale. Between that and the hemangioma images, I now had a small gallery of my own internal oddities stored neatly in my phone. I have surprisingly needed them more often than I would have imagined.

As it was, the removal of the lipoma over my right eyebrow also involved some facial nerves. The result was that my eyebrow seemed to droop. Dr. Gross reassured me that nerve regeneration takes time and I needed patience.

And so, I had no choice but to be.

In addition to referring me for the hemangioma and lipoma, Cory noticed something else: my nasal tissue was swollen. She asked if I'd ever been tested for respiratory allergies.

I hadn't.

I told her I'd complained for years about chronic congestion. My doctors in North Carolina had shrugged it off and suggested a Neti Pot. No one ever recommended an allergy test.

So back I went to Dr. Gross—this time for allergy testing. They pricked both of my arms with a full panel of allergens, and the results were almost comical. I was allergic to everything they tested me for: dust mites, mold, grass pollen, tree pollen, cat and dog dander. Everything.

We started weekly allergy shots immediately—one in each leg.

I thought about all the mornings I couldn't smell the coffee brewing, all the times I'd mentioned it to my doctors, only to be dismissed. Now, back in Yakima, people were actually advocating for me, taking my concerns seriously, and treating the issues instead of brushing them aside.

So, here I am, fifty-three years old, starting a new life on the other side of the US and I feel like I am finally being seen; like the world finally took notice of me.

And it wasn't just the physical observations that people took notice of.

After I made intuitive assessments of some sports situation that my Handsome and I were watching, he would take note and publicly praise me for my insights. Instead of being jealous of my talents, he would lift them up and encourage me to continue. He never saw me as competition for his ego. Quite the opposite. My Dearest seemed quite proud to have me by his side spouting sports wisdom.

In just a few months back in Yakima, more health issues were identified and addressed than in all the years I lived in North Carolina. More than that, I had people around me who genuinely valued my voice.

It felt empowering—strange at first, but deeply healing: to be heard, to be noticed, to matter. I hadn't felt that in a very long time.

It truly felt as if I'd stepped into another world and another timeline.

My thoughts drifted often between my old life in North Carolina and my new one in Washington. The contrasts were sharp: the landscape, the people, and the way I existed within each place. The "old" self I had buried for so long was beginning to surface again, and simply being *seen* made me feel more whole than I had in more than thirty years.

I started paying attention to how good it felt when others acknowledged me, and I was determined to offer that same simple kindness to the people around me. I started making an intentional effort to greet people that I passed on my morning runs or walks. I would offer a quick smile and a gracious thank you to the cashiers and anyone I met.

I'd always taken pride in noticing the small things in others: their efforts, their growth, their quiet wins. Maybe because

I knew what it meant to be overlooked by the very person who was supposed to stand by me. Still, I wanted to be sure that I acknowledged those around me.

Now, as I settled into my new life, I found myself thinking about my friends and colleagues I'd left behind in North Carolina. My departure had been sudden and, for them, heartbreaking. I had fled believing that if MKD discovered my plan, I could be in real danger. Leaving the way I did was necessary for my safety, but I also knew it left my friends and colleagues in a state of emotional shock.

It became clear I had unfinished business from my most recent past.

I needed to offer them closure and to say goodbye in a way I couldn't when I left. So, I wrote a letter. It was generic by necessity, hinting only lightly at why I had to disappear so abruptly. MKD still lived there, and I didn't want my words to define his story or reveal details of the abuse I'd endured. Instead, I thanked them for their friendship, their support, and their impact on my life. I also included how much it meant for me to be back home with my family again.

It wasn't everything, but it was honest. And it was enough to close that chapter with grace.

I made copies of the letter for nearly everyone at Havelock High School and sent them all in one large manila envelope for the office staff to distribute. I mailed a few additional copies to friends in the area and included my new phone number and email address.

It was the best I could do for them. They deserved a final word from me, and I hoped that it helped them gently close that part of their life with mine.

Sending those letters helped me as well. It clipped one of the remaining cords tying me to North Carolina and eased some of the guilt I carried for leaving so abruptly.

The contrast between feeling unseen in NC and being seen in Yakima couldn't have been more striking. I hadn't realized how much my energy would rise once I felt worthy of recognition. That simple shift, being acknowledged as *me*, made me understand how important it was to extend that same acknowledgment to my friends in North Carolina.

Writing those letters gave me a chance to do just that. It allowed me to tell my friends and colleagues that I appreciated them, that they mattered, that I saw the goodness they brought into my life, even if I could no longer remain in theirs.

You will find that leaving trauma often requires leaving behind the entire ecosystem that enabled it; not only the pain but also the people who had no hand in causing it. Moving forward can make it easy to overlook the innocent hearts you leave in your wake. But just because someone hurts you doesn't mean you must hurt others as you go. Sometimes pain is unavoidable, but you must be careful that you don't trample the hearts of others.

When you finally catch a breath on the other side of the trauma and you have the emotional depth to reach back and offer closure to those who were genuinely affected by your departure, then it becomes an act of love for those left behind. It becomes a small gift; a way of honoring the goodness that they were in your life.

And even then, it may still be the most beneficial for your healing to leave them gently in your past and carry forward only their fond memories. And that's okay.

People come into our lives for many reasons. Some are only here for a short time to help us with our journey and we with theirs. When it's time to part ways, let them go with gratitude. Acknowledge their significance, thank them for their part in your story, and then let them continue their own path as you move forward on yours.

I'm reminded of the gentleman sitting on the bench outside Jack's workplace the day I walked past, nervous to see Jack for the first time in more than thirty years. He didn't have to say a single word to me, yet he offered a kind one anyway and, at that moment, it made all the difference. His simple affirmation gave me confidence right when I needed it.

That is a perfect example of someone who steps briefly into your life to nudge you forward. Just a few seconds of kindness, and he fulfilled his quiet purpose: to remind someone that they mattered simply by being in the world.

As people come and go in your life and as you drift in and out of others, be mindful of your impact, whether it's for good or for harm. Notice the gifts they offer, and don't be stingy about giving your own.

Kindness doesn't need to be grand. It can be as simple as offering help to someone who is struggling with their groceries or rolling your neighbor's garbage cans to the curb when they can't. Be sensitive to the pain behind someone's smile and offer a hug without demanding an explanation. Even a warm hello in a grocery aisle can shift a person's energy for the day.

These tiny gestures—these moments of truly "seeing" someone are powerful reminders that none of us are alone, and that for at least one minute, someone cared enough to notice.

Imagine what our world would look like if we all tried to recognize each other's needs before they were spoken.

Feeling the impact of being seen when I returned to Yakima opened my eyes to how essential these small acts are for all of us. What I eventually learned is this: being seen by others isn't the real goal. We can't control who notices us or how deeply they look.

The true turning point, the real sign of healing, is when you begin to see others. When you look beyond your own wounds and become aware of the souls you touch, even while you're still mending yours. That's when you know you're growing and healing.

Whatever you do, let your impact be for the better. Then watch how you move closer towards your own healing as you seek a more peaceful and centered life.

****

There is a stranger out there who still thinks of you because you were kind to them when they really needed it.

Never stop being that person.

Mr. Charles Bell

CH. 10 — Making Up for Lost Time

It's common for survivors of domestic abuse to feel a deep sense of mourning once we finally break free from the emotional and psychological control of our abusers. We grieve the years spent hoping they would change. We grieve the life we might have had if we hadn't been caught in their web of charm and manipulation. And we grieve the parts of ourselves we lost while holding up their fragile egos just to keep the peace.

When we, the 25% who escape and live to tell the story, try to rebuild, we often feel an urgency to reclaim everything we missed. We don't want to waste a single moment on people who might drain our energy again. We try to avoid detours, wanting to fast-forward straight into the good things we were denied, to soak ourselves in every experience we were starved of.

I had completely lost myself in my relationship with MKD. Thirty years of trying to please him had left me emotionally hollow, treading water in a life that revolved entirely around his needs. My world had become very small.

But back in Yakima, living on my own, that urgency surged through me. I wanted to experience everything I had postponed.

My income was only about 40% of what MKD earned, yet I didn't feel deprived. In fact, it felt like abundance because every dollar was finally mine. A few months earlier I'd been scrambling to plug every financial hole he created. Now that I controlled my own money, I began making up for lost time.

One of the first things I did was buy myself new bras: everyday ones, sports bras, even strapless ones for the warm Yakima summer. Then came new panties and sports socks. I couldn't remember the last time I'd brought home a haul just for me. And I didn't stop there.

I treated myself to earrings and necklaces, finding unique handmade pieces at the Yakima Farmer's Market while picking up fresh fruit and homemade soaps. I made several trips to JCPenney and Macy's, refreshing my work wardrobe with fun, colorful pieces. I even splurged on running shorts and tops on sale, because for once, I felt I was worth it.

Music had always been another part of myself that went quiet during my marriage. I'd been stuck listening to whatever MKD preferred. Now, with my own stereo system and the freedom to choose, I bought CDs I loved and filled the turntable, listening to album after album of music that felt like *me* again.

These purchases weren't frivolous. They were acts of reclamation, small but powerful ways of saying: I belong to myself now.

I began cooking the meals I wanted to eat, even splurging on fancy cheeses and nicer cuts of meat. My little propane grill became my go-to for cooking and I used it for nine months of the year. It was easy to step onto my deck, fire it up, and make dinner without heating up my tiny apartment in the summer.

Whenever friends called, I said yes to everything.

"Drinks and trivia night?" Absolutely.
"Pool Day in the sun?" I'm already grabbing my towel.
"Music in the park at Franklin Park on Friday? Picnic basket and a cool breeze?" Tell me what to bring and what time to show up.

I'd even jump in my car and drive to Prosser just to watch my dad and Norma's great-grandson play T-ball. There was no one to guilt me for choosing myself or for being impulsive. After missing so many years of family moments, I wanted to make up for all of them. It felt like a luxury simply to live close enough to say, "I'll be right there."

I rode my bike whenever the urge hit: pedaling all over Yakima, stopping for ice cream, grabbing a coffee, or wandering through Inklings Bookshop on 56th. When my Dearest visited from Ballard, we'd hit the Zillah wineries or drive down to the casino in Toppenish for fun.

My mom treated me to a pedicure shortly after I returned. I had always told myself it was a waste of money, something I didn't deserve. But once I realized how the dark years of my past had convinced me that I wasn't worth it, I was now committed to getting one every couple of weeks. You know why? Because I finally understood I *was* worth it.

I even bought a season pass to White Pass, determined to learn how to ski. I bought the pants and jacket with every intention of taking lessons, but the snowfall that year was thin and the slopes barely opened. Good intentions but it ended up being a dead-end proposition.

I dipped my toes into anything that piqued my interest. Each new experience, big or small, helped me relearn myself.

Through all that experimenting, I began to understand my own preferences, my own desires; the simple truth of what I enjoyed and what I didn't.

Piece by piece, I was rediscovering who I was.

I realized quickly that I didn't enjoy casinos. I had no interest in gambling, the cigarette smoke made me nauseous, and the whole atmosphere felt strangely lonely. People were sitting side by side, but each was lost in their own isolated bubble, absorbed in the machines, without any real connection to anyone around them.

I discovered that quality time mattered deeply to me; that I needed the reciprocal focused attention from whoever I was with. That's what filled my affirmation bucket, and a casino wasn't going to give me that.

That's why evenings at Franklin Park meant so much. Sitting on a blanket in the summer, listening to music with a friend or with my Dearest, I could feel that one-on-one connection I craved. It fed a part of me I hadn't realized was starving.

I also learned how restorative my quiet time was, running through the Barge-Chestnut area, riding my bike wherever I pleased. Those simple routines calmed my nervous system and helped me return to a healthy center.

And I rediscovered how much I loved music and dancing. In my apartment, no one mocked me for breaking into song or moving however my body wanted to. I discovered that I loved to share that joy with someone who appreciated my spontaneity.

I learned it was perfectly okay to "splurge" on a ten-dollar pair of earrings that made me smile when I looked in the mirror. I considered that money well spent, and I deserved it.

I was moving fast; exploring and reaching in every direction to fill the holes I carried from my former life. One of those holes remaining was something that had created a lot of pain for me in the past. It was the fact that I had never experienced an orgasm during my entire relationship with MKD.

That part of my past was steeped in humiliation. MKD routinely shamed me for not climaxing and dismissed any suggestion I offered about what I needed. Every sexual encounter centered entirely on him, and I was expected to somehow reach climax at the same time he did, as if women's bodies worked on command. It doesn't work that way. Women don't work that way.

It takes more intention for women to climax than it does for men. A partner has to care enough to put in the effort, real effort, to help you get there. But MKD had no interest in pleasing me. As a covert narcissist, pleasing everyone else for the sake of coming across as some "wonderful guy", is easy for them to do. They get a benefit from public adulation that fills their weak ego. They do it to fill their ego rather than a genuine desire to help someone.

But pleasing the person who is closest to him...that would be a hard no. Especially if that person knows the truth behind his mask.

With me, everything was one sided. I was expected to meet his needs at every turn, every day. If I fell short of his expectations in even the smallest way, he unleashed his wrath through emotional and psychological attacks designed to make me feel less-than and, ultimately, more obedient.

Sex was no different. He wanted everything from me: submission, passion, praise. I was expected to tell him how incredible he was, even if he'd just finished tearing me down over some imagined slight. Every encounter felt like a performance with impossible standards. I never seemed to get it "right." He even accused me of "just servicing" him, as if he wasn't the one who insisted sex be entirely about him.

The result was thirty-three years of sexual intimacy laced with shame, guilt, and humiliation.

But once I left him and began building a new life, I felt an urgency to reclaim what had been taken from me. Experiencing an orgasm again became more than a physical goal, it was about reclaiming dignity for myself.

MKD had worked hard to convince me something was wrong with me. He mocked me to his pilot buddies, then came home insisting I was the problem. But I always knew the truth: he never created a safe, loving space where vulnerability or honest conversation could exist.

Still, knowing I wasn't to blame didn't erase the reality that the last orgasm I'd had was with Jack, in 1981.

There's a real stigma around women masturbating. For generations, we've been conditioned to believe that giving ourselves pleasure is sinful, shameful, or the domain of promiscuous women. We're told we should be satisfied by our partners, and our partners alone.

But here's the problem: many men don't know how to help a woman climax, and their egos are too fragile to ask what she needs. So, women often forego pleasure altogether, while men experience it every single time.

Not fair.

Acknowledging that imbalance was the first step in reclaiming my own body and my own pleasure. It was time to rewrite a story that had been written for me for far too long.

I started searching online for information about female masturbation and ended up browsing sites like Adam & Eve. I was amazed, almost amused, by the sheer variety of devices available. I had no idea where to begin, but I ordered a couple of things to try.

The companies were discreet when they shipped my order: a plain box, no labels, no return address. It struck me how much secrecy still surrounds something as simple as self-pleasure.

It had been a long time since I'd experienced an orgasm, and I felt strangely nervous rediscovering it at fifty-three. Even in the privacy of my apartment, I was still anxious about this new experience.

It took me several times to figure out how to hit the right spot. When I finally did, the sensation was so intense I had to back off several times. I knew I was close to climaxing, but the overwhelming rush made it hard to stay with the feeling long enough to cross over.

I kept experimenting adjusting the settings, shifting angles, trying to stay patient with myself. Eventually, I called my Handsome Man.

One of the things I cherish most about him is his ability to set his ego aside. From the beginning, he insisted that nothing in our relationship was off-limits, and he proved it repeatedly by offering a space where hard conversations felt safe. Now I was testing that safety in a very real way by discussing something that may challenge his masculine ego with me exploring my own sexuality.

He listened without a hint of discomfort and offered thoughtful guidance. He told me not to fixate on climaxing each time. He reminded me that just the process of exploring myself was a huge step and I should just relax and enjoy the moment.

He also suggested that when the sensation was too intense that I simply lower the intensity by one click and enjoy that level of sensation for as long as I could. He explained that, for him, a sense of calm eventually softens the intensity right before climax and encouraged me to watch for that same shift in myself.

I was sincerely worried before that conversation that he might see my masturbating as a kind of "cheating." Part of me feared he'd feel threatened or assumed that pleasuring me should be his responsibility alone. Instead, he listened with such openness and steadiness that I felt lucky all over again to be with a man who didn't let ego rule the room.

The next few times I tried, I followed his advice. When the sensation became too intense, I eased the power back and simply stayed with whatever felt good. Eventually, my body responded on its own, my muscles tightening, that odd mix of calm and heightened sensitivity rising exactly the way he described and then it happened.

The moment the orgasm hit, I recognized the feeling instantly, even though it had been more than thirty years. I had this silly feeling come over me that I had just proved to myself that I wasn't broken. That all those years without a climax weren't because I couldn't, but because the right parts had never been activated … AND … because I was programmed to believe that a woman who wasn't a slut or a prostitute, shouldn't do that to herself.

As I kept learning, I discovered the truth – masturbation isn't shameful; it's healthy. It relieves tension and stress and, if completed right before bed, it helps with sleep. I also read that it can also strengthen the pelvic floor muscles, boost your mood and ease anxiety.

I know this topic might still be uncomfortable for some of you because of the social and gender programming we grew up with. But exploring my own body was profoundly empowering. It let me reclaim a part of myself that MKD tried to convince me was deficient.

It lifted my self-esteem and sexual confidence. And it made me see just how much nonsense we're fed about female pleasure. We're told men are supposed to "bring us" to orgasm, as if our bodies are puzzles meant only for them to solve. But the truth is, for most women, climax isn't simple – even when we're doing it ourselves. If many of us struggle to reach orgasm with our own hands, how can we expect a partner to magically figure it out?

It's an impossible setup for everyone.

And honestly, why should we wait for a man or any romantic partner, to unlock that part of us?

The idea that a woman should put her own body, her own pleasure, her own sexuality in the back seat until someone else gives her permission to claim it is demeaning to women. My sexuality belongs to me and discovering that changed everything.

Most of us were raised with archaic beliefs that told us not to talk about this topic at all. I certainly never discussed it with my daughters. I didn't know how. I had no model, no language, and no permission. The subject had been so deeply ingrained as taboo that even mentioning it among close friends felt unthinkable.

I debated whether to include this in my book. But the scars I carried from years with a covert narcissist, the humiliation he directed at me for not having orgasms, gave me the courage to say, *this is my body, and I have the right to do with it what I choose.* If that means I pleasure myself, regularly and without apology, then so be it.

I had felt that extraordinary sensation over thirty years ago. I knew exactly what I'd been missing. And I knew I deserved to experience it again. After losing so much of myself with MKD, reclaiming this part of my body and my pleasure rose to the top of my list.

I'll tell you this: I will never again rely on a partner to bring me to climax. If he does, great. But expecting someone else to take full responsibility for something many women struggle to achieve even on their own is unfair to them and unfair to us. Why wait for someone else to do for me what I am fully capable of doing myself?

Healing from abuse means you eventually reclaim every part of who you are. That includes your sexuality, your autonomy, and the quiet voice that once whispered you didn't deserve it.

Knock that nonsense out of your head right now.

You *do* deserve pleasure. It is *not* sinful. It is *not* wrong. It is *your* body, and the choice is *yours.* Always.

If you've been waiting for a partner to bring you to climax or if you have been waiting for permission to stop waiting, then here it is - I am giving you that permission.

There is **no one** on this earth more important to you than you. Don't *ever* let anyone make you feel less than, not even yourself.

Pull your power back into your yourself and own it.

You *are* beautiful. You *are* magnificent. You *are* powerful.

You *are* allowed to do extraordinary things in this life if you choose to. You *are* meant to experience all the beauty in this life. You know why?

Simply because - **YOU** deserve it.

****

Healing isn't about fixing what's broken. It's about transferring authority from the outside world back to your inner universe.

Your heart, your truth, your perspectives: they hold galaxies.

When we heal, we reclaim the pen. We stop letting the world write our story.   We become the author, the alchemist, the sovereign

@quantumlivinglifestyle

CH. 11 — Divorce and Other Annoyances

The primary goal for any victim of domestic abuse is simple and urgent: get somewhere safe, somewhere the abuser cannot reach you or your children. Seventy-five percent of victims who finally escape are still killed by their abuser. Getting somewhere safe is the first and primary goal of any victim.

Once safety is secured, everything else can begin to fall into place. For many married victims, that eventually includes filing for divorce. For me, it was important to start the process before I left.

I had researched how long it would take to get divorced in North Carolina versus Washington State and was stunned by the difference. Washington required only a ninety-day minimum wait after filing. North Carolina required one full year. Since we had married in Washington, I hoped I could file there and move quickly. But when I spoke with a lawyer in Yakima, I was advised to file in North Carolina because attorneys there were more familiar with military divorces. I didn't like it, but I understood. So, I filed in NC, even though every part of me wanted that marriage legally over as soon as possible.

My lawyer in New Bern arranged to serve MKD the divorce papers on the same day I planned to leave. We coordinated down to the hour because I only had a three-day window where escape felt possible. When the date and time were set, I let the office know. That is how the moment of serving papers timed with the moment of my departure came to be.

Now I was back home in Yakima, starting a new life and finally out of his physical reach. I had accomplished two goals at once: getting to a safe place and initiating the divorce.

After I left, MKD continued trying to contact me, flooding my phone with texts. At times I snapped back, exhausted by his rants, but mostly I just wanted him to leave me alone.

I never regretted leaving, not for a second. There were no remnants of nostalgia. I had no happy times. It was all a lie, and it was all dark. Eventually, I blocked him for several months and gifted my soul peace.

I eventually had to lift the block on his number because we were in the middle of selling both the condo in Wilmington and the house outside of Havelock. I had no choice but to communicate with him about the properties.

I was driving home from visiting my Handsome in Ballard, crossing Snoqualmie Pass, when I texted MKD to let him know I had unblocked him. By the time I pulled into my apartment in Yakima, there were more than fifty messages waiting. Fifty. Are you kidding me?

Most of them were meaningless, forced chatter meant to lure me into friendly banter. I could only imagine how many more I would've endured if I hadn't blocked him for those months. I hated every text. Each one was another attempt at control, another reminder that the cord between my old life and my new one wasn't fully severed yet. And with a mandatory year-long wait before the divorce could even begin, I knew that cord wasn't going anywhere for a while.

At around that same time, I learned in my first weeks teaching science at Davis High School that the district wouldn't accept all of my credentials from North Carolina. The news hit hard because it dramatically altered my income. I had expected a twenty-thousand-dollar raise since North Carolina teachers are notoriously underpaid. Instead, I took a five-thousand-dollar pay cut. A net loss of twenty-five thousand dollars.

Here I was, with twelve years of experience, completed my National Boards for Biology, and serving as a clinical teacher for East Carolina University where I trained student teachers to teach, being paid the same as a first-year teacher. When I asked how I could make up the lost income, I was told I could return to school for a master's degree. It would take three years of coursework, thousands of dollars, and then another three years before I'd break even.

I was fifty-three. Six more years would put me close to sixty, and retirement wasn't far beyond that. I needed to maximize my earning power in the years I had left. It was painfully clear that teaching in Washington State wasn't going to make that possible.

I realized this would be my first and only year teaching science in Yakima—and in Washington State. I would honor my contract through the school year, but after that, I knew I'd return to dental hygiene until I could retire.

I hadn't planned for this curve in the road. It disappointed me because I genuinely loved teaching. But when I saw the numbers, reality snapped into focus: working only two days a week as a dental hygienist would earn me the same income I made from teaching full-time. I even discovered that a dental assistant, someone who can be trained entirely on the job without years of education, earned the same salary I was making at Davis High School.

That, my dear friends, is an absolute shame.

And let me add this: I know what is required each year to renew both teaching certificates and medical or dental licenses. Teachers have it infinitely harder. They juggle portfolio reviews, continuing education, and detailed lesson plans, with most of that work happening after hours. Meanwhile, in the medical and dental fields, we sit through a few hours of seminars and walk away with the credits we need.

I have immense respect for teachers. They pour themselves into their classrooms, often unpaid, preparing for the next day.

Have you ever had to give a five- or ten-minute presentation to a group? Think about this: more than seventy-five percent of people fear speaking in front of a group, let alone doing it for only five to ten minutes. How long did it take you to get ready for that five-to-ten-minute presentation?

Now consider this. Teachers deliver forty-five to fifty-five-minute presentations every day, up to six times a day. Imagine the time, energy, and emotional labor it takes to prepare that much content—and then imagine doing it endlessly. If anyone ever claims teachers "have it easy," ask them to sit with that reality for a while.

So, besides having to navigate my divorce for the entire year, I was now facing a career change I never expected. I started searching online for dental hygiene positions in the area just to see what the market was like only to find that there were only a handful available, and most were part-time.

While I was still teaching at Davis High School, I began scheduling "working interviews" with dentists in the area. I used my sick days to do it, days I wouldn't be able to cash out at the end of the school year, so I put them to use. I drove to Ellensburg and Zillah, spending full days in each dental office. It had been nearly twenty years since I last worked as a hygienist, but my skills returned quickly. The interviews went well, but the locations were too far and none of them were full-time.

I had been talking with my Handsome about what it meant for me to return to Yakima after so many years away. My Dearest understood how deeply I needed to stay close to home. He never tried to pull me toward Seattle. Instead, he told me he'd be willing to move from Ballard to Yakima so I could remain near my family. His support was genuine and authentic. He even helped me craft a new résumé and search for full-time positions in town.

I drove around Yakima, dropping off those résumés my Dearest helped me with at every dental office I could find. Most weren't open, so I slipped manila envelope into their mailboxes and hoped for the best.

No one responded. Not a single call, not even a courtesy email.

I was crushed. I'd hoped the transition back into dental hygiene would be smooth and easy. But that wasn't my path. My Dearest, still encouraging me to stay where I felt rooted, offered me a safety net: I could move in with him, work in Seattle, where opportunities were plentiful and continue watching for a full-time opening in Yakima. I wasn't ready to give up on my search just yet, but it comforted me to know I had options.

And through all of this, with the job hunt and the long days teaching, I was still navigating my divorce. Even in the happiness of my new life, I had to carve out time and energy to keep that process moving.

Before I left North Carolina, I made sure I was prepared. After securing a lawyer, I quietly gathered every folder related to our investment accounts and spent hours after school making copies. Then I slipped the originals back into the filing cabinet exactly as I had found them. MKD never noticed a thing.

I am so grateful I made those copies. During the disclosure of our marital assets, MKD conveniently "forgot" to list one of our major investment accounts worth over $150,000. Because I had kept a copy, I caught it immediately and alerted my lawyer. She nudged the other side, and suddenly the account appeared for proper distribution.

If I hadn't made those copies, I would have had no idea that money was missing.

My advice to anyone living in a toxic marriage is this: make sure you have copies of every marital asset in your possession. Especially if your relationship is volatile or abusive and you might need to leave suddenly, with nothing but the clothes on your back.

Have copies of these assets, with account numbers, passwords, and bank information placed somewhere outside of your physical residence. Perhaps at a trusted friend's house, with a family member, or even in your workspace. You can take photos and email them to yourself where your abuser has no access to your account.

You should already have a good idea if you are in a toxic relationship. You feel it in the way you walk on eggshells, constantly monitoring your words and actions to avoid triggering your abuser. Even if the toxic person is a family member, you still know who poses a threat to your peace and safety.

If you are lucky enough to not be in an abusive situation, it's still wise to keep secure copies of important documents and passwords for emergencies, fires, or natural disasters. Preparation is not paranoia, it's protection.

I could have lost a significant amount of money if I hadn't been proactive. MKD claimed the omission was an honest mistake. Maybe it was. Mistakes happen. But preparing for the worst and hoping for the best can keep those "mistakes" from derailing your future.

Eventually, the year-long wait passed, and it was time for divorce mediation. My dad and my Norma wanted to support me, so they drove up from Goldendale and waited quietly in my apartment while I connected with my lawyer via Skype.

The setup was simple: my lawyer sat in a room at the courthouse in New Bern, North Carolina, and met with me online while MKD and his lawyer occupied an adjacent room at the courthouse. A mediator moved between the two rooms, discussing the merits of our case and trying to help both parties come up with a satisfactory resolution.

I had always maintained that I deserved half of everything. I had invested more than thirty years in that marriage, putting my career on hold, raising our children, tending to the home while he was deployed. I had earned my half.

MKD disagreed. He claimed I had "abandoned" him and that I deserved significantly less.

Mediation dragged on for hours. The mediator spoke with me over Skype, then walked next door to speak with MKD, each round of back-and-forth stretching longer than the last. I held myself together until the mediator asked me to detail the abuse.

That part was brutal. The emotional scars were still close to the surface, and I fought to keep my composure. What follows isn't a word-for-word transcript, but it captures the essence of what I relived that day.

I began with November 1994, right after Hurricane Gordon. MKD chased me up the stairs and yanked me down by my ankles, sending me face-first onto the steps. Then he took his gun from the cabinet, loaded it, and threatened to use it, on the dog and himself.

The mediator asked, "Is that when you decided to file for divorce?"

"No," I said. "There's more."

I described how he later accused me of having an incestuous relationship with our own son.

"Ah," the mediator said, confident this was the breaking point. "So that's when you decided to file for divorce?"

"No," I repeated. "There's more."

I told him how MKD threatened to leave me and the kids countless times and take all the money with him.

The mediator tried again, more hesitant now. "Was that when you decided to file for divorce?"

"No," I said. "There's more."

I relayed the second time he pointed a loaded gun at me, how I stood there for over an hour with my hands on the barrel, trying to convince him to put it down.

The mediator's voice softened. "So... this is when you decided to file for divorce?"

"There's more."

In the middle of spilling everything to the mediator, reliving each gut-wrenching memory, I suddenly understood something: any one of those traumatic events would have been enough reason to leave.

And yet I stayed.

A part of me held myself in contempt for putting up with so much more than any logical, sound-minded person would have. In that moment, I felt shame. I started feeling guilty for not leaving sooner and blamed myself. No reasonable person would ever tolerate the extent and duration of abuse that I went through. In an instant, I felt so disgusted with myself.

But I had to remember, years of ongoing abuse had chemically rewired my brain. Trauma conditions a person to survive, not to see clearly. I could not hold myself responsible for what he did to me.

What I did gain, strangely, was validation from the mediator. Each time he asked, "So that's when you decided to leave?" it confirmed what I had spent decades minimizing: each event, on its own, was abhorrent.

Then I revealed the last betrayal, the one I had hoped I wouldn't have to mention.

I told the mediator about MKD's cross-dressing.

The mediator's jaw dropped. He sat there for a long moment, his mouth slightly open, taking it in. Then, in a careful, quiet voice, he asked, "Is it okay if I share this with him?"

Of course, he could. It wasn't a secret between MKD and me. But up to that point, only four people knew: my lawyer, my dad, my Norma, and now the mediator. I hadn't even told my Handsome Man.

It was a shameful part of my marriage, and I viewed it as one of the greatest betrayals by him.

This wasn't about cross-dressing itself; people express themselves in different ways. What made it a betrayal was the deception. MKD never gave me the choice to decide whether that would be part of our life together. He hid it from me before marriage, knowing full well that I would have reconsidered our engagement. The vows we made had been built on a lie.

And he knew it.

And the moment I discovered what he had concealed, the abuse escalated. The secrecy, the rage, the control; it all intensified. He weaponized the truth he had hidden from me.

Of course, I would have backed out. I had the right to make that choice.

As I have said before in my first book, **The Big Dark**, everyone has the right to do whatever they want behind closed doors. If that makes him happy and whole, then he should do it. But not at the expense of someone else's happiness. I had paid the price for his betrayal for decades and I deserved to get at least half of everything in our marriage.

The mediator went directly to the other room to relay what I had just divulged. This time, he came back quickly. He told me that MKD was now willing to settle.

Of course, he was.

At that point, he had nothing to use against me: nothing to leverage, nothing to intimidate me with. Nothing.

The offer was simple: I would receive half of everything, plus...

The "plus" will remain private, but remember, initially, he didn't even want to give me half. Now he was offering me half *and* more. He was clearly afraid I would tell all.

But there was one condition: I could not disclose his cross-dressing. He feared it would affect future employment opportunities.

That was fine with me. I hadn't told anyone in all those years, not family, not friends, not even my Handsome Man. Shame had kept me silent for decades. Keeping one more secret wasn't difficult. It was simply one more piece of my former life that I hid away.

You might wonder why I'm sharing this now, when the mediation required silence. The truth is, I kept that secret for years, long after the divorce. But MKD has since disclosed this part of his life openly to friends, to family, and has even gone full drag walking the malls.

He no longer hides it. If he was concerned about employment security, he would have remained more inconspicuous. In addition, I have used pseudonyms for him and the kids. So, no. I'm not concerned about any legal repercussions.

Mediation ended with an agreement on both sides, but I still had to wait until the end of September 2015 for the divorce to become final. The hardest part was behind me; all that remained was the court date and the judge's signature.

One of the first things I did was legally change my name back to Telford. MKD was furious. He considered it the ultimate insult. But reclaiming my name felt like reclaiming myself.

I didn't care what he thought.

He always made everything about him. He never had consideration for me. There was absolutely no way I would keep his last name. It was just another reminder of the disgusting lie that was our marriage. And besides, everyone in Yakima knew me as "Telford."

Letting his name go felt like shedding a skin that had grown too tight and too toxic to keep.

But the divorce uncovered one last, bitter surprise.

I had been married to MKD for his entire military career. When he retired at twenty years, I assumed, like any spouse would, that I qualified for continued military benefits: medical, dental, and base privileges. What I didn't realize was that I was married to him for one week less than his official twenty years of service. One week.

He had taken his oath and commission seven days before our wedding. His twenty-year mark came and went, and although he retired with full benefits, I fell just short of eligibility because of a date on a calendar. I didn't learn this until after the divorce was finalized, when I sat down to fill out the paperwork to extend my benefits and the clerk politely told me I didn't qualify.

One week.

If he had retired just one week later, everything would have been different. My fate had been sealed back in 2003, and I had never known.

For a moment, I felt cheated. Another insult added to the long list I'd endured in that marriage. It was as if he and the military were giving me one last, well-timed middle finger. But the anger evaporated just as quickly. I was free. I had my name back, and with it, the last tether to that life snapped clean. I refused to let his shadow darken my new, sacred space.

The final irritation of 2015 was more mundane: I still couldn't find a full-time hygiene position in Yakima. After months of trying, I moved to Ballard that summer to live with my Dearest while keeping my Yakima apartment. We agreed to share the expenses for both places while I kept looking for a full-time job opportunity in Yakima.

Finding work in Seattle was easy. I landed a full-time position with Dr. Jeanie Lee in the Medical-Dental Building downtown, right off 5th and Pine. Still, every day I checked the listings in Yakima, hoping something would open up. Nothing did.

Then, in December 2015, another curveball: my Dearest's landlord announced he was selling the house we were renting. Suddenly we were hunting for a new place in the middle of the holidays.

It seemed like my transition back to Washington from North Carolina still wasn't finished. Life was still rearranging itself around me, piece by piece, asking me to follow along.

I had settled into an apartment in Yakima and started teaching science at Davis High School, only to discover that the district's credentialing limits meant I couldn't stay. So, I packed up again and moved to Ballard to live temporarily with my Dearest, taking a dental hygiene job in downtown Seattle, just in time to learn we would have to move once more.

This next move nudged my path farther off course than I'd expected. But that's how life works sometimes. You have a plan, but then the Universe comes along and hands you a different plan.

Still, I knew one thing with absolute certainty: whatever direction I was headed, it was brighter than the one I'd left behind. Even with setbacks and unexpected detours, I trusted I would eventually find my way back to where I was meant to be.

Living in Yakima.

****

Pay attention to the things you are naturally drawn to.

They are often connected towards your path, your passion, and your purpose in life.

anonymous

CH. 12 — How Can I Be So Lucky?

I need to take a moment to say just how lucky I was to find my Handsome Man.

Truly.
Sometimes I still can't believe the timing, or how someone so good could walk into my life right when I needed him most. He is my quiet reward for all the years I lived without real affection or regard. He was most definitely worth the wait.

From the very beginning, when we first met on Match. com and that first long phone call, I felt an immediate connection. He had this effortless way of making me feel worthy and seen. When we talked, he was present. He asked thoughtful questions and waited for my answers. And he was brutally honest from the start: his past, his missteps, and the hard truths about how his marriage ended.

At first, his honesty startled me.

Why reveal the unflattering parts so early?

But I appreciated it. I didn't want to pour myself into someone and then uncover the "bad stuff" after becoming emotionally bonded. Knowing everything upfront meant I could decide for myself whether his past still controlled him or if he had grown beyond it. So, I gave him the benefit of doubt, as I tend to do, and he ended up meeting the standards I held for an intimate partner.

And once we started sharing a life, I discovered just how wonderful it all could be.

After so many years of being shut down, I was ready to make up for lost time. I wanted to experience the fun, the lightness, the simple joy I had been denied. Luckily, I had found a man who wanted that too. My Handsome welcomed me into his world and his circle of friends, all of them devoted to living their lives with passion.

On Saturday nights, a group of us would wander through the Ballard bars and restaurants with music drifting from the open doors. I learned I could actually sing once I had a little liquid courage in me, and I let my "rock star" out for the first time in decades. My Dearest would stand off to the side, smiling, cheering me on. To have someone root for me so openly was its own kind of healing.

One of his friends played in a local cover band called Hall Pass. They played great dancing music from the 70s and 80s and beyond. They had a loyal following so whenever we caught up to their gigs, there were plenty of people our age enjoying the good vibes and good music. It was so easy to just let loose and enjoy the music and dancing.

I was especially inspired by Kathy and her bandmates. Here they were, with full lives and demanding jobs, still choosing to pursue something that lit them up. They weren't content to just sit in the bleachers and watch life pass. They were grabbing life with passion.

And being around all of them made me want to do the same.

I had been restricted from dancing for so many years because of MKD's twisted ego. He couldn't stand the idea that people might laugh at him, so he shut down my joy right along with his own. Dancing had always been one of my purest forms of expression, a way for me to feel alive in my own skin. Finally, at those gigs, with my Handsome by my side, I was free to move again.

Those nights became some of the best of my life.

It was simple, unfiltered joy. Being surrounded by people searching for the same spark made it even more electric. For the first time in decades, I felt like myself again. I loved my new life.

Sundays brought another layer of happiness: Seahawks games with friends.

We'd meet at a local sports bar, someone always arriving early to guard a table from the vultures circling for seats. Finally, I was hanging out with people who really enjoyed sports and friendship so much that they were willing to get up early and fight off others for a table.

I grew up in the world of sports. My dad coached football, basketball, and track, and I played everything available to girls at the time. Sports were part of my DNA. It was such a personal loss to me when MKD actively shot down my sports interests. He hated me watching games and ranted about every athlete being "privileged."

It was such a great internal celebration when I got to actually watch football with people who didn't take it personally if the Seahawks lost. I was reclaiming a lifelong passion, and I was doing it next to a man who was just as excited to share it with me.

My Dearest even joined me on a quick two-day trip to Denver to see the Colorado Avalanche play the New York Rangers. He'd grown up on the upper west side of Manhattan, so the Rangers were in his blood. I was just thrilled to experience my first NHL game with someone who genuinely wanted to be there with me.

We explored Denver, soaked in the city, and simply enjoyed each other's company. The whole trip felt like a celebration of everything I had been missing. And it struck me more than once that this was something MKD would never have done, even though I had begged for small, simple adventures just like this.

My Handsome and I continued to take fun trips on a whim. We traveled to San Luis Obispo twice in less than four months to see dear friends who had moved there from Seattle. The first trip was for my Dearest's birthday; the second was to join their Super Bowl celebration.

They introduced us to California wineries, where we spent long afternoons tasting wine, toasting friendships, and soaking up their generous hospitality. At night, we sang karaoke, danced in the living room, and made wild bets on the game. It was the kind of carefree joy I had been starved for.

We traveled to Las Vegas a couple of times, just because we could. The airfare was cheap, and it was a quick flight, so, why not? I've never been a gambler, but my Dearest and I caught great shows and even watched the UW Huskies play in their conference basketball final. It felt so amazing to take trips just because we wanted to; without fear, without resistance, without asking permission to be happy.

During my time with my Handsome Man, I've had the chance to experience things I never would have imagined.

When MLB's All-Star Game came to Seattle in 2023, my Dearest was gifted two incredible seats behind home plate for the Home Run Derby. He woke up early and made two signs that read "J-Rod Boom Stick" to cheer on Julio Rodriguez, the Mariners' new rookie sensation. When Julio stepped up to bat, the stadium erupted. We stood with the crowd, holding our signs high—and ended up on national television with ESPN and USA TODAY. Texts came in from friends and family across the country who saw us...it was surreal.

Soon after, we were gifted another set of tickets. This time to the Seattle Kraken's Winter Classic on New Year's Day. It was held outdoors at the Seattle Mariners' ballpark. Seeing T-Mobile Field transformed into a winter rink was pure magic.

Then came more tickets to the Mariners' home opener; once again, right behind home plate, complete with a private Root Sports party beforehand at Edgar's Cantina. There were free drinks, swag, and brushing past local celebrities. How amazing was that?

The adventures with my Dearest just kept coming, and I found myself constantly grateful. One of the things I love most about him is his natural state of gratitude. His instinct is always to see the blessing and not the entitlement.

"Isn't this great?" "Aren't we so lucky?" "Don't we have an amazing life?"

He says it with childlike wonder every time and he's right. It is great. We are lucky. And we do have an amazing life together.

And then there were the concerts.

Before my new life with my Handsome Man, the only concerts I had ever been to were the two Jack took me to when we were together. Suddenly, my world opened. We saw Carlos Santana three times, along with Heart, Stevie Nicks, Billy Joel (twice), Sting, the Doobie Brothers, the Rolling Stones, Shania Twain, The Piano Guys, Dire Straits, Cher, Rod Stewart, and others I've probably forgotten only because the list grew so beautifully long.

There were also countless "lawn concerts" around Seattle and Yakima. My Dearest would pack a beautiful bottle of Cabernet Sauvignon, and we'd stretch out on the grass with nothing more to do than enjoy the music and each other's company. Few things feel better than sharing a quiet evening with someone who delights in you as much as much as you in them.

We traveled to New York City to visit his family and caught a Mariners-Yankees game in the new Yankee Stadium. He took me through the neighborhood where he grew up, showed me where he lived, and pointed out the grocery store his father and older brother owned near Columbia University. It was more than sightseeing for me. I was stepping into the roots of the man I loved.

I could imagine him as a little boy, then a teenager, shaped by that busy, vibrant neighborhood and by a family who nurtured him into the incredible man he is now. I loved that he wanted to share those memories with me and the intimate stories of his youth.

I still marvel that someone who grew up so far from my world, in a place so unlike mine, somehow found his way to Seattle and then happen to be in just the right moment in his life where our souls would find each other through a dating app online. It gives me goosebumps every time I think about how every life is entwined and how the Universe seems to wait until you're ready to receive the gift it's been holding for you.

Then there were the day trips around Seattle. We explored North Bend and Snoqualmie Falls, the old fishing village of La Conner where he surprised me with a bed-and-breakfast stay and a couples massage. We would hop onto a ferry to Bainbridge Island where we walked hand in hand with no agenda except being together.

Whenever we visited Yakima, we'd squeeze in as much exploring as we could; touring Open Houses and dreaming about our future home. Or settling into the relaxed atmosphere at Wilridge Winery just west of Yakima. We would head south towards Zillah to take in the wineries of Bonair, Whitman Hill, Two Mountain, Hyatt, and Dineen. We even managed to catch a last-minute show at the Capitol Theatre in downtown Yakima.

And then there were all the breweries: Single Hill on Naches Avenue, Bale Breaker out in Moxee, and the unexpected delight of discovering the Distillarium in Terrace Heights.

Every outing, every sip of wine, every ferry ride felt like another layer of life returning to me; this time with someone who appreciated it right alongside me.

We loved our Yakima outings so much that we bragged about the beautiful area to our friends and family. Our enthusiasm was contagious, because several of his nieces and nephews decided to join us for the annual Fresh Hop Ale Festival in early October. They flew in from Maryland, New Jersey, New York, and North Carolina.

And get this, one of his nephews from Puerto Rico ran into someone he *knew* from Puerto Rico... right there in

Yakima. Talk about the Universe weaving our lives in mysterious ways. We had so much fun that it became an annual tradition, at least until the 2020 pandemic put everything on pause.

Mornings with my Dearest are their own kind of fun. He starts the day radiating positive energy. He'll turn on the radio or queue up Alexa and immediately begin singing as he dances around the kitchen getting breakfast ready. Without warning, he'll grab me, twirl me across the floor, and serenade me with whatever song is in his heart.

If I start singing a line, he jumps right in with the next. Before long, we're holding wooden spoons like microphones, performing our best Stevie Nicks and Lindsey Buckingham impressions as if our kitchen were a Fleetwood Mac concert stage.

Our chemistry is off the charts. We always want to be together, always. At parties or big gatherings, he will scan the room for me and make his way over, slipping his arms around my waist, making sure I never feel alone. The connection between us is so obvious that strangers comment on it regularly. More than once, a cashier has smiled and said, "Oh good. It's the cool couple."

We share the same love language of touch so it's natural for us to rub each other's shoulders, arms, or feet no matter where we are. One friend joked, "Jeez, can't you two keep your hands off each other?" The truth is: no, not really. And we don't want to.

Even when we eat out, my Dearest looks out for me. He watches the wait staff to make sure my meal won't contain any hot spices that will make me sweat, often noticing the details that I miss. It's hard to explain how incredible it feels to have someone so attuned to you who considers your comfort even more carefully than you do your own.

And then there were all the evenings he simply wanted quality time with me, just the two of us, relaxing with a cocktail.

A cocktail.

The first time he asked if I wanted to go out for one, I stared at him completely confused. Cocktail? What's a cocktail?

I had heard people mention cocktails in the old black-and-white movies I grew up watching, but no one had ever asked me to go get one. "Going for a drink" was familiar enough, but a cocktail? That word had an air of sophistication, very cosmopolitan.

So, when my Handsome suggested it so casually, like it was the most ordinary thing in the world, I was intrigued. It felt like stepping into a small experience I had been denied for years, one I suddenly realized I deserved to explore.

We would dress in our casual best: me in jeans and heels, him in one of his bold paisley shirts that only someone with his confidence could pull off. He'd find a table for two, settle in across from me, and hand me the drink menu.

Menus have always stressed me out. I get overwhelmed by too many options and take longer than most people to decide. Now here I was, staring at a slim list of house cocktails with poetic descriptions and ingredients I barely recognized.

I had no idea what gin tasted like.
Or vodka.
Or bourbon.

My "experience," if you could even call it that, was limited to rum and coke. I knew there was a whole world of drinks out there, but I simply never had the chance—or the freedom— to experiment.

So, there I sat, in a cozy bar with twinkling lights and the low hum of conversation around us, looking at a cocktail menu for the very first time.

Since I had no clue what the base for each drink tastes like, I had to rely on my Dearest to help me select.
Nothing too sweet.
Nothing too strong.
Something balanced.
But in the end, it didn't really matter what I was drinking.

What mattered the most was that I had a man sitting next to me who desired for me to be his sole company for the evening. It was just he and I in that busy place. Our eyes fixed on each other as we chatted about whatever came to mind.

I realized I was experiencing more than just my first cocktail. I was experiencing what it felt like to be cherished. To sit with someone who thinks that I am the most important person at that moment to them.

The drink was new.
The feeling of being chosen was newer.
And both tasted incredible.

Having a cocktail with this man was never really about the drink. It was about two people dressing up for each other, carving out time for each other, and choosing to be fully present.

When someone sets aside an evening not for the event itself, not for the food, the atmosphere, or what the night can do for them, but simply to be with you, you can't help but feel that affirmation settle into your bones.

I watched how comfortably my Dearest moved through those evenings. He had clearly gone out for cocktails many times before, while I fumbled through the menu like a beginner. But he never made me feel out of place. Instead, he treated the whole experience as something to share, something to experience together. We could have stayed home with a glass of wine and a TV show, but it mattered to him to make our time special and to show me, in his quiet way, just how much he valued us.

Even though I often felt a rush to "catch up" on all the experiences I'd missed out on, my Dearest sometimes brought a slower, gentler energy to it. He showed me how to enjoy something new without urgency. Those cocktail evenings became one of our favorite ways to reconnect. It put a deliberate pause in the busyness of life, just sitting side by side, honoring each other.

This truly was a tale of two lives.

The contrast between my past and my present was so stark it felt less like separate chapters and more like entire books. As I put distance between who I had been forced to be and who I was becoming, it felt as if I'd stepped into a different world.

And then there are the special occasions. The way he goes out of his way to create magic for me. He would plan entire evenings in secret, leaving me guessing where we were headed next. He once slipped into a restaurant hours before our reservation just to arrange for a bouquet of flowers and glitter, to be waiting on the table when we arrived. These were small details but with big gestures, overflowing with love.

He had "won" me long ago. I was hooked from the beginning. But that never stopped him. Year after year, he kept showing me through effort, thoughtfulness, and consistency, just how deeply he loved me, how much he respected me, and how much he simply enjoyed my presence. It continues to this day.

And then there are the cards. The beautiful cards that he would give me for my birthday, Valentine's Day, Christmas, Mother's Day, and our anniversary. Each one filled with a handwritten message that would show me how much his heart is connected to mine.

How amazing is that? After all the hell I went through, this man is a beautiful gift from the Universe to me. I mean, really...

How can I be so lucky?

****

My Dearest Pam,

I always count my blessings and thank the Universe. You are the Best Blessing I have in my life. We have been so fortunate and lucky that we found each other. I am very aware of the Great Gift of Love I have received from you. I always will cherish this special gift you give me every day of our lives together. You are my Strength and my Biggest Cheerleader. I love you with all my Heart and Soul.

Handsome

CH. 13 — Good Information to Know

Leaving an abusive relationship isn't easy. It takes courage and planning to pull it off. I wish I could tell you that once you walk out the door, everything is easy. It's not. It takes time to fully transition from the hell you were in to get to the full and rich life that you deserve.

Everyone's path out is different. No one way is better than another. We all carry our own circumstances, responsibilities, and limitations. Some of you will leave with young children who require constant supervision; others will have older children who need after-school care. Some of you will be stepping out with a strong support system waiting on the other side. Others will not.

As you read this, remember that my children were grown up and on their own, I had two professional careers I could fall back on, and I had family waiting for me in Washington State. Even with all those advantages, my first couple of years were still full of challenges.

One of the first hurdles was securing medical and dental benefits. Once I left the Yakima School District and began working in a dental practice, I discovered what many people already know; small offices often don't offer health insurance. And if they do, the coverage is usually minimal.

My Handsome saw the stress this caused and encouraged us to register as domestic partners in Seattle. This allowed him to add me to his health and dental insurance through his employer.

It is difficult to move through this world that we live in if we are constantly in fear of getting ill. Medical and Dental coverage gives you another level of safety that allows you to move confidently forward in your life and your life's path. Having medical and dental coverage should be a right to all in our country but, unfortunately, it isn't. Luckily for me, my Dearest was able to include me in his policies so I would have coverage.

The state of Washington is one of the few state that recognizes same sex marriages and grants all the same privileges as heterosexual unions. But domestic partners aren't automatically granted those same privileges. As of June 30, 2014, only couples, where at least one partner is sixty-two or older, can register as domestic partners. The process requires filing a Declaration of Domestic Partnership form (found on sos.wa.gov), getting it notarized, and submitting it with a $50 fee to the Corporations Division for filing.

Why does this matter?

Because, without that legal filing, domestic partners do not receive the same rights as married couples. If your partner becomes hospitalized, you may not be able to make health decisions for them.

For my Handsome and me, we weren't eligible to register as domestic partners with the state because neither of us were sixty-two yet. Fortunately, the city of Seattle allowed us to register through their municipality, which meant I could be added to my Dearest's dental and health insurance. That single step gave me an immediate sense of stability I desperately needed after leaving my old life behind.

Now that we are older, we can register as Domestic Partners with the state of Washington. This ensures we receive the same state-level legal rights, benefits, and responsibilities as married couples. That includes the rights to inheritance of community property and the ability to make medical decisions for each other if needed.

It also means we can legally inherit each other's estates, be named in wills, and consider all the property we've built together as community property. After committing years of our lives to one another, this recognition matters. It gives legal structure to the emotional and financial life we have already created.

Without this legal recognition, you may have problems trying to make funeral arrangements or burial decisions for your partner. Also, if your partner were to die due to a work-related incident, then you may be eligible for workers' compensation benefits that are generally only available to spouses.

My Dearest took care of the immediate issue by registering our partnership with the city of Seattle. Later, once we met the age requirement, we registered with the state. This legislation was designed to acknowledge the legal, emotional, and financial commitment two people make when they build a life together.

Currently, only seven states recognize domestic partnerships statewide: California, the District of Columbia, Maine, Nevada, Oregon, Washington, and Wisconsin. I'm fortunate to live in a state that understands the importance of granting basic protection to all couples. Being added to my Handsome's insurance gave me the health security I needed to move forward without fear.

There are other states and cities that offer varying levels of domestic partner benefits. It would be worth researching the laws where you live and taking advantage of whatever protections are made available to you. When you're transitioning out of an abusive relationship, the last thing you want is to step into a different type of hardship.

After escaping the abusive marriage I was in, I decided I would never marry again. I had lost so much power in my past marriage that I needed to protect my autonomy. You may also have decided that you will never marry again, just as I did. But that doesn't mean you won't want a committed relationship that mutually benefits both of you. In that case, registering as domestic partners may be a wise option.

I encourage you to research what your state or municipality offers. Determine whether the benefits outweigh any drawbacks, and make your decision from a place of information, not fear. Each state handles domestic partnerships differently, so do your homework and find out exactly what steps are required where you live.

It was only a few months after I moved from Yakima to the Seattle area to pursue work in the dental field that we found out that our landlord planned to sell the house we were renting. That meant we had to find another place to live right away.

When we began looking at rentals, we were stunned by the prices. Renting a home in Seattle was going to cost almost twice what a mortgage would. Our budget made the decision for us—we needed to buy. We hoped to find a place in the neighborhood we already knew, but we discovered that dream wasn't going to happen.

Homes in our area were being listed one day and mobbed with buyers the next. Offers poured in at up to $150,000 over asking price, with buyers waiving inspections as if it were nothing. We knew we couldn't compete in that crazy real estate market, so my Dearest started looking outside our desired area.

Because I worked downtown and his schedule was flexible, we had freedom to look almost anywhere within commuting distance. Thankfully, it didn't take long to find a home in Renton that had been sitting on the market since October with no offers.

At that time, Renton had an unfortunate reputation of being the black sheep of King County. Most people wanted to live in West Seattle, Ballard, Fremont, Green Lake, and Shoreline. That left Renton's housing inventory virtually untouched.

Which turned out perfect for us.

That house in Renton turned out to be a win. We found a mid-century home on a hill with a view, and the owners had just dropped the price from $400,000 to $380,000. It needed a lot of work, no question, but our mortgage lender urged us to "just get into a house" because equity was skyrocketing in that market. We offered $350,000 and the owner took it without any counteroffer.

I was stunned by our good fortune. And since we were fully qualified for the loan, we were able to close by the end of February and then move in by the first of March.

Then reality set in.

We realized that we couldn't afford both my apartment in Yakima *and* a mortgage in Renton. I had been hoping for a full-time dental hygiene position in Yakima so we could eventually relocate back, but nothing had opened up by the time we had to move out of our rental in Ballard.

That was a painful realization. I had spent over thirty years away from Yakima while I was married and had just moved back with the resolve that I was there to stay. But the salary at Davis High School wasn't enough to sustain me long-term, and there were no full-time hygiene jobs available. I had kept my apartment with the hope that I could move back instantly the moment a position opened, but it never did. At least not in the time frame that we needed.

Now I was having to let my apartment go along with the faded plans that I had made to be near my family. It was a sad time. I was mourning my abandoned dream of living in Yakima while I was trying to embrace the new dream of owning a house outside of Seattle.

I started calling the house our "life raft" because we needed to find something quick. It had good bones, but that life raft was going to need a lot of work just to keep us afloat.

Thankfully, we had a circle of friends who rallied to help us move in. Only later did they admit they thought we were out of our minds buying the place. It was dirty, it smelled, and it desperately needed updating. But when you have to move, and the real estate market is chaotic, you take what you can get, and you slowly make it your own.

Before I knew it, I was in a deeply committed relationship with this house. I hadn't planned on diving into anything so serious so soon after escaping North Carolina. I was still shell-shocked from the hell I'd lived through with MKD, and the last thing I wanted was to end up trapped again.

But life doesn't always wait for us to feel ready. Sometimes the commitment arrives first, and the healing catches up afterward.

Giving up that apartment felt symbolic, like letting go of the last piece of my independence. I mourned it, even if only quietly. It had represented freedom, autonomy, and the belief that I could choose my own life again.

That is why registering as domestic partners meant so much. Even without being married, I knew my rights were protected. It gave me a sense of stability during a time when everything else felt uncertain.

And if I had to start over under these new circumstances, I was truly fortunate to be doing it with my Handsome Man. He has always felt like a gift from the Universe, appearing exactly when my soul was ready to receive something good. I knew that together we could turn this unexpected detour into an opportunity to grow stronger in our relationship and to be better prepared for the gifts that life was laying out for us.

We simply needed to take it one day at a time, one year at a time; trusting that when the chance to return to Yakima finally came, we would be ready.

****

Life is short, time goes fast, there's no re-play, no rewind, no pause, so make sure you enjoy every moment.

@womenconfidenceclub

CH. 14 — Plugging The Holes

I once read that the fastest way down a river is to stop fighting the current and let the rapids carry you. That's exactly how it felt for us. Buying a house wasn't in our immediate plans. I still pictured us moving back to Yakima, but sometimes you get caught up in the fast-moving current of life and the best you can do is just find a way to go with the flow.

We needed a place to live, and fast. We were fortunate to find this house when we did because only a few months later the Renton housing market took off and homes started selling above asking price.

The house literally became our life raft.

It had good bones and plenty of potential, even if it needed more work than we'd hoped. That's the tradeoff when you're trying to "just get in" to the King County housing market. We didn't have the extra cash to buy a house that was turnkey so we had to look for the potential rather than the polish and trust the return on investment would come later.

Through some internet research, we learned that the original owner, Agnes, had built the home in 1961 when she was in her early sixties. You could tell she invested in touches that went beyond the typical working-class mid-century home.

The house was all brick, on a hill with a view of the Olympic Mountains and part of Lake Washington. It had a living room and a family room, each with its own fireplace, and a sweet little courtyard connecting the house to the detached two-car garage. Agnes even installed an intercom system, central vacuum, and an elaborate in-ground sprinkler system that were luxuries for that era.

Sitting at the top of a curving street, the house overlooked everything. The driveway climbed a small rise and ended at a generous parking pad beside the garage. Inside the garage, a full wall of cabinets and a long workbench stretched across the back, rare for homes of that age, which usually had only a single bay or a carport. We felt very fortunate.

And, in true mid-century fashion, there was a built-in barbecue on the outside of the second fireplace, with both sharing the same flue. This was one of the charming details that illustrated Agnes' pride in the home we were now learning to make our own.

Inside, the front entry had a classic mid-century slate floor, deep green and cool underfoot. A small architectural partition greeted you as you stepped in, with a built-in bookshelf tucked on the far side; a simple, thoughtful design from another era.

The living room fireplace was made of Wilkeson Sandstone from the historic quarry in Pierce County. That stone was first mined in 1886 and used in prominent buildings in Tacoma, Seattle, and the state capital in Olympia. The quarry has been closed for years now, so whatever remains in homes today is all that's left. Knowing that made the fireplace feel like a small piece of Washington history sitting right in our living room.

In the primary bedroom, the original mahogany built-in closets, drawers, and trim were still intact and still beautiful nearly sixty years later. The craftsmanship had held up in a way that felt almost defiant.

The second owner, Betty, had also purchased the home in her sixties. She did what she could to update and maintain it, but dementia eventually overtook her, and her adult children moved in to care for her.

When we bought it, we could see the attempts to modernize the house were   well-intentioned. High-quality materials were used but it was undone with poor workmanship.

It was, as the saying goes, lipstick on a pig.

In the main bathroom, the original double sinks and large built-in medicine cabinets were still in place. The most recent update included beautiful gooseneck faucets: long, elegant, and completely impractical. The medicine cabinet doors couldn't open more than a few inches because the faucets blocked them. It was the kind of mistake I could imagine making myself. I probably would've laughed the first time I tried to open the medicine cabinet doors, then swapped out the faucets for something shorter. But they had left them as-is and simply made do with the tiny sliver of cabinet space they could access.

Little oversights like that were everywhere. And with so much to fix and only limited funds to work with, it was overwhelming trying to figure out where to begin.

So, I devised a process to help us figure out what was the most important project that we had to tackle first. I was keeping to the idea that I was only living in Renton temporarily until the right time came to move back to

Yakima. With that in mind, I asked myself, *if something happened, and we had to hurry up and put the house on the market, what would be the most important thing that a potential buyer would want to have completed in the house?*

There was no shortage of projects demanding our attention. Most people start with the kitchen, but once we assessed what a future buyer would value most, the kitchen slid down the list. Yes, I wanted a better, more functional space to cook in. But if we needed to sell quickly, a coat of paint on the cabinets would make it presentable enough in a hot market. First, we had to focus on the house's integrity and livability; the aesthetics could wait.

So, we strapped ourselves to our little life raft and braced for the rapids. Every project felt urgent, all of them competing for first place, so we tackled whatever screamed the loudest.

The furnace and hot water heater were the obvious starting points, kind of essential if you want to be warm in the winter and have hot water to bathe in.

When the furnace installers crawled under the house to inspect the ductwork, they came back with news that made our jaws drop; only one duct in the entire system was actually connected to a vent. All the heat had been flowing into the crawl space instead of the house. How long had the previous owner lived like that? And to make matters worse, there was no insulation under the house at all.

So, a new furnace went in, with proper ducting this time, and then we hired someone to install insulation under the entire structure.

While the crew was there, we had them check the attic. What they found was totally unexpected.

They discovered the remnants of an old marijuana grow operation and a makeshift bedroom with an air mattress, a portable air conditioner, and even a clothing rod. All stuffed into an attic with barely four feet of headroom before the roofline sloped down to nothing.

"Didn't you catch that during the inspection?" people ask. Not even close. In a hot market, inspectors looked for obvious problems with the integrity of the house, not annoyances of having to deconstruct a grow operation and bedroom in the attic. We were just trying to get into a house before the market sprinted any further ahead of us.

Our little life raft that we had committed ourselves to was beginning to reveal its hidden "surprises" – the kind you get when you're simply trying to "just get in" to a house.

After clearing the attic of all its unexpected extras, we had the old insulation professionally removed. What had once been a measly two inches of insulation was soon replaced with a full eighteen – enough to finally keep the house warm in winter and cool in summer. It was essential for our own comfort and livability and was long overdue.

While the professionals handled the technical work, my Dearest and I focused on whatever sweat-equity projects we could tackle ourselves. We had uncovered beautiful hardwood floors in the bedrooms and closets, so we assumed the same treasure waited beneath the carpet in the living room, dining room, and hallway. But when we pulled up the old carpet, we found no hardwood at all. In fact, none had ever been installed – just plywood and traces of old mid-century linoleum.

Back in the fifties and sixties, wall-to-wall linoleum was standard. With all the open sightlines in our house, I could almost picture how striking that sputnik-patterned flooring must have looked when it stretched seamlessly from room to room. Only the bedrooms and closets ended up having the wood flooring we had hoped would be throughout the house.

Naturally, replacing the flooring seemed like the next logical project. It almost was. But we saw whitewater ahead of the rapids we were riding and knew that we had spotted a bigger and more dangerous task ahead: popcorn ceilings in nearly every room.

Popcorn ceilings are one thing, but we were especially concerned about the possibility of it containing asbestos. My Dearest scraped a few samples and sent them in for testing. Asbestos, a widely used fire-retardant material for textured ceilings back in the sixties, is notoriously carcinogenic. If the ceilings had asbestos, we would be staring at a mitigation bill in the tens of thousands of dollars.

Thankfully, the results came back negative. We could scrape the ceilings ourselves without risking our health.

But the job wasn't as simple as it looked. We watched tutorials, tried different methods, and quickly discovered just how stubborn removing that texture could be. The usual technique of spraying the ceiling with water to soften the material was painfully slow using a regular spray bottle.

So, we dared to pull out the big guns.

Since we had planned to replace the carpet anyway, we dragged the garden hose into the house and used the sprayer attachment to saturate the ceilings. The popcorn texture softened quickly and began to fall off easily after that.

I am sure plenty of you may have dropped your jaw at the vision of us using our hose to spray down our ceilings. But let me tell you...it worked, and it worked well.

We rolled the scraped popcorn texture and all the debris into the old carpet, wrapped it up, and hauled it out in short time.

Next, we needed someone to paint the ceilings before we could even think about installing new floors, another step we had to complete before moving any furniture inside.

We moved into the house in early March of 2015, and it was well into fall before we finished that first round of projects. When winter arrived, the work finally slowed. It seemed that we found a temporary reprieve from the rapids as we allowed the gentle current of our first winter carry us forward.

But, just like the melting snow in spring swells the creeks and rivers with rushing water to start its journey down the rivers again, we found ourselves gearing up for a surge of new demands each spring as we plugged more and more holes in our little raft.

We redid the plumbing and added recessed lighting. We replaced and painted every door, inside and out. We landscaped the front yard and built a deck to capture the sunset and the view, and we had the entire roof replaced.

My Dearest ended up rewiring the whole house, remodeling two bathrooms then built a laundry room, a pantry, and a new hallway that made the whole space flow better.

We installed a heat pump, finally getting the glorious air conditioning we deserved during those hot Seattle summers and re-tiled the courtyard that connected the house to the garage.

Only after all of that, and after years of applying our "what would a homeowner want if the house went on the market tomorrow?" philosophy, did we finally tackle the kitchen. It was the last project, and one of the most expensive, but we were grateful we waited. Every repair, every update along the way subtly reshaped our vision. By the time we were ready, the plan for the kitchen had matured. And when it was finally done, it was everything we hoped for.

The first thing everyone says when they walk in is, "We love the floors!"

My Dearest and I did all the work ourselves except for installing the sink and countertops. The kitchen ended up costing us around $18K instead of the $60K that was originally quoted for just the cabinets!

HUGE savings. HUGE!

People say home renovations will test relationships. For my Handsome and me, we stayed remarkably in sync. No raised voices, no tempers, just steady work, quiet determination, and genuine appreciation for each other's effort.

If you're riding rapids in a raft full of holes, the journey becomes far more dangerous when the occupants can't work together to get through the toughest parts. But my Dearest and I moved through eight exhausting years of repairs, giving up countless weekends and summers, only to end up with a deeper gratitude for who we were together. Eventually, we reached calmer waters, and the life raft we'd once scrambled to keep afloat was now in the best shape it had ever been.

It wasn't long after I had restocked the kitchen cabinets and drawers that my Handsome, once again, showed me why he is the most amazing guy I know.

At some point, he had slipped into the kitchen, and with a pen and a stack of sticky notes, he wrote some beautiful words of praise in recognizing my work. When I opened the knife drawer, a note read, "This is *awesome.*" In the dish cabinets above it, I found *"You rock"* and *"You are amazing."*

Who does that? Who takes time to celebrate the small, unseen things their partner does? My Handsome Man does. I couldn't have chosen a better companion for this journey. I got it right the moment our profiles linked on Match.com nine years earlier.

Of course, the river of life didn't stop tossing challenges our way. As the house demanded more of us, life did too. First, I eventually had to change jobs; my former commute was wearing me down with nearly two and a half hours a day on the road. Now I work for Dr. Pawandeep Kaur in Renton, just fifteen minutes from home. Close enough that sometimes I walk.

Second, I endured the loss of my beloved father to Glioblastoma, an incurable brain cancer, in December 2018. Then, my Handsome was diagnosed with prostate cancer and underwent successful surgery in 2020, and I faced my own breast cancer diagnosis and surgery in September 2021.

This is life.

No one plans for life's hardest challenges, but they arrive all the same – often nudging you off your carefully plotted course. My Dearest and I were fortunate, we had each other's support, and every hardship seemed to bind us even closer.

Outside of our health challenges, we experienced unexplainable little "signs" we believe came from the two previously deceased owners of the house: Agnes and Betty.

One evening, we were sitting quietly in the family room with no tv on, just Dearest and I enjoying the earned stillness of a long day, when we heard the strangest sound. Do you remember the iconic sound from the old tv show *Dark Shadows* from the 60's or sometimes from the other show, *The Twilight Zone*? The one that makes the hairs on your neck rise as if a spirit has slipped into the room; that eerie, wavering tone? That's exactly what we heard.

We turned to each other with matching wide eyes. "Did you hear that?" And then, almost in unison: "Wow... that was cool."

There were other small things too. Doors would close on their own and lock from the inside. Items we thought were long lost would reappear in plain sight on the counter.

We never got spooked by any of it. We thought it was cool that we had energies from our beloved past owners still attached to the house. It felt like the lingering presence of the two women who had loved this house before we did. We would often talk to them during renovations, and we always thanked them for being such good early stewards of the house.

It had been eight years since I had to take life's detour and move away from Yakima, with seven of those years being spent navigating the rapids of home renovations. Finally, we were gliding into calmer waters, comforted by the thought that life might ease up as we prepared to have a much-deserved relaxing summer.

But calm waters can be deceptive. They look still – soothing even, lulling you into believing the hard parts are behind you. Yet sometimes those still waters hide something deeper and darker waiting below.

And so, I found out one night in March of 2023 how deep those dark waters and hidden currents run in the back of our minds after years of trauma.

In the quiet of one night, the trauma of thirty-three years of abuse and the nine additional years I'd spent suppressing its aftermath began rising from the depths.

It didn't come gently. It surged to the surface like an angry boiling pot, reminding me that the "dark work" has yet to come.

Those long-quashed emotions over the thirty-plus years re-emerged in the darkness of that night and hit me unprepared. Like a sudden tsunami, the dark waves tried to pound me down and drag me under while my heart pounded in terror as I literally gasped for air that night.

That terrorizing image in my dream left me panicked and shaking, as if a demon in the night had come for me.

What is this malevolent darkness that has left me emotionally shredded?

What does it want with me and where did it come from?

****

> Life is like the river, sometimes it sweeps you gently along and sometimes the rapids come out of nowhere.
>
> Barry Campbell

CH. 15 — The Dream

Having C-PTSD is like having pop up ads in your brain
for a horror movie based on a true story.
@amandagullettlpcc

You know how life can slip into a rhythm, almost like muscle memory? You wake up, go to work, come home, take care of the chores, sleep, repeat. Sure, there are birthdays, sick days, small surprises but mostly the days glide by without much shifting under your feet.

That's where I was.

I had begun a new life with a new love and a new career. For nine years, my Handsome and I built a world together, one filled with small adventures and steady joy. We poured ourselves into restoring our little "life raft" of a home until it had nearly regained its former beauty. That summer we were finally ready to rest and enjoy what we had created.

I was living a good life. *We* were living a good life. Everything felt like it was moving forward until … it wasn't.

It had been nine years since I escaped MKD. I was one of the 25% who escaped and survived. I was happy. I was safe. And I thought I had put enough distance between the woman I used to be and the woman I had become. I believed I was healed.

But my body knew better. The body always keeps score.

Just as I had described in ***The Big Dark*** about the hair loss, the ambulance ride, and the abdominal pain that had no name, my body began speaking again in the only language trauma gives it.

I never imagined that nearly a decade after breaking free, that old darkness would find a way back in, pulling me down into the deepest parts of myself.

It began in the middle of March 2023 with a dream.

Not the beautiful dream from March 2014 where Jack appeared and told me I didn't have to live like that anymore – the dream that finally allowed me to leave MKD and his narcissistic abuse behind.

No. This dream was nothing like that.

This one wasn't beautiful. It was dark.

It brought back a single shard of memory that I had spent years tucking safely away. It was a dream of one of the countless acts of intimidation that MKD would direct towards me – in private and alone so no one saw or heard.

And of course, this terrifying glimpse of a memory took place in the kitchen. The room where I had spent so many hours alone, paying bills, grading papers, reviewing volleyball films and doing chores while he chipped away at me.

In the dream, he stood in the doorway between the kitchen and the small hallway that led to the front door. His fists were clenched at his sides, his eyes hard and hateful with his shoulders tense and menacing. He said a few words that I can't remember but the tone and the threat underneath them were unmistakable.

And that was all it took.

It's strange, isn't it? How something that isn't real, something that exists only in the drifting landscape of a sleeping mind, can ignite such immediate, physical fear. Sleep should be the one place where the body is safe. Yet this dream delivered the same jolt of danger I had lived with for years, as if the past had slipped its leash and returned in real time.

Even now, it's hard to explain the depth of the darkness that came with it: the trembling fear, the sense that his silent, simmering rage would spill over at any second and give way to physical harm.

He didn't touch me in the dream, but my body reacted as if he had or was about to. Fight-or-flight rushed in before I even opened my eyes.

I woke suddenly, bolting upright. My heart hammered against my ribs and my body shook so hard it felt like it might come apart. My throat tightened until I could barely pull in air. The room was still wrapped in early-morning darkness, which only fed the panic gathering in my chest.

My Dearest jolted awake, startled by the sobs and the shaking beside him. His voice was full of worry before he even knew what was happening. He wrapped his arms around me instantly, trying to steady me. I could feel the fear in him too – fear of whatever brought on the sheer terror that was flooding out of me.

I tried to speak, but my throat seized every time I attempted to breathe. Only high-pitched sounds came out. Nothing close to words. Each breath stung, and the more I struggled to breathe, the more frantic my body became.

And still the image stayed with me: MKD standing in the kitchen doorway, fists tight, shoulders set, radiating that quiet, familiar threat. A single frozen moment, looping in my mind.

Why that dream? Why then?

There had been no movies, no conversations, nothing in the days before that could help to explain this visceral reaction. There was nothing I could point to and say, *that is why I had that dream.*

I sat upright in bed, sobbing and shaking, wrapped in my Dearest's arms as he held me close and spoke softly to remind me that I was safe. Together, with his arms around me, he succeeded in anchoring me while my body continued to tremble uncontrollably.

Slowly, my breathing began to deepen, though my insides still felt as if they'd been shot out of a burning rocket. I could still feel my heart pounding against my ribs and my blood burning through my body while trying to convince myself that I was safe.

As my mind finally started to quiet enough for me to take in the room around me, I realized I was drenched in sweat. I may have intellectually told myself that I was safe, but my body didn't believe me. It was still locked in the aftermath of the dream and still reacting as if the threat had been real.

It took a long time before I felt brave enough to close my eyes again and claim what little sleep I had left before I had to get up and go to work. You don't know how much I wanted to call out for work. My body was limp with exhaustion and mentally wrung out. I was still emotionally connected to that brief terrorizing image in my head.

I had survived so much in those thirty-three years with countless moments of intimidation and threats from MKD. I had survived the two times he brandished a gun with clear intent to harm. I had survived the physical pain he directed towards me, the humiliation, the bullying and the threats of abandoning me and the kids. All of those I survived without the complete collapse of my body the way it did after this single, fleeting image of him in my dream.

I was spent. Every part of me wanted to stay in bed, wrapping my arms around my body until the trembling passed. But I couldn't. I had patients counting on me being there. I had a dental office who counted on my production to help pay the bills. I had no choice but to climb out of bed and somehow put on a smile to face the day.

How did I ever do it before? How did I make it through all those years of abuse and not have the physical collapse that I just experienced? Why now, after all these years is my body turning inside out?

I started having so much more respect for myself for all the years that I was able to carry that secret; for how I masterfully endured the abuse so no one suspected the hell that I was living.

But now...it seemed so much harder to pretend. Why?

In the days that followed, I moved through life in a fog. The shadows of the dream hovered just behind my eyes and settled heavily in my chest.

I cried without warning. A sudden wave of sadness would roll over me at the smallest, most ordinary things. Songs would come on the radio, and I would feel this deep sadness. Songs that usually made me happy were now a trigger for sorrow. I had to pause and try to figure out why.

I would go back into my past and try to remember all the memories tied to these songs. But my sadness was so deep that it kept me from finding the answers.

It felt eerily similar to the grief I experienced in March 2014, when I finally gave myself permission to leave MKD. It was a familiar sense of mourning, but this time I didn't understand what I was mourning for.

Wasn't my life going great? The sadness that was consuming me was so deep that I couldn't understand where it came from. *Haven't I already reconciled my past?*

I knew I regretted marrying MKD. That much had always been clear. It was the most destructive decision of my life. But as these waves of sadness kept pulling me under, I started to wonder if there was more beneath the surface, something I hadn't yet faced.

I could feel myself edging toward a personal reckoning. The sadness was dark and isolating, a heaviness so complete it felt as if I were disappearing inside of it. It frightened me. The only place lower than where I was headed, it seemed, was to end it with self-harm.

That, I wasn't going to do. But for the first time, I truly understood how people could lose the strength to keep showing up for their own lives. I could see how the mind convinces someone that the kindest thing they can do for themselves is to stop the pain altogether and end their life.

That realization shook me.

I was making it through every day. Making conversations and interacting with people all with a smile. But I was sinking and disappearing inside. I had felt small and lifeless when I left MKD nine years ago.

But *this* feeling *this* time was more profound, and I intuitively knew that what lie ahead of me was even scarier than anything I had faced before.

****

"Most people who have Complex-Post Traumatic Stress Disorder don't have it because they were hurt, they have it because they encountered someone who wanted to hurt them. So it was that glimpse of that malevolence that fractured them. People can go through all sorts of horrible things and not be traumatized. You wait until you tangle with someone who is malevolent, boy, you will not be the same person at all, assuming you were able to put yourself back together at all."

Jordan Peterson

CH. 16 — Triggers

According to the Cleveland Clinic, the primary difference between PTSD and Complex PTSD is the duration and nature of the trauma. PTSD often develops from a single, short-term event: a car accident, a house fire, witnessing violence. CPTSD, however, grows out of long-term, repeated trauma where escape is difficult or impossible, such as domestic abuse or sex trafficking.

People who endure prolonged trauma often carry additional symptoms and may take longer to regulate their emotions because their bodies have learned to anticipate danger from multiple directions over many years. There was no doubt in my mind that what I experienced that night was a form of CPTSD.

But why did it take nine years to surface?

The Cleveland Clinic explains that survivors of long-term abuse often use suppression as a survival mechanism. The mind tucks away the emotional weight of the trauma to protect the person in the moment, especially when facing the reality that the abuse is too overwhelming or too dangerous. This is one reason why it can take years for the trauma to finally manifest; the mind has tucked it deep in the subconscious.

That had been true for me. When I was still married to MKD, I regularly shoved the trauma into a little box deep in my subconscious because reconciling the two versions of him, the charming one and the cruel one, was too painful. And when pieces of that trauma started to leak out, I became skilled at pushing them back down. It was easier than facing the truth that the person who was supposed to love and protect me was the source of so much harm.

CPTSD also builds through cumulative stress. For me, financial strain was always present. I was constantly expected to shore up our depleted accounts without any sustaining help or commitment from him. Every payday, I braced myself for his venom when he discovered there wasn't money to spend when he wanted to spend it then he would expect me to somehow magically come up with a way to cover our basic bills.

Then there were just the normal changes in our life that MKD couldn't handle, like the birth of each of our children. He would put enormous amount of pressure on me to keep the babies from crying so he could study or sleep. Never considering how much his unrealistic demands were crushing me, nor caring when I expressed how exhausted I was.

In other words, the impact of the trauma was more than my nervous system could process in the moment it happened. Pushing it deep into my mind was the only way I could protect myself and keep functioning.

Because of that, CPTSD often takes years to work its way back to the surface. And when it rises, it doesn't come quietly. It comes like pressure building behind the walls of a dam, then finally breaking through with all its force and fury to destroy whatever is in its path.

That ugly, dark, menacing image of MKD standing in the doorway had burned a hole in the wall of the "dam" that I had spent decades in constructing. The entire load of repressed traumatized emotions was released and penetrated every cell in my quivering body.

How was I supposed to manage this dark, dark energy that had just escaped?

It was too big and too powerful to pack it up and put it all back at once. It was loose and running wild, swirling around my being, taunting me with its dark message.

Suddenly, everything became a trigger.

If a TV show or movie hinted at domestic violence, especially anything involving a gun, I recoiled and walked out of the room. The connection was immediate: MKD and the way he used his guns to torment me with his so-called "suicide threats." Even now, I refuse to watch any film that includes violence, especially against women or children. I can't do it. My body won't let me.

If a show included even a hint of condescension toward a woman, even in a sitcom where the "joke" depended on someone being gaslit, I felt my insides start to shake. A dark veil would fall over my consciousness, pulling me straight back to the countless times MKD cut me down with his words, trying to make me feel stupid, small, or incompetent just to feed his fragile ego.

Television stopped being a source of entertainment. Even commercials became landmines. A product he used would flash on the screen, and suddenly I was back in that old life.

I quit eating peanut butter because I associated it with him. He always had to have raspberry jelly on his sandwiches or he would blow. It was its own kind of torture having to add that same jelly to my grocery list because it also happened to be my Handsome Man's favorite.

I never told my Dearest about that association. It didn't feel fair to make him give up something he genuinely enjoyed because it carried pain for me. Instead, I tucked the jar at the back of the refrigerator where I rarely saw it. I never used it to make him a sandwich. Even now, it disgusts me.

Music was no different. If a song from the eighties came on, I changed the station instantly, especially anything by Boston. MKD played their one worn-out CD constantly in his truck. I used to like their music, but now the association was too much for my nervous system to handle.

Nearly the entire decade of the eighties became unbearable. I spent all but two years of it with a monster. Music that once held meaning now carried the residue of fear, loss, and the loneliness I lived inside.

With each trigger came back a flood of dark memories. And with the memories came a flood of emotions that caused my anxiety to spike. I felt myself drowning in a deep, bitter hatred towards him. Sometimes the words, *"I hate him"*, slipped out before I even realized I had spoken.

It didn't matter where I was or what I was doing. A sudden image of him would pass through my mind, and I'd hear myself say it out loud: *"I hate him."*

At first my Handsome thought I was talking about him. His startled, "Excuse me?" would jolt me out of the memory long enough to apologize and explain that it wasn't about him. But as soon as the moment passed, I would slip right back into the darkness, punishing myself for ever being with MKD in the first place.

The outbursts happened so often that eventually my Handsome stopped reacting. He understood that the words weren't about him; they were echoes from a past still clawing its way through me and he let me process it however I could.

For years I believed my life was moving along smoothly. I thought I had navigated my escape from MKD masterfully. I couldn't understand why, after nine years of peace, these small triggers suddenly held so much power.

But then I started remembering the little emotional stings I had brushed aside, convinced they meant nothing. Maybe I hadn't been "fine" after all. Maybe these moments were the warnings I ignored, the first cracks in the dam long before the dream finally shattered it.

These were the early triggers that I almost forgot about. The ones that I just shoved to the back of my consciousness thinking they would stay there. These were most likely the precursors to the hellish dream that I just had that sent me into an emotional spiral.

Like one beautiful fall day, eight years before, my Dearest and I took our bikes out around Ballard and down toward Golden Gardens and Shilshole Marina. We flew down the winding hill with the breeze drumming our hoodies against our chests. I loved the exhilaration of the ride with the company of someone who held my wounded heart so close to his.

It was a beautiful day, a beautiful moment until...

It wasn't.

When we reached the marina, my Dearest wanted to stop and look at the boats. We stood there with the frame of our bikes between our legs, looking out at the boats tethered in the water. Then he started wistfully reminiscing about the years when he and his daughter's mom (HDM) lived in Arizona. How they had a beautiful house on a lake with a boat tied up to their private dock behind their home.

He told me how, almost every weekend, the neighbors would meet out on the lake with their boats tied together to create a safe place for the kids to swim. He spoke about how, even though he and HDM were now divorced, they still had good times, and those days out on the water were among the best.

When he was done reminiscing, he climbed back onto his bike and started down the path again.

He didn't notice he had left me behind.

I had been listening to him retell the stories of the good times he had when he was married, and I marveled at how he was able to walk away from his own toxic marriage with such good memories and little emotional baggage.

I tried to go back into my own marriage and see if there were any moments that I could recall with similar fondness the way that my Dearest just displayed.

But when I looked back, there was nothing.

It was all dark.

Even moments that might have held happiness were quickly overshadowed by MKD's brooding, unpredictable mood swings. Then came the memories of the lies. The betrayals. How he manipulated me from the start. How he hid his cross-dressing so I wouldn't leave him, how deception was woven into the foundation of everything.

I stood there with my bike between my legs, staring out at the boats bobbing gently in the water, feeling myself drop into a familiar emotional pit.

My Dearest had pedaled far ahead before he realized I was no longer behind him. I stayed rooted in place, watching the water rock those tethered boats, while the realization set in once again that I had wasted thirty-three years of my beautiful life to a selfish, self-absorbed man.

I forced myself out of the trance and onto my bike, catching up with my Handsome so we could finish our ride. But the lightness of the day was gone. A shadow followed me – the kind that doesn't lift, even in good company.

I tucked that trigger away and nearly forgot about it.

There were other little moments too, subtle warnings from my body that I had not fully processed the pain. Like the time I missed a road my Handsome asked me to watch for, and I instinctively recoiled, shrinking into the corner of the passenger seat, bracing for the vicious rebuke MKD would have hurled at me.

I had not experienced anything obviously significant before that dark dream, but looking back, my body had been giving me warning signs for years, small flashes of unprocessed trauma and subtle tremors in my nervous system. Those little triggers stacked up until the dam I'd built in my subconscious finally gave way and released everything at once.

And the triggers continued.

I've always had a special relationship with my patients, and they know it. I don't just clean their teeth and send them on their way. After surviving decades of abuse, I learned to read someone's mood and seeing beyond their smiles and hearing beyond their words. It was a survival skill I mastered being married to MKD; I had to always be vigilant to monitor his mood and state of mind so I could anticipate and protect myself.

In my new life, it became a gift. I could sense when someone was hurting and I could offer a safe space where they could unload and feel heard. I am humbled that they feel safe to share their vulnerabilities and I honor that by keeping their confidence.

Because I authentically care about my patients as beautiful and deserving beings, I try to help them see how worthy and deserving they all are as I send them off with a clean mouth and hopefully, a clean spirit.

But after the dam burst in mid-March, my patients' stories started hitting me harder than ever before. A couple of times, their pain mirrored mine so closely that I found myself sobbing and hyperventilating right there in front of them.

One patient told me he had just gotten engaged and then his fiancé suddenly left him for another man. He was stunned, blindsided; trying to make sense of something that made no sense at all. And in an instant, I was back in 1981 pulling the rug out from under Jack's heart.

I tried to comfort my patient, telling him maybe his fiancé was confused, maybe she made a mistake, maybe she didn't know how to come back to him just like I didn't know how to get back to Jack.

Instantly, the old memories of me realizing my mistake with MKD coupled with my mom chastising me that "Jack won't take you back", flooded back to me and cloaked me in shame and guilt for what I did. And then finding out thirty-three years later that he *would* have taken me back was only a bittersweet truth.

It was a flood of regret, shame, and guilt. The lowest emotional energy that you can feel – and it all seem to come at once. I couldn't stop the tears. I couldn't stop the dark sadness that broke open inside me.

Usually, my patients rely on me to support their emotional needs. But now I found myself comforted by them. Somehow, I made it through each appointment. I could tell they felt honored to offer me the same support I had given them for so many years. They would give me the biggest hug when they left, and it helped me to compose myself before I saw my next patient.

Then there was the woman who confided that she had just discovered her husband was a cross-dresser and didn't know what to do, especially with two young children. You can imagine how that one hit me. Her story ripped open an old wound that I had worked hard to pretend didn't exist.

I am usually a warrior when it comes to showing up for my colleagues and my patients. But this time I couldn't hold it together. I broke down in front of my dentist, trying to give her the smallest glimpse of the life I had escaped and how I needed to go home early because I was about to mentally collapse.

Dr. Kaur looked taken aback by my emotional frailty and she immediately okay'd my early exit for the day with a compassionate plea that I seek therapy to help me through this darkness.

She was right.

So was my Handsome who had already been urging me to get some help.

Maybe I should have. But it hurt so much to just have a glimpse of one of the memories come back to me, I couldn't imagine how deep the pain and scars would go once I opened the door to *all* of them. I didn't know how deep the scars went, and I was afraid of finding out.

Plus, I had witnessed my two daughters struggle to find a good fit with a therapist. I couldn't imagine cutting myself open so deep just to find out that the therapist couldn't help me. I would end up having to start all over again and I couldn't imagine the depth of the pain I would have to endure all over again.

No. I wasn't going to go to therapy.

I was going to take control of this monster, just like I did all those years when I was would force myself to box it all up and shove it deep inside where it couldn't hurt me.

It was the only survival method I had ever known.

So, when a trigger started to come over me, I would say, *look forward, look forward, don't look back, don't look back, look forward.* And it actually seemed to work... for a short while.

Then it would come back and I would have to repeat the same thing in my head, *look forward, look forward, don't look back, don't look back.*

I did this for a couple of weeks and then realized, *the dark monster is winning. My way is not working. I have to turn and face it. I have to put on my warrior armor and face it...*

I have to face the dark

****

I want to be clear that I am not advocating that you go it alone without a professional to help guide your healing process. This is what I chose for myself at the time, and I may still seek professional help in the future. I had been used to digging my own way out of any emotional debris from the thirty-three years of abuse that I had endured, and I know that it played a part in my decision not to seek professional help.

It is great if you can find someone you know who is capable of hearing your trauma, but it is a BIG ask of anyone who isn't a professional to do that for you. Just like I didn't want to place an emotional load on my friends in NC by telling them of the abuse before I escaped, this is too much for anyone to hold in their being. Plus, you just don't know what the other person has had to endure in their own life. You retelling your traumatic stories could trigger them to experience their own CPTSD when they may not be ready to deal with it themselves.

When you get a professional therapist, they remain emotion free and can offer a non-judgmental space for you to be totally honest, which is necessary if you want to heal. The therapist doesn't have any agenda with any pre-conceived outcome for you other than to help you process your pain the best way that you can.

Plus, a therapist is bound by law to keep everything you say to them private. This should give you even more confidence to offload your emotional scars honestly, knowing that you will not be judged and the information you share will not leave the room.

So, as you move through the rest of my story, please do not think that I am encouraging you to do what I did. My method most likely prolonged my suffering, which, in turn, kept me from being whole sooner.

Most health insurance policies will cover a certain amount of mental illness counseling appointments. Check with your insurance provider to see what your policy covers for you. And if you don't have insurance, then contact the National Domestic Abuse hotline @ 1-800-799-7233 for their guidance on where you can get help in your area.

You need to know that you are not alone and there are resources available to you. Unfortunately for me, I had burned a long path of not relying on anyone for help. My hyper independence was due to the trauma and abuse that I endured for a very long time, and I didn't feel like help was an option.

But you deserve it. I know that now. So go get it.

****

THE TEARS AREN'T ABOUT THE COFFEE SPILL…IT'S DEEPER THAN THAT.

Be kind – always.

@riseinsilence

CH. 17 — Facing the Dark

I had shoved all the trauma I had endured deep inside for decades as a survival mechanism. I thought I could simply move on. I was so, so wrong.

People love to say, "The past is in the past. Just move on." I tried and it didn't work. I smiled, pushed through each day, and pretended I was fine. But the pain didn't go away. It circled back again and again, tightening its grip. No matter how hard I tried to "let it go," it still came back as a tormenter and refused to release me.

Enough. I had enough.

No more dodging the pain.

I needed to face it if I ever wanted peace. I was still murmuring "I hate him" at random times. The words would slip out without any conscious awareness of him. But I didn't have to be thinking of him - he was lodged in my subconscious, torturing me as if he were still standing in front of me.

So, I stopped pushing the memories away. If I was going to fight these demons, I would have to meet them head-on.

I bought a spiral notebook and gave myself permission to write whatever came to mind. I would lie in bed at night and just let the anger spill out. Once I started, my pen refused to stop. Every emotion I had buried clawed its way to the surface.

It felt like lancing an infection swollen with puss and watching the putrid contents ooze out. I had so much hate for him it was incredible how fast and how much poured out of me and onto that paper.

Up to then, I was still telling myself that his untreated depression was the reason for his cruelty. I wanted to believe it. I wanted there to be a reason. But almost a year later, I learned just how intentional that cruelty had been.

For now, in those early days of trying to reclaim my emotional health, it was enough to simply name what he had done. Depression or not, it was enough for me to hate him just for the hell he put me through.

For several weeks, I pulled that binder out at night, lying in bed and venting the pain I had carried for so long. I knew I was only skimming the surface, touching the edges of the memories that had nearly destroyed me. I just wasn't ready to go deeper yet.

Regret and guilt washed over me again – guilt for marrying MKD and regret for breaking up with Jack in the first place.

I would go on long walks with the intention of working through this logjam of shame in my mind. All I accomplished was beating myself up for staying with him.

How could I be so stupid to have stayed that long?
Why didn't I leave when his tantrums made me feel unsafe?
Why didn't I see that the endless purging of our bank accounts was reason enough to leave?

Why didn't I walk away after he traumatized all of us with the loaded gun after Hurricane Gordon in 1994?
How could I do that to the kids?
What was I thinking?
Why did I stay?

Seeking answers to these questions, I decided to go through my old photo albums to see if any of them could help me to recall what my state of mind was at the time.

As it was, I was lucky to have any photos at all. Before I escaped MKD nine years earlier, I had carefully chosen a small collection of pictures to take with me. I left the bulk of them behind because I truly believed he would be devastated if he didn't have meaningful photos of the kids. Once again, that was me giving him more consideration than he had ever given me.

I was wrong again. Here I was, still giving him the benefit that deep down family was important to him. I should have just taken all the photos with me.

Soon after I left, MKD went on a tirade, throwing things out and giving the kids almost no notice to retrieve their belongings. Craig and Clair were out of state. The youngest two had no way to get to the house in North Carolina before his arbitrary deadline. And poor Jillian, living in a tiny apartment nearly three hours away, didn't have the space to take everything.

Still, she raced down to Havelock weekend after weekend, trying to save what she and her siblings wanted before their unhinged father disposed of it all. She rescued as much as she could, but he still managed to throw plenty away before she got there.

I could use this moment to express how disgusted I was that he couldn't set aside his wounded pride long enough to see how his actions were traumatizing the kids and how little he cared about the memorabilia they might have wanted. But honestly, it's just too exhausting.

Thankfully, Jillian had managed to salvage the photo albums. When she moved to Seattle after finishing her second master's degree, she brought them with her and eventually gave them all to me. I had tucked them away in a closet, waiting for the day when I felt ready to look through them. When the darkness returned, I reached for them, hoping that somewhere inside those pages, there might be a memory that could help me get through this dark period.

But almost every photo carried phantom shadows of MKD as each image seemed to have a connection to something dark. It was no wonder I hadn't taken them with me when I escaped nine years earlier.

I made the decision right then that I would go through every album, separate the photos into piles, and send them to the kids so they could decide for themselves what to keep and what to let go of.

When I told Jillian my plan, she was grateful for two reasons. First, she wanted the pictures so she could have her own library of memories. Second, she reminded me of something most of us don't think about; the burden we unintentionally place on our children to handle our belongings after we die.

"Thanks, Mom," she said. "That's one less task I'll have to take on when you're gone."

She wasn't wrong.

I had already given the kids much of what I felt belonged to their own history. The photos were the last piece. I created five piles: one for each child, one for me, and one for their dad. Even after everything he did, I still wanted him to have the option to keep or toss whatever he wished.

It took a couple of weeks to sort them all, place them into albums, and prepare the packages. I mailed a large box to him, another to Craig and Claire, and Jillian, who lived on Capital Hill in Seattle, came by to pick hers up in person.

Going through the photos was emotionally brutal. I was already fighting off the dark cloud trying to swallow me, and each picture triggered another painful memory. Still, it became a symbolic shedding, another layer of the past I didn't realize I needed to release. Unfortunately, the photos didn't bring me any closer to answering the deeper questions that haunted me.

My Dearest struggled watching me twist in so much pain. Every now and then I'd share a flash of a memory that ambushed me, and all he could do was hold space while I vented. And that meant everything.

Still, I kept a lot from him. The pain felt bottomless, and I didn't want to burden him. So, I walked long, fast, furious walks where I had heated conversations with myself. People driving by, seeing me shake my fists at my shadow, probably thought I was high on something. I didn't care. Walking fast and with a lot of power helped me to physically pound down a bit of my suffering.

I would routinely have my Handsome drop me off at work in the morning and then I would walk the three and a half miles home so I could be alone with my shadows. It took a little over an hour to get home. By the time I got home I was physically and emotionally worn out and ready for a diversion. After these "therapy walks", I felt like I could put my heavy baggage aside and be more present with my Dearest. Unfortunately, it didn't always work.

I knew my inner struggle was bleeding into our relationship. I tried so hard to be present with him and give him the attention that he deserved. It would be a lie to say that it was easy to do. The darkness was all through me and I had to stay vigilant as to where it was trying to take me.

I kept circling back to Memorial Day of 1981. Those days and the weeks before that remained pivotal. How could I have been so foolish as to think I could take a brief break from my relationship with Jack, have sex with another guy, and then simply slip back into the life I had with him? Even now, the memory makes me sick.

It was inescapable: MKD and Jack would always be linked in my mind.

How many of us can look back and point to the one choice that splits our life in two; the decision that sets us toward something better or something far worse? For me, that moment is unmistakable. It feels surgical, as if a knife sliced straight through the reality I was living, leaving a clean dividing line between two worlds. On one side of the blade was Jack – on the other was MKD. But they were still part of the same blade, forever fused.

I hate that the short, beautiful life I had with Jack will always carry the shadow of the long, dark, painful life I had with MKD.

The shame and regret over what I did to Jack tangled tightly with the traumatic flashes that kept rising from my subconscious. Each emotional cut pulled another memory to the surface. I cursed myself for my foolishness. I even convinced myself that Jack's failed marriages were somehow my fault; that my decision had reverberated through both our lives like a curse we couldn't shake.

I found myself whispering, "I'm sorry. I'm so, so sorry," just as unconsciously as I had muttered "I hate him." Two sides of the same blade. Two realities. One heavy knot of regret that refused to let me go.

Then I decided to do what I had done so many times before when I was at a low point; I would pull out my pictures of Jack and try to reconnect to a time that was happy and full of light. Looking at these pictures always helped me to remember that my life had once been amazing and that Jack had also held me close to his heart.

I went to the closet to get the album, but it wasn't there.

I told myself it had to be somewhere. I hadn't needed to look at those photos in years because my life with my Dearest had been so good. But now, I couldn't remember exactly where I'd tucked them. I started digging through my bedroom closet, pushing clothes aside and pulling down boxes.

Nothing.

I moved to the other bedroom and tore through that closet; the one crammed with things we didn't use but hadn't decided to part with. I emptied shelves, dug through corners and checked the top and bottom.

Still nothing.

I went back to my own closet, this time with panic rising in my chest. My hands were shaking. I kept searching even though some part of me already sensed it was pointless.

I needed those photos. I needed that physical reminder of beauty and love and safety. I needed the proof that, before my life with my Handsome Man, there was another place where I had been truly loved and seen.

And now I couldn't find it.

My past was so dark except for Jack. I only had two years of beauty before I destroyed it, and those photos were proof that the light had been real. I had leaned on them and on the memory of him to survive the years of pain and torment with MKD.

I needed them now. I wanted them in my hands.

As my thoughts spiraled, a faint image flickered through my mind – me throwing the pictures away.

Did I do that?

Could I really have done that?

At some point in the last nine years since I'd last seen Jack, I know I had considered getting rid of them. I thought that maybe letting go of the photos would force me to move on. Jack had been such a powerful presence in my life, and the bond we shared was still there, even after decades and even with the full love and devotion of my Handsome Man. That connection never faded.

Sometimes I worried that thinking of Jack was a kind of betrayal. He surfaced in my consciousness almost every day. I'd find myself sending up a silent prayer for his happiness. I tried more than once to push him out of my mind. But he always returned, like a guardian angel brushing a hand across my shoulder.

I vaguely remembered telling myself I needed to cut every cord, and that included the photos. But it wasn't clear in my mind if I actually did it. My memory usually doesn't fail me so why was it so hard to pull this one back?

I couldn't make sense of it. Why would I discard something so precious, something that symbolized strength during the worst years of my life?

But I must have done it. I couldn't find them anywhere.

A fresh wave of sadness hit me.

I must have thrown them away, believing it would break the tie and keep Jack's memory from resurfacing.

I asked myself facetiously, "So… how did that work out?"

I had tried to tuck my life with Jack into a far corner of my mind because there was too much pain attached to the beauty. And I had tried to bury all the trauma from MKD for the same reason—to avoid feeling the enormity of the pain.

But both returned anyway. The trauma came charging back, waving a flag and blasting a horn so loud I couldn't pretend not to hear it anymore.

The darkness from my years with MKD came roaring back at the same time the memories of Jack's light resurfaced, two forces forever linked in my mind.

I was beginning to understand that you can't simply "cut the cord" with someone that special. You can't. Their influence is woven into who you are. They don't disappear; they continue to live inside you as a quiet reminder of the immense influence they had on your life. You realize that they are one of the biggest reasons that you are who you are.

But in the present moment, I had no tangible connection to that part of my past. And I needed it desperately. I needed some reminder of the light to counterbalance the darkness pressing around me.

So, I decided to reach out to Jack.

I hadn't contacted him in years and had no idea if he still had the same phone number. But the need to feel anchored again outweighed the hesitation. I sent a text and waited.

It didn't take long, and he responded.

He seemed surprised to hear from me after so long, but his tone was warm. My heart brightened just from getting his text. He asked how I was and how my mom was doing. I kept the exchange light; I knew not to ask personal questions. But I did feel comfortable asking how his mother was.

To my surprise, he said that she was living just ten miles away from me in an assisted living facility. Barbara, who had played such a vital role in helping me reconnect to my past life in Yakima when I was still in North Carolina, was only a fifteen-minute drive away. Jack gave me her number but warned me that her memory was failing.

Barbara and I had reconnected nine years earlier, when I first returned to Yakima, but I had drifted away after meeting my Handsome Man. I had intentionally decided to stay away from Barbara since I wasn't sure how my new relationship would handle the complexity of my past. Plus, Jack's girlfriend, Celina, was giving Barbara a hard time for spending time with me and I didn't want her to feel like she had to choose sides.

I had no idea she had moved over the mountains from Yakima. Now she was just fifteen minutes away. I was hoping she would remember me regardless of her dementia. I didn't have any photos of Jack to connect to my past, but I at least had Barbara. Fingers crossed.

I dialed her number and listened to the ring.

The phone picked up. I recognized Barbara's voice immediately and said, "Barbara, this is Pam Telford. How are you doing?"

My fear of her not remembering me evaporated immediately when she excitedly replied, "Pam! I have so much to tell you!"

****

Trauma makes you obsessed with understanding everything.

Trauma re-wires the nervous system to prioritize safety above all else.

When you've been through experiences that left you feeling powerless or blindsided, your brain learns that understanding everything is the only way to stay safe. Because not knowing once led to pain.

It is your nervous system trying to protect you.

@healwithfrancesca

CH. 18 — Barbara

When I first began searching online for help in healing from the traumatic abuse, all I could find were technical explanations on the phases and stages of recovery. I read everything I could, but the approaches varied, and none of them felt like they fully matched my experience.

The one point every source agreed on was this: in order to heal you must first be in a safe place that is stable. Without a secure, predictable environment, real recovery is almost impossible.

I could at least check that part off my list.

My life had been safe and stable, ever since returning to Washington state nine years earlier. My life with my Dearest had been a solid eight years in this home, with a total of nine years together. Whatever storms I carried inside, the external foundation was steady.

But the rest confused me. The next "official" step in trauma recovery is often described as "Remembrance and Mourning"; the phase where a survivor begins deliberately processing the trauma through journaling, self-reflection, or therapy.

I didn't start journaling until nine years after I escaped, triggered only by that emotionally scarring dream I had in March.

So what about all the time in between? Wasn't I healing during those years too?

I saw myself more clearly in what some sources list as step seven: the "Rescue Phase." In that stage, the survivor focuses on immediate needs, survival, and basic functioning while slowly starting to accept what happened.

Maybe I hadn't fully come to terms with everything I'd endured over those thirty-plus years, but I had been addressing my immediate needs from the moment I escaped, and I'd been doing it ever since. In many ways, that was my third step, not my seventh. My recovery wasn't following anyone else's chart. It was following me.

I was beginning to understand that each individual path to healing from trauma was different. My healing was different. It had to be, because nothing about my path resembled what I'd found illustrated online.

So, before I go any further, let me say this plainly: everyone's healing is their own. Your journey will be as individual as you are. If you're worried you've skipped a phase or don't match the "official" stages, please don't be. If you're moving forward, facing your own darkness in whatever way works for you in the moment, you are doing just fine.

For me, I needed to reconnect with the brightest part of my past. And since I could no longer do that through photos of Jack, I was grateful I could still do it through Barbara.

We arranged for me to visit her after work on Wednesdays. I usually started my day around six a.m. and was finished by three. Barbara liked me to come at four since her favorite TV program ended at that time. The timing was easy. I'd sometimes change my clothes, swing by Trader Joe's near her place to get her flowers, maybe grab a coffee, catch up on texts, and then head over.

I always called before I arrived. I didn't want to catch her off guard if she forgot our plan.

Our first meeting in nine years was beautiful. Barbara was standing in the hallway outside her room, waiting for me, and she wrapped me in the warmest hug. She was now shorter, more fragile, but her blue eyes were still bright, and her smile was unmistakable.

She loved the flowers. While I found a vase and arranged them, she moved carefully through her little space, easing herself into her favorite chair.

Barbara had lived a grand life in gorgeous homes, and now everything she owned had been condensed into two small rooms and a bathroom. She had surrounded herself with the pieces that mattered most: portraits of wild horses her father had painted decades ago, pictures of her beloved husband who died twelve years earlier, and a family photo of her and her four children from 1979, the year Jack and I first found each other.

It was hard to see her life distilled into just two rooms. But what touched me most was how limited she'd become. Her balance issues kept her inside unless one of her children came by to take her out. This woman who once rode horses, water-skied, and tended a lush rose garden, was now confined to a fraction of the vast world she had lived so fully.

My heart ached for her. I couldn't imagine losing my freedom to move and to explore – to wander and to feel the world expand around me. The thought of such a narrowing of life felt devastating.

I realized quickly that my visits with Barbara were going to matter just as much to her as they did to me. I wanted every moment to be happy for her, especially knowing she didn't have much time left on this Earth.

Once she moved back to her chair and we got past the polite catch-up you exchange after years apart, Barbara got right to the point. She had that way about her. She would ask pointed questions that could make some people feel uncomfortable, but they were always honest and valid.

She wanted to know why I had come to see her after all these years.

Where was I supposed to begin?

I had already told her about my abusive marriage when I moved back to Yakima in 2014. But her dementia had wiped those conversations away. So, I started again. I explained the terrifying dream that sent me into a spiral after nine years of relative calm and how all the old triggers were resurfacing and pulling me back into the trauma I thought I had outrun.

I told her that when I looked behind me, all I could see were dark years and that seeing her was helping me reconnect to one of the few bright chapters of my past.

And I admitted that I still couldn't forgive myself for how I ended things with Jack.

She tried to comfort me. "Oh, Pam. You two were so young."

But her answer felt too simple. I didn't feel "too young" to have loved someone that deeply. And I couldn't accept that decades of torment with MKD were just the consequence of a youthful mistake. It didn't seem fair that one choice at twenty could condemn me to more than thirty years of suffering. If the pain had lasted that long, surely there had to be another explanation – some missing piece that would finally let me off the hook for what I had done to Jack.

One question I kept circling was this: *What was lacking in me back then that made me capable of hurting someone I loved so much, and then staying with someone who hurt me so deeply?*
How could I claim to be a good person and yet cause such damage not only to Jack, but also to MKD?

Because of Barbara's dementia, she didn't remember the details of my toxic marriage, so I had to retell the story. This time, though, her questions were sharper.

The first thing she asked was, "Why didn't you leave?"

This is one of the worst questions you can ask a survivor of domestic abuse. It reduces years of manipulation, fear, and psychological captivity to a false choice as if leaving were simply an option you declined. It puts the victim on the defensive, forcing them to justify why they didn't run when, in truth, their ability to leave had been stripped from them long before.

People who ask that question don't realize what they're implying. What it tells me is this: these people were lucky enough to not have experienced the abuse that we victims did. If they had, they'd understand, it's not easy to "just leave."

Let me try to explain why.

Most victims have personalities that make breaking away incredibly difficult. We are empathetic, compassionate, and forgiving. We look for the good in people. We give without limits. Many of us were programed early on to put our own needs last and that our worth came from making others happy.

When an abuser first enters our lives, they paint themselves as loving, compassionate and empathetic; they mirror our own traits back to us. They present themselves as gentle, loving, and deeply understanding. But they also act wounded so that the victim believes they are the only one who can help them heal. It feels like a soul match.

But as the relationship progresses, the mask slips. The abuser grows weary of pretending to be compassionate and empathetic – it gets harder to keep up the charade. You will discover that it was all an act, and the darker parts of them begin to surface. The shift blindsides the victim, creating a mental and emotional whiplash known as cognitive dissonance – an actual dysfunction in the brain where two competing truths cannot both be real.

Is he really the kind, loving partner he was in the beginning, or is he the cruel, dismissive person standing in front of me now? The victim has real memories of when their abuser was kind and loving towards them. But now they are presented with this cruel opposite version of them.

To reconcile that contradiction, the victim searches for explanations that feel safer than the truth: *He's tired. He's stressed. He must have had a bad day at work.* These stories are easier to believe than accepting that someone who has professed to love them is intentionally cruel.

So, one of the reasons victims don't leave is they are still hoping that, with enough patience, love, and compassionate understanding from the victim, that the abuser will return to being the loving person they were in the beginning. It often takes many years before the victim realizes that the abuser will never change.

And then comes the next barrier: money.

Most victims of abuse are women, and many have been financially controlled long before they realize it. They are encouraged not to work and not to seek independence because, after all, their loving partner insists that *he* take care of her. Who doesn't want to be cared for.

But dependence becomes captivity.

Now that time has passed, and you see your partner's cruelty truly has no end, that they are not going to change, you realize another truth: you don't have access to money, or maybe you no longer have a career to stand on. And if you have children, multiply the difficulty by ten. Which is the third reason it is hard to leave: having children.

How do you escape an abusive relationship with children? Do you simply say, *I've had enough. The kids and I are leaving?* Good luck with that.

Abusers build a climate of fear and intimidation so thick that any act of independence feels like a provocation. The idea that you deserve a better life becomes dangerous. And let me remind you - 75% of victims are still murdered by their abusers *after* they leave. That is an annihilation.

So, reason number four is simple and brutal: the fear for your life.

Number five follows quickly behind it: fear of traumatizing your children.

And there may be other reasons why victims don't "just leave". But let me be clear. If not done surgically, the fear for your life is real and is validated by the statistics of 75% of victims being killed.

A well-known real-life example of a surgical escape is Katie Holmes and her daughter, Suri Cruise. If you don't know their story, look it up. It unfolded in real time for the whole world to see. My heart goes out to her for the precision and courage it took to break free from the immense control she lived under.

So, there I was, sitting with my dear Barbara, who innocently asked why I didn't "just leave." I held my breath and finally said what I had spent years refusing to say—to her, and to myself.

I told her about the fear. The isolation. The way his cruelty seeped into every corner of my life until I couldn't see daylight. I told her how I blamed myself—not only for what he did to me, but for the ripple effects of choices I made long ago. How I still carried guilt for hurting Jack, for the end of his marriage, for all the broken pieces that I had felt responsible for sweeping up.

Pulling those memories up was like dragging stones from the bottom of a lake. I sobbed as I spoke. Barbara could feel my pain and realized how deeply tormented I had been. She listened with such grace. She didn't rush me, didn't flinch. When I finished, she lovingly said to me, "I wish I had known, Pam. You could have come and lived with me."

What a beautiful thing to say from a beautiful heart such as hers. But I shook my head. I didn't want her to take on any of my pain as her own. And realistically, I reminded her, I could not have left—not with the danger, not with the paralysis that abuse carves into you.

She understood. She wrapped me in the biggest hug, and for a moment, I let myself soften into it. Her hug felt like understanding and forgiveness.

This meeting with Barbara was not how I imagined it would go. I only wanted to sit with her, enjoy her presence, talk about the weather, reminisce about her husband who had passed in 2011, and share our mutual love for Yakima. But Barbara had a way of opening the door to harder conversations, and she was genuinely curious about why I had come to see her and why I hadn't left my marriage sooner.

I would visit her every other Wednesday and bring her flowers. And each time, because of her dementia, she would ask again about my abusive marriage, the same questions repeated.

It hurt every time I had to answer them. Yet, something unexpected began to happen. The more I pulled those memories out and the more honest I became about what I had lived through, then the less power the memories held over me. I still had so many unanswered questions for myself, but I was getting a bit stronger. I was finally learning to face my past instead of flinching from it.

I also discovered that the journaling I did each night in my spiral notebook wasn't enough anymore. If I wanted to heal, I was going to have to dig deeper. I needed to examine each memory the way you might pause a film and study each frame. It terrified me. I knew it would hurt. I knew I would uncover things about myself that I might not like.

But I also knew I had to do it. I wanted to free myself from the guilt and shame I had carried for so many years.

Barbara helped me pull the pain to the surface. Now it was my turn to sift through it, to understand what had been happening in my poisoned mind during those dark times, so that finally, I could find some peace in my soul.

****

Sometimes, people will look at your life, your patience, and your positivity, and assume you've had it easy.

They haven't seen the countless times you've resurrected yourself when feeling dead inside, or how close you've come to giving up.

They aren't aware of the discomfort you've endured while confronting your demons and fears. They haven't witnessed your entire journey.

Vex King

CH. 19 — Looking for Answers

My visits with Barbara continued throughout the summer of 2023. I always brought flowers, and she always returned to the same questions about my abusive marriage. I never said, *"I already told you,"* or *"We talked about this last time."* It was painful for me to have to relive my story to her each time, but it felt cruel to make her feel the weight of her own disease. So, I just kept retelling my story.

Eventually she would pause, tip her head slightly, and say, "I think I remember you telling me about that," and we'd move on to lighter things. But each retelling shook something loose in me. I kept trying to understand how I had stayed in a life that hurt so much.

At home, I pulled out memories one at a time and wrote down every detail I could recall: the season, what was happening around us, what the world outside our home looked like. It mattered to me to place each episode in context. We don't live in a vacuum; the forces shaping us are always larger than the moment itself. Online timelines, old calendars, even historical weather reports helped me fill in the backdrop. Each small confirmation steadied me. *Yes, this happened. Yes, I remember it clearly.*

But the work was painful. I wasn't glancing at memories anymore, I was watching the full reel, frame by frame, and stepping back into the feelings I had spent years trying to escape. The emotions could slice through me without warning. I'd find myself asking the same impossible questions:

How could I have allowed myself to stay with such a cruel person? Why didn't I realize sooner that he wasn't going to change?

Some days the pain was too much. I would shut my notebook and realize I needed air and the open sky. I had to back off and look for some balance. I knew I could find that balance in Yakima, so I decided to return for the weekend to let my heart breathe.

Yakima always had a way to boost my mood, especially Franklin Park. I had endless great memories woven into that place, and I was counting on it helping me to find some peace in all the darkness that was shrouding me.

Dearest couldn't join me, but I didn't need him to. I needed to go by myself. I needed to walk my old streets, run the routes my younger self once relied on, and find my center again. I needed solitude for my own healing, and I was grateful he understood.

I made it to Yakima on Friday evening just in time for the summer concert at Franklin Park. The city had been hosting these concerts for years, and I wanted anything that might lift me out of the heaviness I'd been carrying.

The park was crowded in that comforting, familiar way. I settled under the trees and let the music and chatter move through me. I loved watching the mix of people who came out to enjoy the simplicity of the evening. There were older couples in lawn chairs arranged in inviting half-circles so they could visit with each other easily. There were the younger couples sharing picnic blankets and families letting their children run loose on the playground. And then there were people like me, sitting alone and enjoying the soft July evening under the shade of Yakima's big trees.

I knew I had come to the right place, and I was looking forward to the next morning to reconnect.

My plan was to be at the park by seven and go for a run through the cool air. Then I would refresh myself with cold water and a simple breakfast of yogurt and berries that I would have with me in the car. After that, I planned to walk wherever I wanted to go: Barge-Chestnut, Summitview, the old neighborhoods, even past the house where I'd lived in high school and while I was in dental hygiene school at YVC.

I wanted a weekend of all-things Yakima, and I was counting on having my spirit cleansed a bit from the darkness that was following me everywhere.

But my subconscious had other ideas.

It all started as soon as I lay down to sleep. All the darkness came back to judge and mock me.

Why is it that our brain won't allow us to let go of the regrets from the past when we lay down to sleep? Nighttime has a way of stripping away distractions, leaving only the day's truths and in my case, the truths of decades for me to ruminate. With me, I found myself ruminating against all the good things from my past that ended abruptly when

I made that decision to break up with Jack. There they were…the good memories tethered to the dark ones.

I tried to separate them, but those memories came as a pair; the beauty stuck to the ugly – the dark parts clung to the light. With them came the familiar weight of shame, guilt, and regret; the lowest forms of emotions you could ever conjure for your soul to endure.

I lay in bed crying—crying for the life I might have had if I hadn't made that fateful decision on Memorial Day weekend in 1981. One moment of youthful misjudgment had opened the door to thirty-three years of hell, followed by nearly a decade of silent suffering afterward.

In the dark, the blame returned in full force. I blamed myself for the pain I endured during my marriage, and even for the pain Jack must have felt because of what I chose all those years ago. How could someone like me, someone who tries so hard to be good, hurt a person she cared about with one impulsive decision? How could such an innocent desire unravel into the darkest chapter of my life?

The sobs came so hard I was grateful my Dearest wasn't with me. I didn't want to frighten him. And still, sleep wouldn't come.

By two in the morning, I gave in and took a Benadryl just to take the edge off. I thought about taking two, but I didn't want to sleep through the run I'd been counting on. I needed that morning at Franklin Park. Somehow, I finally drifted off.

By 5:30 I was awake again, two hours of rest at best. Not enough to function, but lately that has become my new normal. I still don't know how I moved through my days without people seeing how hollow I felt inside.

But the morning came anyway, whether I slept or not. I lay there scrolling on my phone, gathering the energy to face the day. I was still looking forward to the healing powers of Franklin Park and the walk that I had planned.

Fingers crossed.

I reached Franklin much earlier than I thought I would. As usual, the park was nearly empty at that time in the morning. Just the way I liked it and just like it used to be when I was a teenager on those early summer mornings.

I took off for my run, earbuds in, letting a '70s playlist carry me back to the girl I was before everything darkened. The music helped. Those songs were stitched to good memories, ones untouched by shame or regret. The music allowed me to break free from some of the darkness that framed my existence.

But somehow my seventies songs got hijacked by some early '80s tunes, and with them came the memories of Jack; how good things once were, and how abruptly I had unraveled them. The contrast hit hard.

Now I found myself sobbing again and not being able to finish my run. The tears and the mucous would flow relentlessly and I was running out of room on my shirt to wipe my eyes and nose.

I went straight to my car and sat there, sobbing. I'd learned there was no point in trying to suppress the pain, but I also didn't want anyone to witness me breaking apart. So, I just sat in the car, with the front seat reclined a bit, and I let the dark pain flow over me again.

When would it end?

Eventually I ate my small breakfast, gathered more tissues, and set out for my therapy walk hoping that it would calm my inner self.

I walked all the way up Chestnut, cut over to Barge at 32nd, then headed back toward 16th before looping around again. I wove through as many side streets as I could, letting my feet take over when my mind couldn't.

These streets had once been a comfort: the canopy of trees, the quiet neighborhoods, the sense of belonging I used to feel here. But now the memories they stirred were too painful. Instead of recalling what had been beautiful, I saw only what I had lost in the thirty-three years with MKD.

I grieved for the life that I might have lived here. A full life. A loving partner. My children growing up in a home filled with support instead of fear. I grieved for the *"what ifs"* and *"might have beens"*, and for the version of myself who went searching for something shallow when I already had so much with Jack.

I walked and walked along both sides of Tieton Drive and Summitview; through familiar neighborhoods, down my old street on 23rd Avenue to the dead end at Lincoln Drive and back again. But instead of comfort, all I saw was opportunity lost. The beauty felt out of reach.

A fear crept in: *What if I can't move back here? What if Yakima hurts too much now?*

I had a beautiful life with my Handsome in Renton, but it wasn't my true home. And yet, standing in Yakima, the place that once held the best of me suddenly felt like a stranger, a dark stranger that didn't want me anymore. It felt like the part of my past that had been filled with light had turned on me, leaving nothing good to hold onto.

What do you do when even your good memories start to betray you?

The thoughts turned darker and heavier. After so many years spent packing the pain away, hiding it where I didn't have to look at it, the pain was now unpacking itself, pushing me to face it directly. I didn't like where it was taking me, but I understood: the darkness was as much a part of my story as the brief light I'd had with Jack.

My walk through the old neighborhoods didn't soothe me. It amplified the ache, showing me all that I had missed in those thirty-three years with MKD.

I kept asking myself the same impossible question: *What did I feel I was missing? What gap in me—or in my relationship with Jack, made me think I needed to "experiment" with MKD?*

And with that, the darkness shifted into self-loathing. How could I have left someone as genuine and kind as Jack for a man so selfish and self-centered? I slipped back into blaming myself.

My mind returned to that Memorial Day weekend in 1981, climbing the three flights of stairs to my dorm room with Jack beside me, knowing I was about to break his heart. I replayed it over and over, searching for the moment that explains everything.

Just two months before that fateful moment, Jack had taken me to Dunbar Jewelers on Yakima Avenue near the Downtown Mall to look at rings. I can still see the emerald-cut solitaire I chose. He took me there so casually, without explanation, supposedly just to look. I remember feeling both thrilled and confused; wondering what it meant, waiting for him to say something he never quite said. We left the store, and life went on or so I thought.

It was March of 1981. Jack's good friend Rob was getting married in mid-April, and Jack was a groomsman in the wedding. Spring felt full of promise, and I was excited for what the season might bring for both of us.

At the wedding, Lori, the bride, asked if I would manage the guest book. It was a kind gesture, considering we barely knew each other outside of our guys. I had sewn myself a beautiful royal blue crepe-de-chine dress for the occasion, and Jack looked handsome in his tux. I felt proud to be on his arm.

The reception followed immediately with the DJ playing all the current hits. At one point Lori sought me out to hold her dress while she used the bathroom. She had bridesmaids who could have helped her, but she chose me. It made me feel important, as though she saw Jack and me as the couple who might be next.

Jack and I danced exactly once in the nearly two years we had been together, and it happened that night. I can still picture his dance moves, even though it was just that one song.

Later, a girl I didn't know, one of Lori's guests, kept drifting toward me for small talk. She seemed lonely, swaying to the music by herself. Jack, meanwhile, spent a lot of time talking with some of the male guests. I tried not to take it personally, but I felt a little deflated. I had hoped he would want to be close to me that night.

When the reception ended, I was still in a romantic mood, and I had not spent much time with Jack at the reception. Instead of driving straight back to his mom's house, I suggested we go up to Scenic Drive and look at the city lights. Back then, there were still quiet patches along the road where couples could park, talk, and share a little privacy.

Jack agreed easily as he always did. But once we parked, I immediately detected a sense of distraction with him. I wanted to savor the sweetness of the evening, maybe even talk about what the day meant for our future. Instead, Jack kept both hands on the steering wheel and stared blankly out the window.

I tried to engage him in an intimate conversation, but he just sat staring out the window. It was evident that his mind was miles away. Wherever his thoughts were, they weren't with me.

Suddenly he said, "Let's go."

No explanation. No shift in tone. He just backed the car up, pulled away from Scenic Drive, and drove toward his mom's house in silence.

His distance stung a bit. I'd never felt insecure with him before, but that night something shifted. He barely acknowledged me, and I sat quietly beside him, wondering what his silence meant for me, for us.

That Sunday we went our separate ways again, me back to Ellensburg at CWU, him to Seattle.

Only six weeks later came the weekend when I "temporarily" broke up with him, the decision that changed every direction my life would take. Not much time at all between Rob and Lori's wedding and that moment I made the biggest mistake of my life.

In those weeks, Jack and I managed one more weekend together. It was around the time Rob and Lori returned from their honeymoon. We stopped by their new apartment for a quick visit. I don't even remember why we went since we didn't take our jackets off or stay long.

The month of May became a blur. I had three interviews scheduled for entry into dental hygiene programs, each one falling on a weekend and each one pulling me away from Jack. It meant we wouldn't see each other again until the end of the month.

The first interview was at Shoreline Community College, just north of Seattle. My mom was hoping that I would get accepted there so I could live at home and commute from Camano Island. That was my last choice for obvious reasons. I'd just spent two years away at college and the last thing I wanted was to return to the constraints of my teenage life. Still, I went through the motions and took their short exam and made sure that they had my current CWU transcripts.

I wasn't impressed with Shoreline's "qualifying test." They handed each candidate a bar of Dove soap and a carving knife, along with a sheet of written directions. The idea was to carve the soap into a specific shape to demonstrate spatial awareness. I remember thinking it was silly.

Worse, they claimed I was missing prerequisites that were clearly listed on the same transcript they had already reviewed. I pointed out their mistake, but they insisted I was wrong. At that moment, I knew I wasn't interested in attending a school that couldn't even read a transcript correctly.

My next application was to the dental hygiene program at Fort Steilacoom Community College. I stayed with my Great Aunt Vy nearby and took their qualifying exam. This one made more sense, a spatial reasoning test with flattened box shapes. You had to choose which assembled box matched the example. Apparently, I did well because they invited me back for a verbal interview.

But my heart was set on Yakima's Weston D. Brown Dental Hygiene Program at YVC. Of course, I would want to return home to finish my final two years. My only memory of that selection process was a simple interview with a panel of instructors with straightforward questions and answers. I left feeling hopeful.

The responses didn't take long. Both Fort Steilacoom and YVC accepted me. I declined Fort Steilacoom's offer and happily accepted YVC's. I was ecstatic that I was going to be in Yakima for the next two years, and Jack would be home around the same time, after finishing his own program in Seattle. It was exactly what I had hoped for.

Everything felt like it was lining up. I was focused and driven, checking each box on my two-year plan. Getting into the Yakima program was the final confirmation that I was exactly where I was supposed to be.

So, what happened? How did I go from being thrilled about starting my life in Yakima with Jack to suddenly feeling this strange "mood" that led me to temporarily break up with him and "experiment" with someone else?

This was the missing link I couldn't shake. I became consumed by it. And in that obsession, I turned every bit of self-loathing, shame, and guilt inward. I punished myself for what felt like the destruction of not just my own life, but Jack's as well. I convinced myself that my decision that weekend in May had set off every loss he later endured in his marriages.

I told myself that if I hadn't broken up with him, we would've still been together. I know that Jack had dispassionately told me when I first came back to Yakima in 2014 that we probably would have gotten a divorce. But I knew better. *If I could stay with a monster for over thirty years, surely Jack and I could've weathered any storm.*

But that life I had imagined with him never happened. And I kept blaming myself, not just for my pain, but for any that he may have gone through in his life.

I know some people reading this might think my emotions were extreme, that my logic had twisted itself into knots. You're right but that's what trauma does. I wasn't thinking like the person I used to be. My mind had been shaped and distorted by decades of psychological and emotional abuse from someone who was supposed to love and protect me.

That kind of betrayal forces your brain into a war with itself. The cognitive dissonance can break you. When the person who should be safest becomes the source of terror, your sense of reality collapses. You learn to trust no one, not even your own thoughts. All you're left with is your own damaged mind trying to interpret a world that no longer makes sense.

I was very well aware that I had an amazing man in my life. My most Handsome Man, who I loved more than I have ever loved any other man, including Jack. But that didn't erase the fact that I had spent over forty years in pain because of the one decision I made back in 1981.

I had placed myself in a kind of mental prison, and I kept wondering why the sentence felt so harsh. Other people committed worse crimes and seemed to walk free long before I did. Why was my punishment lasting decades?

How much more of this punishment was I supposed to endure? How do I get my light back? How do I put on a smile for the world to see and yet battle this dark force that kept tightening its grip on every part of me?

Coming back to Yakima didn't give me the answers I was looking for. It only pulled me deeper into the shadows.

I knew I had to keep facing the darkness. I had to keep fighting it. I didn't have any choice but to keep moving forward in my fight unless I wanted to just end it all. That, I wouldn't do, but I could see how others could give into that sweet relief of pain because the darkness was so thick and deep.

I needed to go back to Renton and be with my Handsome Man. His arms were the one place where the heaviness loosened, even if only for a little while. I needed to feel his love wrapped around me where there was no demand that I be anything other than what I was in that moment.

I would have to find another way to fight the darkness. Returning to Yakima wasn't the answer; it only unearthed more hurt. I needed to find the way out of these shadows and have my questions answered so I could feel like I deserved to be happy again.

****

Anything unresolved within our energy field will keep manifesting itself into life until we heal it.

Nadia Gledhill, QHHT, Past Life Regression

CH. 20 — The Toll It Takes

I don't think many of us truly understand how destructive long-term, chronic stress can be to the body. And this stress doesn't have to come from the outside. It can manifest itself from our own minds, old thoughts, old images of past traumas that resurface from a brain that has never fully processed the event of the past.

When the original trauma occurs, the body reacts instantly. Specialized brain regions and glands surge into overdrive, flooding the system with hormones that were meant to protect us. But in that extended emergency state, the hormonal balance that normally regulates the body becomes chaotic instead.

Once the immediate danger has passed from the consciousness of the person, the hormone levels eventually settle. But the memory of the trauma doesn't disappear. It stays locked in the brain waiting to be released and, when it finally resurfaces, the onslaught of a hormonal war kicks in and the body reacts as though the threat is real and present in the moment – as if it is happening again.

The brain doesn't distinguish between what is real or what is imagined. It only recognizes danger. So, the glands react accordingly, even if it is just a dream or a memory. Sometimes those glands release too much hormone and sometimes too little. Over time, this imbalance can cause real and lasting changes in the brain of a victim of prolonged abuse.

Cortisol, the primary stress hormone, is produced in the adrenal glands, which sit on top of the kidneys. When the brain perceives a threat, cortisol surges, converting glycogen stored in the liver into glucose. That glucose fuels the muscles so the body can respond instantly in a classic "fight-or-flight" mode.

But when cortisol stays high for too long, the consequences become serious. It can cause weight gain, weaken your immune system so you get sick more often, and can increase your blood pressure.

Prolonged elevated cortisol can even lead to hair loss by disrupting the immune system that protects hair follicles. I wrote in **The Big Dark** about discovering two shiny patches of scalp behind my right ear. This was one of my first clear, physical signs of what the stress had been doing to me. The hair loss traced back to a specific traumatic event six months earlier when MKD threatened suicide. It was only then that I started to understand the toll those years of fear had taken on my body.

The hippocampus, which is not a gland but a structure deep in the brain, is responsible for memories and learning new things. It's also highly vulnerable to cortisol. Studies show that prolonged traumatic stress can actually shrink the hippocampus, which makes it harder to recall things clearly and contributes to the brain fog that so many victims experience. This happens because your brain has been forced to constantly scan for threats, so your survival becomes a priority over memory storage.

When a victim seems confused, struggles to learn new information, or has trouble forming coherent sentences, it isn't weakness or dramatics. It's the physiological impact of cortisol on the hippocampus.

I lived this. There were countless moments during my marriage to MKD when I knew exactly what I wanted to say, yet the words came out jumbled and tangled beyond my control. I was shocked that I couldn't even control my own words or make sense of them.

If you or someone you know has this same experience of jumbled words when trying to speak, know that you have no control. And understand that it is the overload of stress hormones that is causing it.

The amygdala, another structure of the brain, is located just in front of the hippocampus. It processes emotions, especially fear and anxiety. It aids in decision making and it is responsible for identifying external threats that would trigger the fight-or-flight response.

Under long-term stress, the neurons in the amygdala actually change in structure *and* behavior. This restructuring of the neurons contributes to the intense emotional responses to psychological triggers. This, in turn, plays a major role in the development of PTSD and Complex PTSD. Those changes in the amygdala heighten emotional responses and make psychological triggers feel like fresh danger.

The amygdala's constant vigilance of looking for threats explains why the victim has a quick trigger to snap and get angry. This usually follows with a wave of guilt that they "over reacted" to a situation.

Again, you have no control over this emotional response. The poor amygdala's shape has been altered and thus alters its functions. Your uneven emotional responses are a product of this altered shape and function from this part of your brain.

My intense reactions to anything tied to the trauma and their memories that I endured for over thirty years may look dramatic or irrational to some, but they are, in fact, predictable neurobiological responses to prolonged abuse.

Then there's the prefrontal cortex, the area behind the forehead, responsible for executive functions like reasoning, problem-solving, and emotional regulation. This part of the brain is important for abstract thinking and allows us to make connections from past experiences and plan appropriately for future events instead of reacting impulsively. This is the part that is actively engaged in our conscious thoughts.

Interestingly, this part of the brain will also shrink under prolonged stress. When that happens, logical thinking becomes compromised. Brain fog intensifies. Decision-making becomes clouded and distorted. Parts of the brain stop communicating with each other.

These are reasons why victims of abuse often can't think rationally. It's not because they don't want to – it's because they are physiologically unable to do so. These are the other reasons as to why victims don't "just leave" their abuser – they don't have the mental capacity to see their way out.

I couldn't comprehend at the time that MKD's threats to abandon me and the kids and take all the money were just manipulations. Today, I can see that clearly. But back then, I believed that his threats to abandon us were real. My traumatized brain was incapable of sorting the real from the coerced. I couldn't see beyond the threat for me and my children due to the heightened levels of stress hormones flooding my body and brain. Because of that, he successfully coerced me to be obedient.

Now that my hormonally scrambled brain has finally settled, I can see what I couldn't see back then. I know now that the military never would have allowed MKD to abandon us without recourse. He would have been legally required to support his children. But in the fog of prolonged, intense stress, I couldn't recognize my own leverage. My logical thinking had been bent out of shape by years of trauma.

When the prefrontal cortex isn't functioning properly, emotional regulation falters. And when the amygdala's neurons have reorganized themselves under prolonged fear, emotional responses become amplified. The two systems team up: one weakened, one overactive creating a perfect storm of heightened reactions.

That's how something so simple, like pulling a sentimental mug from the dishwasher, could send me into tears. Or, how putting socks in the underwear drawer by mistake could spark anger far beyond what the situation calls for. These aren't "overreactions." They're the result of neurobiological damage layered on top of emotional scars.

Then there's the breakdown in communication between the different brain regions. Even when the individual parts are struggling, they still need strong neural pathways to relay information back and forth. Under prolonged trauma, those pathways fray. The brain begins to feel like it's swirling inside a hurricane – chaotic and disorganized, spinning without direction.

And then there are the physical signs people rarely talk about.

Premature graying, especially before thirty, isn't always genetic. Research shows it can be linked to prolonged, intense stress. Looking back, it makes sense. I carried a lot of stress early in my life while I was working at a young age and contributing financially just to survive. That pressure only intensified once I married MKD and had to absorb the consequences of his spending habits.

I was once embarrassed by a dentist that I worked for early in my marriage who was shocked when he stood over me in my operatory and could see gray hair forming in the back of my head and he let me know it. "Pam. You have gray hair already? And you are only 27!"

Thanks Doc.

Oh, and I loved how he made that comment right in front of my patient as well.

There were other stressors early in my marriage to MKD beyond the financial ones. His emotional and psychological control took a toll long before I realized what was happening. No wonder I began graying in my mid-twenties and have been coloring my hair ever since.

When someone falls apart and collapses in front of you, when they sob so deeply that they feel the emotion vibrating through every cell, they're not "overreacting." They're not being dramatic. Cortisol has been running wild in their body for years, reshaping their brain chemistry, shrinking key structures, and stripping away their ability to regulate their emotions.

I didn't know any of this while I was falling apart during the summer and fall of 2023. I didn't realize what I was going through was a normal but serious physiological response to decades of traumatic stress. I didn't realize just how compromised my brain had become.

But it all makes sense now.

At the time, it was terrifying. I didn't know if I would ever conquer it. And it was dark as I became drenched with these immense, heavy emotions that ran through my veins along with the brain fog that re-emerged that made rational thought nearly impossible.

I felt like I was drowning inside my own mind.

These are the unseen scars of domestic abuse; the intense psychological and neuro damage that victims develop, long after the traumatic abuse ends.

And the damage doesn't stop when the abuse stops. It continues to silently build until something finally forces the survivor to confront it. That unpredictability is why the reckoning can arrive years later, without warning, and flatten the very soul of someone who thought they were safe.

Remember, it didn't come back to destroy me until nine years after I had escaped.

Be warned: if you have escaped the torment and torture of long-term abuse, there *will* be a reckoning. It will bring you to your knees and crumble your very being. There will be no escape. And it *will* happen; it's only a matter of when.

When this reckoning does manifest, remember this; what you're feeling is normal. It will hurt more deeply than anything you've known, but the same strength that carried you out of the abuse will be the strength you draw on to face it. You can't bury it anymore. It will keep surfacing, again and again until you finally turn toward it and begin to heal.

I was worn down from my poisoned brain refusing to set the darkness down long enough for me to rest. I could count the hours of sleep I managed to get each night on one hand.

Four hours of sleep seemed to be my average. Many nights, I didn't sleep at all. Was it menopause? Unresolved trauma? Most likely both. It often felt as if my body and mind were fighting two different wars at once.

Rest is essential. We need it to recharge and to meet the physical, emotional, and mental demands of the day. Without it, our response time to external stimuli is slowed. You see the light turn green, but you sit there, unsure what to do next. You struggle to recall your computer password. You will count yourself lucky to make it to or from work without running a red light because you won't even remember the drive at all.

Sleep is so important that in the updated hierarchy of human needs, it comes right after water and before food. That shocked me when I first learned it. I grew up believing our basic needs were air, water, food, clothing, and shelter – in that order. Added to that list now is sleep, right before food, and it makes sense. Sleep deprivation is literally used as a method for torture and without sleep, the human body begins to shut down within a week.

My lack of sleep pushed me into a downward spiral. On top of the physiological changes already happening in my brain from trauma, I began seeing changes in my face. My eyes were puffy. My skin sagged. The area over my right eye, where I'd had the lipoma removed in 2015, drooped even more because the nerves never fully regenerated.

Feeling empty inside was one thing but watching that emptiness show up on my face created its own kind of grief. It became a negative feedback loop. I became more depressed about my appearance – which manifested in my face and neck – which caused me to become even more depressed. The vicious cycle continued.

I realize now that the dratted stress hormone, cortisol, is also to blame for this. The long-term elevated cortisol levels deplete collagen, the protein that gives skin its structure and resilience. When collagen drops, your skin loosens, sags, and separates from the muscle beneath it.

Aging is natural, but I felt as if mine had been pushed into fast-forward. Thirty years of chronic stress, followed by nearly a decade of unprocessed trauma, left their marks on my face long before time intended them to be there.

I started to become self-conscious wherever I went. I wore sunglasses almost everywhere so no one could see my drooping eyelid, and I tried to limit interactions with anyone outside of work.

Eventually, I decided to look into cosmetic surgery. If I could correct what I saw on the outside, maybe I could begin feeling better on the inside. Living just outside Seattle and

Bellevue meant I had access to world-class specialists, so I searched online, read reviews, and scheduled consultations. My goal was to restore my drooping eyelid caused by the lipoma removal eight years earlier.

I found a specialist in Maple Valley and went in for a consultation.

The doctor was nice enough, though I felt nervous simply being there. Women are often criticized for wanting cosmetic surgery, and somewhere in the back of my 63-year-old mind I could still hear my grandmother calling it vanity. But after a lifetime of pleasing others and placing myself last, I pushed past that old programming. I sat tall on the exam table and let him give his assessment.

He told me I could do this and that, then if I wanted to, I could also do this – all while pulling gently at my skin to show the potential results. He explained the procedure, the recovery time, and how much work I would need to miss. Then he left me with his assistant to discuss cost.

It came to nearly $18,000 for the procedure that I had inquired about. Yikes! I had no idea it would be that expensive and insurance wouldn't cover any of it.

I thanked them and took the folder of information home to think it over. Eighteen thousand dollars was a lot to consider, especially out of pocket, and his proposed approach for my eyelid involved more procedures than I'd expected.

But I knew one thing for certain: I *would* have the surgery eventually. It was simply a matter of timing and saving the money. I decided to take my time and explore other specialists before making a final decision.

Around this time, I received an invitation to my high school reunion at the end of September, an all-class event, with alumni from the 1960s through the eighties. I wanted to go, but it fell on a Saturday when I was scheduled to work.

In our dental practice, we typically work Tuesday through Friday. We put in long nine-hour days. Once a month we open on Saturday to accommodate patients. But it seemed that every Saturday we worked, something meaningful in my life was happening too. After Covid, finding a temp became nearly impossible, so I was constantly missing family gatherings, celebrations, and chances to reconnect with friends because I was working on that Saturday.

I am always a supportive team player, and I am aware that everyone was sacrificing something to work on those Saturdays. But now, with my emotional reserves running thin, I needed that day for myself. I was growing resentful of how much of my waking life was obligated to others when what I truly needed was rest, and a chance to reconnect with myself, good friends and family.

I had already missed so many high school events over the years because they landed on our work Saturdays. When I learned the reunion would be another casualty, I had a small meltdown.

It happened early in the morning before patients arrived. A group of us were gathered at the front desk reviewing the day's schedule, and I finally let the frustration spill out. I vented about always having to miss important life-moments because of our Saturday hours.

Too many nights with little sleep had taken their toll and I had become fiercely protective of my weekends. I needed that time to rest and tend to my mental health. After nearly fifty years in the workforce, it was becoming clear that I had to scale back.

So, I told Dr. Kaur right then that I couldn't work Saturdays anymore. I needed that one day each month to reclaim myself.

Fortunately, she understood. And just like that, my Saturdays were mine again, free from conflict, free from guilt, free from feeling torn between work and missing out on important events.

Making that decision was a profound step for me. I had been conditioned for so long to never let anyone down, to always put others' needs ahead of my own. That mindset is part of what led me into MKD's abusive orbit in the first place. I put his needs and wants way above my own so that I started to become less of me. I was convinced that I didn't have the right to prioritize myself.

Even though I'd escaped nine years earlier and believed I had healed, the truth was obvious: I still didn't value myself enough to have opted out of those Saturdays sooner.

It was time to put myself first and to stop apologizing for it. I deserved that extra day each month. Such a small thing on the surface, yet such a tremendous move forward in rebuilding my self-worth.

Gaining back my Saturdays became a win in my quiet battle against the darkness that tried to convince me I was unworthy and at fault for all the years of pain. It was also a necessary step for my health. Decades of stress had taken a real toll, and this choice wasn't indulgent, it was survival.

I still had a long way to climb out of the toxic neuro-soup of shame, guilt, and regret swirling inside me.

But for now, I have my Saturdays. And that was a meaningful start.

****

Neuroplasticity *(neu-ro-plas-tic-it-ty) — n.*
The brain's ability to form and reorganize synaptic connections, especially in response to learning or experience or following injury.

Neuroplasticity, also known as brain plasticity, refers to the brain's remarkable ability to change and adapt throughout life. The brain can change its structure and function in response to new experiences, learning, or even injury.

CH. 21 — Sophie

Life doesn't unfold one clean event at a time. We are constantly dealing with layers of events that happen all at once: the weather, chores, obligations, work, interactions with friends and strangers, returning calls, paying bills, squeezing in a workout, figuring out dinner, tending to our children's needs, finding time to rest. All these events and more are going on around us and through us in the course of just one day causing our brain to always be in the state of multitasking whether we like it or not.

Our minds are constantly shifting gears, adjusting to whatever needs attention in the moment while monitoring the other tasks waiting their turn. One priority rises, then another, and we move with it almost without thinking.

And so it goes with me.

My visits with Barbara overlapped with my own internal search to try to understand how I had become entangled with MKD. At the same time, my body was reenacting old trauma in the form of triggers that manifested a physiological response in the form of grief, shame, guilt, and a sense of heavy internal darkness. All of this was happening while I worked full-time, managing a home and intimate relationships.

Everything was happening at one time, all the time.

Sensing how overloaded I was, my Dearest suggested we spend our ninth anniversary weekend camping at Whispering Pines in Cle Elum. We could take in the summer concert at Swiftwater Cellars, then drive to Yakima for an afternoon. He is always so good about planning something special for our anniversary, and he could tell I needed space to disengage from the usual. My Dearest has always been in tune with my emotional needs, and I am so very fortunate to have him by my side.

Camping sounded perfect. It was a chance to step out of the noise of daily life and let my nervous system breathe. Whispering Pines offered exactly that: quiet, shade, and room to reset.

We rode our bikes along a nearby trail that morning, then headed to the small pond with our floaties to cool off before getting ready for the concert. I had a almost forgotten how therapeutic water can be. Just drifting together and holding hands while the water's gentle movement kept us suspended helped to make the darkness that I had been carrying feel lighter and less noticeable.

We were so relaxed we considered skipping the concert altogether. But eventually we mustered the resolve to climb out, dry off, and get dressed for a relaxed evening of celebrating us.

In the realm of quantum physics, time doesn't exist – only the moment you're in. You don't move through time. Time moves through you, one experience at a time. So here we were, nine years into our relationship, and it felt as if we had simply blinked. How lucky we were to have found each other. How blessed to be sharing the last chapter of our lives side by side.

The day's sun was drifting down around us at Swiftwater Cellars causing gentle shadows to start growing around our feet while the day's heat fell away to a sweet coolness. We set up our lawn chairs with a clear view of the stage and settled in for a night of music.-

The evening was deeply healing for me with my Handsome Man holding my hand and making me feel like I was the most important person in the world to him. Here I was with the man who made me feel the safest and most loved by my side.   And here we were, celebrating us, in this place and at this moment. It was exactly what my soul needed.

The first band to play covered the best of The Eagles. Soon we found ourselves tapping our toes and keeping rhythm with the one hand that wasn't holding a glass of wine. People of all ages sang along to the music of the seventies. It felt like one big karaoke fest. I allowed myself to simply enjoy the moment, letting the past stay where it was.

Then came the next band, *Petty Thief*, which covered music by Tom Petty. It happened to be one of my Dearest's favorite performers so before I knew it, and before the band could play the first full measure, my Dearest grabbed me by the hand and pulled me up to the dance floor.

It was impossible not to be swept into Tom Petty's music. The energy around us was pure joy. My Dearest spun me gently, then drew me in close, wrapping his arms around me, capturing my eyes and singing every song as if each word was a personal message from him to me.

There are few people like my Dearest who let themselves be fully carried by the music, feeling it all the way down to their soul. Anyone watching could see how infectious his joy was as his energy radiated outwards to anyone nearby.

And standing there with him, held in his arms, I felt some of that joy seep into the places that had felt dark for so long.

How could I not love and adore this man? He is the greatest blessing the Universe has ever given me, and I am forever grateful to have him by my side.

So why, then, did tears start sliding down my cheeks while I was dancing with him?

As we held each other close, I couldn't stop thinking about how wonderful my life is now and how much I had missed out on a connection like this for more than thirty years.

MKD never danced with me, *and* he didn't want me dancing without him either. Because of this, I wasn't allowed to express my joy through dancing for a long time. I had lost so much joy being married to him. I was forced to always be on the lookout for whatever mood he was in. I had to be careful not to be too happy in his presence. He would always find a way to punish me if I was happy when he wasn't.

Narcissists can't tolerate emotions they don't control. They don't like it if you have your own emotions. If they're miserable, you're expected to be miserable too. If you dare to feel joy, they twist it into proof that you don't care enough about their unhappiness. Over time, you learn to dim your own feelings just to keep the peace.

Narcissists are sick, manipulative people.

And now here I was, on a beautiful summer evening in the Cascade Mountains, dancing with the man who absolutely adores me and celebrating nine years together – feeling all the beautiful love he has for me. And yet, the darkness of my past wanted to have center stage.

I know now that I have always deserved this kind of connection, even when I was married. But MKD was incapable of giving it. He pretended at first, but pretending to be something that you aren't is exhausting. Eventually the mask slipped and I saw the real man that I had married; a man who didn't care if he hurt me. In fact, he took pleasure in the power that it gave him.

That's when the real terror lodges itself deep in your brain.

When the person who vowed to love and protect you becomes the one person you fear the most, your mind has to contort itself just to survive. You try to create explanations because the truth is too cruel and too destabilizing. This is where cognitive dissonance takes over, and your brain dissolves into a fog of shock, denial, and confusion.

Imagine having to walk on eggshells and navigate your whole nervous system around the one person who should have been the source of your calm, safety, and grounding.

My Handsome Man was the complete opposite of MKD. And here I was, face to face with that stark contrast of what I had endured and what I now have. I was crying for the part of me that was lucky enough to have this human soul connect with mine and I was mourning for the part of me that had lived in heightened fear and anxiety for more than thirty years.

The tears were all thanks to my amygdala and hippocampus being distorted due to the increase flow of cortisol as a result of the traumatic memories flooding back.

I was trying to heal, to move beyond the darkness of my past. But healing is messy. It can look like stagnation even when something deep inside is slowly shifting. I knew I was moving forward, but I had to fully grieve for the me who was lost, hurt, and alone through those thirty-three years of hell before I could move into the whole, healthy life I was meant to have.

I hated MKD for the darkness he brought into my life. And I was so mad at myself for the part that I played in it.

For the rest of the evening, I held my Handsome a little tighter. Maybe I needed to reassure myself that he was truly a safe place for my heart. Maybe I wanted him to know how much he means to me. And maybe some part of me still believed that the dark energy of my past was real and could come and take me if I didn't hold tight enough to my Dearest.

I found it hard to fall asleep again. The dark energy swirled inside me, making me feel as though I had to stay vigilant during the darkest parts of the night where I felt the most vulnerable. Much like all those nights when I endured the wrath of MKD and still had to climb into bed beside him. There had been so little sleep back then because sleep meant letting my guard down. Even now, with him miles away, my nervous system struggled to believe I was truly safe.

So, I lay there with tears in my eyes and heavy clouds in my mind, trying to give my body the rest it needed.

The sleep finally found me and the morning finally came. My body felt depleted and exhausted from the emotional toll of the night and the lack of rest. I had become used to running on very little sleep, but it meant barely functioning during the day.

My Dearest suggested I try CBN gummies to help me relax at night. We had a day trip planned to Yakima, and we decided that one stop would be at a cannabis store so I could find something to help.

Whenever we go to Yakima, one of our favorite things to do is to go through open houses and dream about moving back. The idea of returning was a bit mixed for me after my last visit when the city felt more hostile than welcoming. But I was willing to go if I had my most Handsome Man with me for an emotional buffer.

I tried hard not to pull my Dearest into my emotional journey. There wasn't anything he could do to make the darkness disappear; this was a path I had to walk myself. He was already doing so much simply by being there for me and creating an intimately safe and stable place to be. That, alone, is one of the most essential ingredients in recovering from trauma; having a space where you can work through your psychological demons without fear of judgement.

So off to Yakima we went. From Cle Elum it was only an hour's drive, and we chose the Yakima Canyon instead of the interstate over Manastash Ridge.

The canyon road is one of my favorite routes into Yakima. It winds gently alongside the Yakima River; a two-lane road carved through ancient volcanic rock. The basaltic columns rising from the canyon walls are remnants of massive lava flows that shaped the region nearly ten million years ago.

To take the canyon road, you have to be content driving 45 miles per hour. If slowing down frustrates you, then you will want to stay on the interstate. But for me, that slow pace was exactly what I needed. It calmed my nervous system and gave me a chance to spot some unique wildlife like Big Horned Sheep, Bald Eagles, and deer. In the summer, the river is full of people floating on inner tubes, fly fishing, or zipping along on jet skis.

The beauty of the canyon with its basaltic columns makes it easy to drop out of your thoughts and simply exist in the moment. And on a clear day, when you emerge from the south end, you're met with a spectacular view of Mt. Adams on the horizon.

Mt. Adams is the quiet sibling of the more famous Mt. Rainier to its north and the infamous Mt. St. Helens to its south. Mt Adams was that same mountain that blew me a kiss nine years earlier as I drove west on I-82. It was my first silent "welcome home" after escaping MKD.

Here I was with my Dearest, heading back to the city that has always held me the closest, and I wasn't sure how I was going to handle it. Would Yakima embrace me, the way it once had? Or would it feel cold and rejecting the way it did on my last visit? I didn't know. But I was deeply grateful to have him beside me.

We stopped at Starbucks for coffee and looked over the Sunday open houses so we could plan our route as efficiently as possible. We wanted to be sure to still have enough time to meet up with a high school friend of mine and a former neighbor who had moved to Yakima a few years earlier.

My Dearest had grown up on the upper west side of Manhattan in an apartment above his dad and older brother's grocery store on 109ᵗʰ Street and Amsterdam Ave. which is now a pub called Amity Hall. He used to believe that anyone who grew up in an actual house had to be rich. So, he loved wandering through Yakima's neighborhoods with me, imagining how "rich" we must be to live in one. We both fell in love with several little pockets of neighborhoods that each had its own kind of energy.

There was the Barge–Chestnut neighborhood for obvious sentimental reasons where I had spent my teenage years. But beyond nostalgia, the tree-covered streets also offered a sense of protection with the branches forming a green canopy that softened even the hottest summer day.

Still, I reminded my Dearest that those same leaves would eventually fall. Since he despises yard work, the raking would be left to me and at this stage of life, climbing ladders to clean out gutters and hauling bags of leaves had lost its charm.

Then there was the Lincoln–Gilbert Park area. We love the single-story brick homes and the welcoming sidewalks that encourage daily strolls and neighborly conversation. A single story meant easier roof access; a practical detail we couldn't ignore. And because my Dearest thrives on connecting with people, the idea of sidewalks would make that easier to greet others on our walks.

We also meandered through Englewood and the Scenic Drive area, enjoying the eclectic mix of architecture and the changing views of the city and the rolling hills in the distance. I pointed out houses where I used to babysit or where high school friends once lived. Eventually, the homes gave way to orchards with the apples already beginning to mature.

Somehow, having my Dearest by my side made Yakima feel kinder. I found myself believing that maybe we could move back someday. I started to imagine the beautiful life we would have together; one filled with more time for living and less time for the daily grind of work that had claimed nearly fifty years of my life.

We stopped by the home of our former neighbor who had recently moved to Yakima, but he wasn't in. No worries. We still needed to pick up some CBN gummies for my sleep, and we were still planning to meet my high school friend, Sophie, later in the afternoon. So off we went to find a cannabis store.

I was surprised to find that Yakima's cannabis shops are tucked into the most obscure pockets of the city. One sits off 16th and Fruitvale, pulled back from the street and almost hidden. Another is on the far east end of Yakima Avenue, close to the interstate.

Why wasn't there one in West Valley? Or near Nob Hill and 24th? There are plenty of people in Yakima who use cannabis for recreational and medicinal purposes and it's legal. And yet the city seems to have pushed these stores to the fringes as if embarrassed by their existence.

When I was young, the area where the Yakima Tennis Club now stands on Fruitvale, used to be full of outdoor movie theaters. Remember those? They were magical. Sometimes my siblings and I would climb on top of the car with our sleeping bags and watch movies under the stars. I still remember seeing *Mary Poppins* at the Sunnyside outdoor theater.

There was at least one outdoor theater off Fruitvale that played X-rated films. As teenagers, we would drive past slowly, craning our necks and hoping to catch a forbidden glimpse of the screen. I had always thought of Fruitvale as the place where the city put businesses that were not considered mainstream.

So, when I saw the cannabis store tucked back off Fruitvale, it gave me the same impression—that the city was a bit ashamed of this commerce and wanted it camouflaged, the way they once tried to hide the adult movie theater. It's funny, considering how many Yakima residents quietly slip in to get their stash.

I guarantee that as more younger generations become eligible to vote, the city will eventually loosen these restrictions and more of these stores will pop up all over just like any nail salon or auto store.

In the meantime, my Dearest and I stopped at Yakima Weed Co. North on 16th and Fruitvale and were lucky enough to find one remaining pack of 3:1 CBN/THC gummies. The clerk told us they're incredibly popular and hard to keep in stock. Clearly, I wasn't the only one in Yakima struggling to sleep.

But I was relieved to have a bag in my hand. I had big hopes that tonight, finally, I might get the rest my body so desperately needed.

We were planning to head back to Cle Elum and our campsite in a couple of hours, but first we drove to the River Ridge Golf Course in Selah to meet my high school friend, Sophie Boucher. We had kept in touch off and on since I returned to Yakima nine years earlier, often running into each other whenever I was in town. She is one of the few friends in Yakima who has met my Handsome Man. He has always enjoyed Sophie's energy, so when I suggested a meetup, he was genuinely looking forward to it.

River Ridge Golf Course sits just to the right as you enter Selah. They have a fun little bar and restaurant that my Dearest and I have taken advantage of in the past when I would reconnect with some of my friends. By the time we arrived, Sophie was already waiting for us.

It's always great to be in her presence. She is an authentic soul. You know that the attention that she gives you is sincere and focused while she seeks to connect at the level just like my Handsome and I do.

We started with light conversation, checking in on one another and talking briefly about the upcoming class reunion. Then my Dearest got up to grab us a couple of drinks. The moment he walked away, Sophie's empathetic antennae went up. She knew something was off and asked me a direct question.

Sophie is one of those people who has the ability to "hear" beyond the words and "see" past the smile just as I do. As an empath, you may recognize that someone's energy is off. Part of being an empath is that you also know when to say something to someone and when to just give them a hug and a knowing look that shows your silent understanding. Sophie has that same gift. Due to our closeness, she knew she could bridge that knowing and ask directly what she already sensed.

"How are you really? The last time I saw you, you were struggling."

That was all it took. The floodgates opened, and I just began to sob. Sophie didn't flinch or rush me. She simply sat with me, compassionately allowing me to bring it all out at my own pace.

I told her about the dream I'd had in March and the torment I'd been living with ever since. She understood without my having to explain much at all. She reminded me that when I returned to Yakima nine years earlier, I had hinted at things I couldn't talk about. "I knew," she said softly, "that whatever it was had to have been really bad for you."

And then the dam broke. I let everything spill out—the years of emotional abuse, the betrayal of discovering his cross-dressing only after we were married. Sophie understood instantly. She didn't need details. She began naming the truth before I could.

"I can imagine that once you found out he was a cross-dresser, you must have been so confused about what to do. And you had little ones to consider. I'm sure that's also when he increased the abuse, because you knew his secret and he was afraid you would give him away. He must have bullied and tormented you so you would be obedient. It wouldn't be easy to get away, especially if you have kids and then are expected to be the sole provider. You went through hell because you didn't have a choice."

Holy crap! How did she know all of that? She was spot on— every part of it. And for the first time, someone understood the full cost without me having to justify why I stayed with a monster. Sophie knew.

She just sat there with the most compassionate eyes that told me I was not invisible.

I had felt invisible for so long. The pain had been too much for me to face, and too much for most people to hear without them being overwhelmed themselves. But Sophie "saw" me, even though I was putting on a good front.

That's what empaths do. We sense the smallest shifts in tone, expression, and body language and instantly understand the emotional terrain. I developed that ability from living on high alert for so many years. It was a survival mechanism that I mastered so I knew what mood he would be in so I could put on the right armor to protect myself.

I have no idea how Sophie honed her skills. Some people are simply born with them. But the ability to read a room so acutely comes at a high cost. We empaths become overwhelmed quickly by the energy around us. Even joyful energy can be too much. We absorb it all, every emotion, every shift, until our own system is overloaded. Then we have to slip away from the group or find a quiet corner where we can minimize the overload.

Up to this point, the only person who had been able to help me was Barbara. But she helped by asking difficult questions I needed to confront. Sophie, on the other hand, didn't need me to say much of anything. She already understood. All I had to do was sit in her compassionate presence and let the tears fall. She was going to stay there with me until I was ready to stop.

My Handsome Man returned to the table with our drinks and saw that I had melted into a sobbing mess. Sophie looked up and said matter-of-factly, "It was me. I asked her a question, and she needed to let the pain go."

My Dearest, always the steady support, simply replied, "Good. I'm glad she has someone like you to talk to. My baby has had a hard time processing this pain."

And there I was, held in the presence of two loving, patient souls – neither trying to fix me, neither urging me to "get over it" the way so many well-meaning people do. They just let me cry. They validated the depth of the wound by witnessing it without turning away.

I want you all to know this: people who are hurting do not need you to solve their problems. They need you to be there. To hold them. To offer a hug. To sit quietly beside them while they feel what they need to feel. What they do *not* need is to be rushed out of their pain or be told to "move on."

Those with deep scars cannot simply decide to heal on command. The body will heal when it's ready. True healing from the deepest, darkest wound requires turning toward it and doing, as they say, the dark work - the shadow work.

There are no shortcuts.

You must create space, real space, for the brain to slowly rewire itself out of the fight, flight, freeze, or fawn state it lived in for so long. Those states may have protected you once, but over time they reshape the brain in ways that create even more pain.

Remember, the brain can't distinguish the difference between what is real and what is imagined. With the flood of these traumatic memories also comes with it the suppressed feelings of real danger. The subconscious mind then pumps the stress hormones of adrenaline and cortisol throughout the body in an attempt to protect it. The result is unregulated emotional outbursts and the inability to process the emotions logically.

Victims would like nothing more than to be able to "just get over it", but their subconscious and their hormonally poisoned body won't let them.

That's why victims need a safe, stable environment – free from extra pressures and expectations, while they process the trauma they've spent years surviving. They don't need to be told they're exaggerating, taking too long, or being dramatic. They already feel "less than." Why would anyone with a heart add to that weight by suggesting their healing is too slow or not being done the "right" way?

Having Sophie see me, the real me, was a transformational moment. It gave me permission to feel sad and to grieve the life I could have had. It told me that the pain was something that I was allowed to feel.

I want to emphasize this: feelings are never wrong. People respond to trauma differently because no two lives are the same. Even siblings raised under the same roof experience life uniquely.

The oldest child often grows up with parents who are usually younger, just starting out, and have less money and more stress. The middle child may get lost in the shuffle of a growing family, their needs met more slowly. The youngest might encounter the most relaxed rules because the parents are exhausted or have simply softened over time.

We each grow into adulthood with our own emotional toolkit, one shaped by circumstances only *we* lived through. So, you cannot criticize someone's emotional response just because it's not the one you would have. That isn't empathy; it's judgment. And judgment wounds someone who is already in pain.

Often, the best and only thing you can do is give people the space to feel what they're feeling. Offer a hug. Say, "You're amazing. You're worthy. You're beautiful. I got you."

That's it. Just be there. Truly be there. Not fixing. Not rushing. Not minimizing.
Because, remember, physiologically, people cannot help their emotions.

The drive back to the campsite with my Handsome Man was quiet as I sat with the aftershocks of that unexpected emotional release. I had cried before, of course but usually in private. Rarely had I let myself unravel in front of someone else, aside from my Dearest, who always allows me to show my pain without judgment. Being witnessed like that was profoundly healing.

I felt a small lift in the darkness, but the heaviness wasn't gone. It was still waiting for me to face it; to understand why I endured so much, for so long. I knew I was moving forward in my healing process, even though I still had a long way to go.

I had taken back my Saturdays for my mental health. I had reinforced how extremely lucky I was to have my Handsome Man by my side. And I just had a loving and compassionate soul "see" into my pain and make me realize it was ok to "feel" the pain.

I was determined to dig deeper into the darkness and find out what happened to me so that I could cleanse myself of the guilt and shame that I was wearing.

I knew I could do it.

Just knowing that Sophie witnessed my pain without judgement gave me the belief that I deserved to find the peace that my soul needed.

Who would have thought that social media would pave the way towards answering those questions that still haunted me.

****

What people don't talk about much is that to heal trauma, you have to grieve a lot. You need to grieve the life you didn't have, the love you didn't get, the years lost, the way you treated yourself and others.

We don't like to feel this way, that's why most people avoid it. They suppress it. They dissociate. They will stay frozen in their grief for years and they won't even know it. But it will show up in their lives as depression, stagnancy, and disconnections from their emotions and relationships.

It's some of the most difficult emotional work that a person can ever do. But it's the only way through, because without that grieving, without that letting go, the trauma stays with you. It poisons your body, your mind and your spirit. And it makes you keep reliving and recreating the past as if it is still present.

The only way out of this is by going into the emotions that weren't safe for you to feel when the trauma happened. If you can feel those emotions, it's a sign that you are already healing. "You can't heal what you don't feel" has a profound truth in it.

When we feel, we remember our souls again. We regain connection to life and all that is. When we grieve, we heal our connection to God and every other living being.

Underneath all the feelings you don't want to feel is your aliveness, your vitality, your laughter, your love for life and your love for others and your soul.

Grieving is a soul retrieval where you dive into the darkness to recover the truth of who you are.

Dr. Natalya Fateyeva

Therapist, Doctor of Behavioral Health, Holistic Practitioner

CH. 22 — Instagram

I've never been a big fan of social media. It always felt like too much work to keep up with people, and most of my free time is already spent taking care of myself and my small family.

I did take a chance on Twitter years ago because I wanted to follow my two favorite artists, Steve Perry and Pink. But the app kept feeding me posts I didn't want, and eventually the cruelty and negativity became too much. I already had enough darkness in my life for several lifetimes, and I wasn't about to add more. So, I quit in November 2022.

I joined Instagram in June 2023, a couple of months after that terrifying dream in March. I thought it would be a gentler way to stay connected with Pink and Steve Perry. I had no idea how quickly I would come to appreciate the momentary escape from my darkness with the lighthearted clips of babies, toddlers, and animals.

Aside from sports, I had stopped watching TV because every channel seemed steeped in negativity. So, Instagram became my harmless distraction, a simple way to disengage from the intrusive thoughts that followed me everywhere.

I eventually learned how to create folders on the app and busied myself finding cute things to save so I could lift my own spirits whenever I needed to. Soon I was finding great workout routines and healthy recipes I wanted to keep so I created more folders for quick access. It surprised me how genuinely enriching the app became for me.

Whenever I visited Barbara, I would open the "cute" folder and play the videos for her. We would laugh and laugh together. There were toddlers mispronouncing words and animals doing ridiculous things. It felt so good to laugh. And it felt even better to see her laugh and enjoy herself.

Seeing her every other Wednesday gave me time to gather new videos to share with her. Before long, I had more than fifteen folders, each one holding different kinds of joy. I would spend my entire visit with her just laughing at the videos.

One thing I appreciated about Instagram was the lack of snarky comments from sad, angry people. It was much easier for me to navigate the app without having to dodge the bullies and the hate mongers. Mostly, it was just lighthearted, fun content.

And I discovered something else: the longer you linger on a kind of post, the more the algorithm feeds you similar content. So naturally, I kept receiving more videos of babies and animals, exactly what I needed. On nights when I couldn't sleep because the dark energy was swirling in my brain, I would turn to Instagram and scroll through those gentle images, trying to replace the negativity with something softer.

I know it isn't good to look at your phone late at night. The backlight gives off short-wave "blue" light that suppresses melatonin, the hormone that signals your body to sleep. Staring at a phone before bed or during the night, activates the brain's alertness system and makes falling asleep much harder.

I understood all of that. But I also knew that the dark thoughts and the relentless ruminations about my past were keeping me awake anyway. If I was going to be up, I decided I might as well fill the time with images that made me smile, hoping they would override the negative ones.

And they did. At least for a little while.

But when I finally put the phone down, the darkness would rush back in and fill the empty space in my mind with shame, regret, and old memories I didn't ask to revisit. I kept chasing the "glimmer" of the sweetness that Instagram offered and it helped me to soften the emotional damage that hovered behind everything I did.

Then, somewhere around October 2023, a single word on a post made me stop scrolling and go back for a second look: the word was "abuse". I wanted to know what kind of abuse they were talking about, and whether it resembled anything I had experienced.

I want to be clear. Up to this point, I had only identified two forms of abuse in my marriage to MKD: physical and emotional. Physical abuse is easy to detect. We are all conditioned to spot that kind of abuse. But emotional abuse takes longer to identify. It creeps in slowly and teaches you to doubt your own reality.

There were only a couple of times in my marriage when MKD was physically abusive. I had always wondered if I would have escaped sooner had there been more of the physical abuse since it is easier to identify and to prove. But emotional abuse? That's trickier.

He made me feel "less than," unworthy, stupid, ashamed, confused, scared, intimidated, and discarded. All the harm was there, but because it didn't leave bruises, I convinced myself it wasn't abuse.

I was so incapable of recognizing the different kinds of abuse that I didn't even acknowledge the emotional abuse he was dishing out until right before the prophetic dream I had in March 2014, the one where Jack told me I didn't have to live like that anymore. By then, we had been married for thirty-one years.

I remember the exact moment it hit me. I was walking down the hallway toward my bedroom when it came over me like a flash. I stopped dead in my tracks and thought, *It's emotional abuse.*

A wave of sadness and betrayal washed over me, consuming my whole body, as I realized I had been emotionally abused for decades and hadn't seen it.

What I didn't realize was that there was so much more.

I scrolled back to look at the post on abuse, and it detailed the twisted control of financial abuse. I didn't realize there was such a thing as financial abuse. The post went something like this:

Financial Abuse Looks Like This…when money is used to control, manipulate, or trap you – that's abuse. @djtamayo Joyce Tamayo

A simple post like that one made me realize that all the stress that I underwent trying to pay the bills and plug all the financial holes that MKD made with his reckless spending was another form of abuse: financial abuse. I had felt trapped because I didn't have the money to get away.

I started getting more posts on financial abuse like this one that blew me away:

Financial abuse is never just about money. It's about control, isolation, and fear – silent weapons used to keep you small, obedient, and stuck. And the worst part? They'll still call themselves the provider while robbing you of freedom.   Healing_withkellynicole

That was it. It was about control. And I was isolated. How many times did he threaten to leave me and the kids and take all the money because after all, he said, "It's my goddamn money".

One of the biggest reasons I could never leave him sooner than I did was because he always spent most of the money that was in our checking and savings account. We would be lucky to have two thousand dollars in our account. Then, he would usually drain us down to almost three hundred in our piddly little savings every pay period. And I was left to try to pay the bills with the little money that was left.

When I dared to push back against his spending, I would get a verbal lashing combined with the intimidation in the way of his physical posturing that made me feel unsafe. It was perfectly clear that I endured financial abuse in addition to the emotional abuse all those years that I was married to him.

That discovery didn't end there. Instagram continued to send me more feeds on domestic abuse and now I was beginning to understand that there were many more types of abuse other than just physical and emotional.

There is mental abuse and it includes: name calling (he'd call me stupid or gullible), gaslighting (tried to make me believe that I didn't hear or see what I heard or saw), making threats (threatened to leave, take the money, kill the dog, kill himself), withholding affection (when I was crying he just yelled at me), dismissiveness (when I complained about his friend grabbing my breast and he did nothing), criticism (when the laundry wasn't done on his timeline), humiliation (telling the guys in the squadron that I don't have orgasms), blaming (said it was my fault we didn't have money because I insisted that we invest some money), giving you the silent treatment (how many times did I chase him down and beg him to tell me what was wrong), belittling (making me feel stupid and saying I was incapable of reading a map), and trivializing (telling me my problems at work aren't worth his time).

I was stunned. Was there more?

I looked up online the different forms of domestic abuse and found that in addition to what I had already discovered, there were a few more: psychological abuse, sexual abuse, and verbal abuse.

This revelation cut right to my core. I had endured every one of the abuses that I had found online. Some were more prevalent than others, but I definitely experienced every one of them.

How did this happen? How did I allow this to happen? Why didn't I recognize the abuses at the time that it was happening?

I knew that I had lived a hollow, sad and lonely life in my marriage to MKD. What I didn't fully understand until now, nine and a half years after I escaped, was how pervasive the abuse was.

But it made perfect sense. Every one of those different forms of abuse ignited a trauma response by me. He succeeded in coercing me to be obedient and not to hold him accountable for his cruel behavior.

At the time I just thought he was acting out due to the stress of his job. He always made me believe that his life was on the line if he didn't get his rest, if he didn't study and pass his flight checks, and if he wasn't able to have peace and quiet so that he could decompress before the next day.

I was manipulated into believing that his demands were reasonable and that my reaction to them was out of line. Now I saw his treatment of me in a whole new way.

My higher self, my subconscious, had always known that his behavior was a threat. No wonder my body reacted the way it did. I'd tense up instinctively, shrink back, walk on eggshells; terrified that anything I said or did might ignite his anger. Now I understood why there had always been sadness just behind my eyes.

As this new understanding settled, it pulled me into another layer of darkness, this time fueled by anger. I was furious that all the classic tactics of domestic abuse had been used on me, and that I hadn't recognized them for what they were.

But in my defense, I didn't know how to recognize or research any of it. Most of us are programmed to identify only one kind of abuse: physical. I suppose MKD believed he had a pass, since aside from a few incidents, he could say he "never touched me." If society only associates domestic violence with visible bruises, then of course he could justify his cruelty.

And because I didn't realize that the other behaviors counted as abuse, I simply told myself I was married to a cruel man. It never occurred to me that cruelty itself *is* abuse. Now that I was finally informed, I felt both devastated and enraged.

My new obsession was to learn everything I could about domestic abuse. And suddenly, answers began appearing to questions I didn't even know I had.

It didn't take long before my late-night Instagram scrolling began feeding me posts about narcissism.

Up to that point, the only type of narcissist I knew about was the grandiose kind; the flamboyant, boastful person who needed constant attention – the one sucking all the oxygen out of every room. But the posts introduced me to something far more insidious: the covert narcissist.

What I was reading stopped me cold.

It was as if the authors knew MKD personally. The covert narcissist, the "wolf in sheep's clothing" type. Every description, behavior, and pattern - he matched them all. That was him.

Here are some of the character traits of a covert narcissist:

> Appear shy or introverted.
>
> Play the victim to gain sympathy.
>
> Are passive-aggressive and subtly controlling.
>
> Feel superior but hide behind modesty.
>
> Has fragile self-esteem.
>
> Silently resents other's success.
>
> Guilt – trips and emotionally manipulates.
>
> Avoids direct confrontation.
>
> Lacks genuine empathy but will mimic it.
>
> Destroy holidays and celebrations that are not about them.
>
> Huge sense of entitlement and doesn't respect boundaries.

Nice to everyone outside of their home.

Tend to put themselves down.

High sensitivity to criticism.

Grandiose fantasies.

Feelings of depression, anxiety or emptiness.

A tendency to hold grudges.

Blames others for their failures or mistakes.

Exaggerating problems, dramatizing them.

Every one of these characteristics was right on target with MKD. I finally had a label for his personality disorder. And with that clarity came the painful understanding that my forgiving nature was no match for his manipulative ways. No matter what I might have done differently in the beginning, I was doomed from the start.

He had presented himself as a wounded soul, someone the world should feel sorry for. And because I was drowning in guilt and shame for what I had done to Jack, I was desperate to redeem myself by trying to help MKD be a better person.

What a colossal waste of time because...

My further research revealed that covert narcissists are incapable of change because they lack empathy and self-awareness. They cannot self-reflect and see their accountability in any situation. They never sincerely apologize. Instead, they flip their shortcomings back onto you until you are the one apologizing. I did that countless times just to keep the peace and avoid triggering his fiery temper.

Once I connected with MKD back in 1981, I had no chance of getting away until I finally built enough strength to believe I deserved the same love, compassion, and empathy

I had always given to everyone else. I had to establish clear and strong boundaries of behavior – expectations for how I deserved to be treated by others. And I had to recognize those boundaries as a right to my autonomy and not as a selfish or conceited trait.

But when I met him, I was nowhere near owning those basic rights for myself.

I was doomed from the beginning.

Realizing who he truly was and how perfectly my lack of self-worth made me an easy target hit me hard. I fell into a wave of self-disgust; hating that I had been so "weak" and so easily caught in his web. But at the same time, I was finally beginning to understand why I hadn't walked away early on.

I didn't believe I deserved better.

I believed it was my responsibility to fix people, to make them whole.

That is the unfortunate toxic side of empathy and people-pleasing: you give and give without boundaries until there is nothing left.

One detail that grabbed my attention is that one of the characteristics of a covert narcissist is depression.

MKD claimed to have depression for most of our marriage. I convinced myself his demeaning behavior was the result of his untreated mental illness. That belief became one of the reasons I stayed. I told myself that if I could help him conquer the depression, he would return to the "great guy" he had pretended to be in the beginning.

I lived on hope, not for who he *was*, but for who I thought he could become. I dismissed his cruelty as symptoms of his depression; still clinging to the fantasy that once he got better, everything else would disappear.

But none of it was depression. None of it was temporary. It was who he was all along.

My brain had been poisoned by the contrast of personalities: *Is he a nice guy who is also cruel? Or is he a cruel guy who pretends to be nice?*

This cognitive dissonance that I had developed over the many years was still raging inside of me nine years after I had escaped and up to this point, I had continued to believe that it was his depression that caused his cruel behavior.

Then came a **huge** turning point in my reconciliation of this duality dilemma.

I came across this post on Instagram from a survivor of domestic violence that made everything so clear:

> *If his behavior towards me was really because of his depression, then he would have treated everyone the same way. But he didn't. He only treated me that way, which told me that his abuse was intentional. He waited until no one was around to witness the abuse and then he lay in on me.*
>
> *@bea_you_t_ful*

Holy cats!

My eyes opened and immediately I saw the truth.

It was intentional. He meant to hurt me. He knew he hurt me and yet, he kept doing it.

Do you know how utterly cruel you must be to intentionally manipulate, gaslight, bully, coerce, intimidate, threaten, undermine, humiliate, betray, shame, criticize, and belittle the one person in the entire world that you have pledged to love and support for ever?

This is one of the lowest forms a human being can take. Only someone deeply sadistic, selfish, and self-involved would betray the intimate trust of their spouse just to feel powerful; to prop up their own weak ego at the expense of someone else's mental health.

And suddenly everything became clearer at warp speed.

I realized he never loved me. Not at all. He only loved having me as a constant supply of fuel for his ego. He was never a "nice guy who could also be cruel." He was always the cruel one pretending to be nice. He manipulated me from the beginning because I had a huge heart and I didn't know how to say no to someone else's selfish needs.

Listen: when you genuinely love someone and you realize you've hurt them, you will rush to apologize and you will *never, ever* say or do that same thing again. It would personally hurt you knowing that you hurt the most important person in the world to you.

MKD knew he was hurting me. He knew it and he still didn't stop or apologize to me. He did it repeatedly with no remorse. He took pleasure in hurting and humiliating me. ***And****... he purposely waited to unleash his cruelty when* no one else was around.

His depression had **nothing** to do with it.

The realization hit me hard: I had endured thirty-three years of marriage to a monster who intentionally abused and tortured me. If he despised me so much, why didn't he let me go? We could have both started a new life. We could have both had a better chance to be happy. You would think that he would have wanted it as well.

But he didn't let me go because I knew his secret. I knew about the cross-dressing. I knew the real man behind closed doors. He needed me so he could cloak his shame of cross-dressing behind the public image of having a beautiful family life – so no one would suspect his secret obsession. He knew that the reality he had so carefully crafted would crumble. He was terrified people would discover that he truly was a fraud. A cruel, despicable fraud.

The awareness sent me sinking into another wave of deep, heavy sadness. My entire adult life had been manipulated and controlled by someone who felt no remorse for the pain he inflicted.

My heart could never bend that way towards another being. I cannot fathom treating another human being that way, especially if they were the one person in the entire world who was supposed to love and protect you from someone just like themselves.

It made me sick to realize how long I searched for the good in him, how many excuses I made, how often I gave him the benefit of the doubt that he would change. What a cruel joke life played on me. I wasted decades and cried so many tears alone only to discover that he never loved me and that he was incapable of any authentic love for anyone other than himself.

I gave him social credibility. With me by his side, he could put on a show to the world that he must be a wonderful person to have such a great wife.

That was it. That was all I was to him.

Just an accessory. Just someone he could control. Just someone to help create his false image.

Now my deep sadness was suddenly overtaken by anger.

I could feel my body boiling inside of me. I cursed him over and over again.

I cried for the intentional cruelty that he directed towards me, and I got so, so angry that I *ever* gave him any allowances for *any* semblance of having a good heart.

How could I have *ever* been so blind?

This was a **HUGE** turning point for me. Most of the darkness that I had been carrying for so long had now turned into anger and the most intense hate for this man.

To think that I ever let him touch me made me physically sick.

So now the big question I had was, why me?

Why did such a good person as I go through so much pain and hell?

Was I being punished for what I did to Jack? Surely what I did to Jack couldn't be worth the punishment of enduring over thirty years' worth of hell with this a**hole. People go to prison for worse things and are let out long before I ever let myself out of this prison. The length and extent of my punishment was too extreme for just breaking up with someone when I was twenty years old.

Maybe I was an a**hole in a previous life and this was my payback.

I was so angry and so hurt that God would punish me so severely for breaking up with Jack. There had to be more.

There had to be a good reason. I couldn't believe that God would allow me to hurt just to hurt.

I want to know **WHY?**

WHY ME?

****

Healing will make you angry. And if it hasn't yet, you probably haven't gone deep enough. There is a rage that lives beneath survival. A rage that builds when you realize how much of your life was shaped by someone else's dysfunction.

How much of your personality is a byproduct of having to survive chaos? How many of your choices were never really choices at all, just coping mechanisms disguised as decisions?

And when you finally see it, when you feel it fully, it's not pretty. But it's necessary.

Because anger is clarity. Anger is boundaries forming in real time. Anger is the nervous system screaming, "I'm not safe yet."

Let yourself feel it.

It's not the end of healing.

Sometimes it's the beginning.

@healwithconsciousness

CH. 23 — Healing Isn't Pretty

That fall of 2023 was a turning point for me. I discovered that the abuse from MKD ran far deeper than I had ever understood. It wasn't just physical and emotional abuse—it was verbal, sexual, financial, mental, and psychological. And I finally accepted the truth: it wasn't his depression that caused his cruelty. For decades I gave him the benefit of the doubt, believing his behavior came from untreated illness. But now I knew the truth, his cruelty was intentional.

My dark energy transformed into intense anger. I was seething at the thought that I had ever married him. Any image of him that flashed across my mind made me recoil.

The real him was finally revealed.

Any grace I had ever extended, any credit I had ever given him for being a "good man deep down" I took it all back. I see now that it was *my* compassion, *my* empathy, *my* loving heart that had made him appear good. I had projected my own goodness onto him because I believed everyone had a good heart.

I wanted so badly to prove to myself that I wasn't a bad person for what happened with Jack that I overlooked MKD's flaws, his inability to empathize, his lack of humanity. And he couldn't believe his luck, that someone as wonderful as I didn't see through him. So, he kept up the pretense, shaping himself into whatever version of a man he thought I wanted.

Then I began to realize something painful: all the "good" qualities I thought he had were simply mine that I had projected on to him. He was never capable of being empathetic or compassionate, he only mimicked those qualities after watching me.

When our neighbor lost her husband, I went to console her. He never visited her and only offered kind words when he ran into her and only after I initiated the compassionate gesture.

When one of Craig's Boy Scout moms was struggling financially, *I* invited her and her children to spend Christmas with us. I bought all their gifts and made sure the kids woke up to joy on Christmas morning. MKD stood there looking dazed by my generosity yet gladly soaked up the gratitude this woman directed toward both of us.

He rarely initiated help for anyone in need. He could see someone struggling and feel nothing, not even the impulse to offer a moment of emotional support.

But if someone asked him for help, he would jump at the opportunity, even if it meant abandoning prior commitments to his own family. Helping others gave him a chance to score admiration points, to appear generous and selfless. He loved the praise too much to turn it down. But he rarely offered help on his own, only when there was an audience to applaud him.

Now that I understand what narcissistic personality disorder looks like, I can see exactly how he gained approval from others. He didn't help people because they needed help, he helped them because it was a public *performance* of generosity. A way to collect external validation not only from the person he assisted but also from anyone who happened to witness it. There always had to be something in it for him. Otherwise, he wasn't interested.

External praise was his lifeblood. It propped up his fragile ego, kept the illusion alive that he was a wonderful man. His image meant everything to him. He constantly worried about how others perceived him, even while loudly insisting he didn't care.

But the moment he walked through our front door, the mask came off. He would complain about being inconvenienced, about how no one else knew what they were doing at work and how lucky they were that he had stepped in to fix things. Then he'd grumble about how tired he was and insist I not "bother" him, yet he fully expected me to drop everything and meet his needs immediately, without gratitude, without acknowledgment, and without the slightest concern for the disruption it caused me.

There was a brief period when MKD announced he wanted to "change." He said he would start going to church with the kids and me. I didn't ask about his motivation. I simply welcomed the chance to do something as a family for once.

But the impulse didn't last.

A group of adults often met before or after the service to study passages from the Bible with our priest. MKD joined me one day. The priest, noticing that MKD was new to the group, tried to make him feel included and asked him to read a passage aloud.

I could see the instant discomfort. You might assume a narcissist would relish being singled out, but covert narcissists are different. He loved appearing superior, but only in ways he could control. When he struggled to pronounce a few words, his insecurity flared. Because he hated looking anything less than perfect in front of others, he refused to go back to church again.

That's when I realized the only reason he came with us in the first place was to look good to outsiders. It wasn't about spiritual growth or family togetherness. It was about ego and image.

For years I felt sorry for him. I thought I could prop up his low self-esteem by offering constant affirmations throughout the day. I would offer compliments on whatever I could think of in hopes that he would eventually move past the sad, self-deprecating image of victim that he had created for himself.

But it didn't matter what I said or did. He continued to be morose and gloomy. And somehow, he always made me feel bad for not joining him in his misery. *How dare I be in a good mood when he wasn't.*

He thrived on being the victim. It was his favorite posture, his sick way of getting attention by having people work extra hard around him to make him happy.

Ick.

Ick. Ick.

I now know that it didn't matter what I said or did to try to make him whole. He was incapable of change. He only hung onto me and our marriage because I made him look good. And I, who convinced myself that my beautiful, compassionate and forgiving heart could save him from himself, only succeeded at heaping pounds and pounds of sugar on top of his stinking pile of sh*t; not realizing that no matter how much sugar I poured on it, it would still just be sh*t.

Too harsh for you?

As far as I am concerned, it's not harsh enough.

I gave and gave with the most authentic intentions, and all he did was take and then make me feel like whatever I gave still wasn't enough.

I kept giving him the benefit of the doubt, telling myself his depression caused him to act this way. I tried to compensate by doing more and being more. I was destroying myself for him and he couldn't see any of it. All he could see was what he didn't have, what he wanted, and what he thought the world owed *him*. He painted himself as the perpetual victim of a cruel, unfair life: entitled to more, deserving of more, and never satisfied.

When I escaped nine years ago, I did it with the very real fear that if he discovered I was leaving, he might snap and pull a loaded gun at me, as he had before. I believed his untreated depression had twisted him into the person he was. I believed I had stayed long enough, tried hard enough, and given enough of myself to help him get better. I did my best, but it was destroying me, and I had to go.

I knew he had physically abused me in the past, but I made excuses for it and stayed to try to help him anyway. I had only just become aware, right before I escaped in 2014, that all those years of manipulation was a form of emotional abuse.

And still, I credited all of it to his untreated depression. I told myself he couldn't help it. But I also knew I would not survive if I stayed. I was at the point of having an extreme mental crisis if I didn't get away.

So, I escaped.

I escaped to salvage what was left of me after thirty-three years of giving everything to someone who was never getting better; someone capable of killing me if he emotionally snapped under the slightest pressure.

Depression or not, I did what I could.

But now I know the truth: his depression wasn't the reason he abused me. He used it as an excuse. His behavior was calculated, purposeful, and intentional.

And with that realization, I saw the true depth of his cruelty and the depth of his disregard for me.

And I was **ANGRY.**

I may have been disgusted with him before this realization, but now I was just spitting angry.

I would go on my "therapy" walks and just verbally beat the crap out of him. I was consumed with questions: Why hadn't I seen it sooner? Why did God and the Universe allow me to go through that much pain for as long as I did?

This was now November 2023, and the Seattle rain and dark days were starting to appear more consistently. The holidays were approaching, and I had to bring my therapy walks indoors. I tried to burn through the anger by chipping golf balls into a net in the living room and practicing Pickleball volleys against the only bare wall in the house.

My Handsome would often hear the thud of pickleballs hitting my paddle...then the wall ... then the floor ... then my paddle again - as I tried to replace my negative emotions with something that once brought me joy. I was tired of sitting in the darkness, and I decided I had to make myself get up and do something I used to love.

The distraction helped, but the anger toward MKD didn't go away. And soon, I was forced to confront and manage that anger head-on when my daughter Claire asked a favor.

She and her family had been stationed in Japan for three years. They had hoped for orders back to the U.S., but the Navy was sending them to Guam, a tiny U.S. territory southwest of the Philippines. That meant another three years overseas.

Recognizing the strain such extended deployments place on families, the Navy allowed them to fly home to visit family for the holidays.

It had been five years since I'd last seen Claire, her husband Jeff, my granddaughter Amelia, and my grandson Perry. Now they were going to come back to visit family for the holidays and Claire wanted to know if her dad could come and visit them at my house while they were there.

The moment I read her text, my body began to tremble. I was at work, and I had to quickly check my emotions so my patients and coworkers wouldn't see the panic rising in me. I didn't respond to Claire right away - I reached out to my Handsome first.

"Claire wants to know if her dad can come to visit them at our house while they're here," I texted. "What do you think?"

I was secretly hoping he'd say something like, I don't think that's good for your mental health. But he responded, in his usual generous way: "That would be fine."

I didn't want to be anywhere near MKD. But I also knew that if I said no, Claire and her family would have to rent a car, drive two hours south, and get a hotel room because her dad didn't have space for them at his place. I didn't want them to be inconvenienced – financially or emotionally, just because *I* couldn't stomach the idea of being in the same room as him.

Claire had no idea about her dad's abuse. When I escaped nine and a half years earlier, she and her siblings had gathered in North Carolina to support him. It was during that time that he disclosed his cross-dressing to them but conveniently left out the part about the decades of abuse he had inflicted on me.

So, in Claire's eyes, I left because of his cross-dressing. She had no clue about the emotional, psychological, and physical abuse. And over the years, she had even challenged me a couple of times, believing I was being "intolerant" of his cross-dressing obsession.

When I tried to tell Claire about the emotional abuse in the past, she would shut me down almost instantly. "I don't want to hear it. I don't want to hear it." So, I never had the chance to share even a fraction of why I truly left him. She cut me off every time.

Now I was faced with a double bind. No matter what choice I made, I would suffer. If I said no, Claire and her family would be burdened with the inconvenience, and I would look "intolerant" of her dad's obsession. If I said yes, then I would have to endure his presence in my home for several days, silently, without anyone knowing.

I had suffered for over thirty years without anyone knowing. But back then, I thought his cruelty came from untreated depression. Now I knew better; his cruelty had been deliberate, calculated, and intentional.

Jillian, now living on Capitol Hill, had planned for her dad to stay with her. They would drive over each morning and back each night. He would accompany us on outings and sit at our table for every meal I prepared. I convinced myself I could manage by staying out of his orbit – if he was in the family room, I'd be in the living room. I told myself I could minimize my interaction with him and allow him to visit Claire and her family as much as they wanted.

I texted Claire that it was okay and then I began preparing myself for the reality of having this evil, despicable man in my presence again.

I recognize now that my anxiety of letting Claire down by not allowing her dad to come over was just my old programming of putting everyone else first and compromising myself. The power of toxic programming from our youth is so powerful that it was still governing my actions well into my adult years and I was still new at allowing myself to set boundaries that protected me.

A week before Christmas, Claire and her family arrived at Sea-Tac from Japan. I was beyond excited to see them. Five years is a long time, especially when you see how much the grandchildren have grown.

The last time I saw them was the summer of 2018, when my dad was diagnosed with Glioblastoma. Amelia had been seven and Perry was just two. And now, suddenly, Amelia was twelve and Perry was seven. They had grown into entirely new people while I was only able to witness it from photos and video calls.

When they finally came through the overseas customs gate, I couldn't hold back. I screamed with joy and started running towards Perry and Amelia.

Perry seemed a bit unsure of me at first, but then he mimicked my excitement as he came running towards me jumped up into my arms, wrapping his legs and arms around my body. Amelia followed close behind, and I hugged and hugged those sweet children as if I could make up for five years in one embrace. Then I pulled Claire into the biggest hug I had.

I had missed them all so deeply. Military life demands so many sacrifices, and one of the greatest is the loss of consistent contact with extended family. My own children grew up without holiday gatherings full of aunts and uncles; without that built-in network of cousins to grow up alongside. They never truly knew what that kind of family connection felt like. Now Claire's children were living in the same reality.

If you haven't experienced military life, then you don't understand the number of sacrifices that are made. It's not just the servicemember who makes the sacrifices – but also, the family. The inherent sacrifices of that life can alter forever how the next generation engages with their extended family.

These children will never fully know what they missed in having extended family close by because distance became their normal. They may grow up believing isolation from extended family is simply how life works. It is a personal loss that they won't recognize until much later in their lives.

But for now, I had Claire, Jeff, Amelia and Perry with me and I was determined to savor every moment of it even if MKD was present.

Speaking of him. He had made his way up from his home two hours south and was at Jillian's tiny Capitol Hill apartment. The next morning, after breakfast, he and Jillian arrived.

I kept myself busy with chores, all the while watching the driveway through our RING alerts. I didn't want to be anywhere near the entryway when they came in. When the camera chimed, I slipped quietly into my bedroom so Jillian and MKD could greet Claire and her family without my presence adding tension.

I stayed there until I heard the commotion drifting towards the living room. Once I knew they were settled and distracted, I emerged into the kitchen and family room area, staying alert for any movement in my direction. If they headed my way, I planned to simply relocate to another part of the house. My only goal was to give Claire and the kids their time with him, while keeping myself as safe, invisible, and distant as possible.

It worked for the most part, but it didn't take long before I found myself face to face with MKD in the family room, with only Perry there as a witness.

Perry had come into the room upset and climbed into one of the recliners, pouting. When I asked him what was wrong, he said, "Papa Mike won't play chess with me. He says he doesn't know how."

Okay… that was a crock of bull.

He absolutely knew how to play chess. When we were married, he insisted on buying a chess set, and we played often enough. I'm just an amateur and I know the rules and basic strategy, but I could still win a fair number of times. It was one of the few games where I had any edge over him.

And he hated that.

I usually hated playing any game with him because he was always a poor winner. He would taunt you and make sure you felt small whenever he won. But if *you* beat him, you couldn't celebrate – you had to act like it was no big deal because he couldn't handle what he dished out. He despised losing to me, and eventually he stopped playing chess.

And now, here he was with his seven-year-old grandson whom he hadn't seen in several years. Instead of simply playing with his grandson and allowing Perry to feel important because his Papa was choosing to spend time with him, MKD wouldn't play with him because he told him he "didn't know how."

His ego was terrified of losing to a little kid. So, what if he did? This was his chance to praise his grandson's skills and be proud of him instead of protecting his own ego.

But he couldn't. Not even for his seven-year-old grandson.

So, there we were. Perry and I alone in the family room and he looked up at me with that disappointed little voice, telling me his Papa Mike refused to play because he didn't know how.

I simply said, "Why don't you teach your Papa how to play chess?"

Just then, MKD wandered into the room alone and heard what I said to Perry. Perry got so excited at the idea of being able to teach his Papa the game of chess that he immediately changed his mood and jumped up out of the recliner to find his Papa. All Perry had to do was turn his body and there was his Papa Mike, looking at me with daggers in his eyes.

He clearly didn't want to play chess with his grandson and now I have encouraged Perry to "teach" him how to play. I could see the anger in his eyes as if he was saying to me, *"How dare you encourage Perry to teach me how to play chess. Now I don't have any excuse to not play with him."*

What an a**hole. Here is this super sweet little boy who had just learned how to play chess and all he wanted was to spend time with his Papa, sharing with him a new game that he had learned. And all MKD could think was how much he didn't want to play chess with this little boy in case he gets beaten by him.

MKD couldn't see that he was depriving Perry of a beautiful gift of his time and his companionship. Something as simple as playing a game with a child makes them feel valued and worthy. But that was something that MKD was incapable of doing. He always wanted to know, "What's in it for me?"

A now happy and excited Perry grabbed his Papa Mike's hand and eagerly guided him toward the living room, thrilled that he would teach him to play chess. Meanwhile, MKD kept his disdainful gaze fixed on me a little longer as they left the family room just so I would know how much he despised me for suggesting that his own grandson "teach" him how to play chess.

This man didn't deserve a family. He is so selfish and so self-centered that he can't see the worth of interacting with anyone unless he stands to benefit. Once the veil lifted and I finally saw who he truly was, I was in disbelief that I had ever thought he was worth my time. As I mentioned earlier, any good qualities I once attributed to him were only mine that I had projected onto him. I could see none of his own.

Now here he was, standing in my home, after I had only recently uncovered the full depth of his intentional cruelty, trying to keep his dark energy from penetrating me any more than it already had.

I tried my best not to interact with him during his visit. But MKD kept attempting to get me to engage with him and reminisce about the "good ole days."

He would say, "I see you have the two Adirondack chairs that I made on your front deck." "You guys have the same dining table I do. Where'd you get it? It's the same as mine." "I see you have a Coleman pop-up camper. Good for you guys."

It made me sick that he was trying to get me to go down memory lane with him and to try to make some sentimental connections from our past.

When he mentioned the Adirondack chairs, I said nothing. When he commented on the dining table, I replied, "It was Handsome's. I don't know where he got it." When he brought up the camper, I said, "We're selling it."

At that moment, I realized I didn't want to own a single thing he could claim as any kind of link between us. We sold the camper the next year. And when we move back to Yakima in 2026, I'll offer the Adirondack chairs to Jillian if she wants them and I will chat with my Dearest about replacing the dining table as well.

The visit continued, and MKD accepted every bit of hospitality my Dearest and I extended. He ate the meals I cooked, helped himself to my refrigerator, and he rode along in the huge van that I rented to accommodate everyone on our outings.

The first evening, Handsome pulled me aside and whispered, "Did you see his nails?"
I hadn't. I was making a conscious effort not to look at MKD at all.
"He has long fingernails," my Dearest said quietly, "and they're decorated for Christmas."

I finally saw them when we sat for dinner that night. And while I honestly don't care what he chooses to do with his appearance, those nails were a symbolic slap in the face. They reminded me of his colossal betrayal; how he hid his cross-dressing from me before we were married and how the foundation of our relationship had been built on lies. They were symbolic of the thirty-three years of hell I went through at the hands of his intentional emotional and psychological abuse.

Those acrylic nails were a visual reminder that the darkness and pain that I was going through was because of him. His fragile ego, his lies, and the way he twisted my empathy and forgiveness into a weapon against me. They represented everything I lost during those dark years.

I looked away quickly, finished my dinner in silence, and swallowed the disgust rising in my throat.

One of our outings that week was to Top Golf where I had rented two bays so the whole family could play. I kept myself in one bay, deliberately facing away from MKD, and spent my time helping Perry and Amelia swing the clubs and watching them have a great time. Food and drink were ordered, and we spent two hours swinging the clubs.

Perry loved it. Jeff loved it. I loved it. We all seemed to be having a good time.

MKD attempted one swing, missed the ball completely, and immediately gave up. He couldn't tolerate looking bad in front of anyone. So instead of trying again or laughing it off, he slunk away to sit down and refused to participate. I didn't care. I kept my back to him and stayed in my own safe bubble, pretending he wasn't there.

When it came time to pay the bill, I could see that MKD wasn't going to make any offer to help. There were no gestures, no reaching for the check, no offer to contribute. I wasn't surprised.

Every day when he and Jillian came over to the house, he never brought anything: no flowers, no food to share, not even a simple carton of eggs. He just came over and took but never gave. He was always that way – always a taker and never the giver. He was incapable of giving anything without a prompt and without him getting something out of it.

Jillian told me that she thought about suggesting to her dad that they bring something when they came over, but she wanted to see if he would recognize the importance of the gesture on his own instead of her initiating it. Of course, he didn't. And here we were, both parents enjoying the rare visit of our daughter, Claire and her family, and he couldn't see his way of helping to pay for any of the activities.

So, I paid for everyone, including that sloth of a man who I used to think that I loved.

Ick, ick, ick.

Jillian had been confiding in me that every evening, as soon as she and her dad walked down my driveway toward his car, he would slip into a dark mood. The moment they were out of my sight, he started descending into his familiar victimhood, complaining that the day "wasn't fun," sulking, dragging her into his emotional pit.

When I escaped in 2014, Jillian was the one left to absorb the brunt of his morose moods. She told me he once said it was because she reminded him of me. I felt awful for her. She had allowed this moody, emotionally stunted man, her father, to stay with her during Claire's visit, and he repaid her by dumping his self-pity on her every night.

Fortunately, Jillian had more self-worth than I did at her age. She refused to be pulled into his pity spirals. She simply ignored him.

So, it didn't surprise me when he suddenly decided to cut his visit short by a day. What surprised me was that he left Jillian's apartment without even saying goodbye to Claire or her family.

Claire was deeply hurt. And she told Jillian that it was my fault.

In her mind, I "wasn't hospitable enough." Somehow, she had built up a fantasy that having her dad and me in the same space with her family was going to be like a "Hallmark Christmas."

I don't know how she imagined that two divorced parents, especially *these* two, would create anything resembling a Hallmark moment. She was living in a story where her dad and I were old friends who shared warm memories, and the only thing that ever got in the way was his "depression." She expected a reunion full of smiles and mistletoe with a sprinkle of tinsel on top.

I felt bad for her misplaced expectations. But I also resented that she blamed me for her dad leaving early. She didn't know who he really was, and she had refused every attempt I made to gently explain it. Whenever I tried to respond to her challenges about my attitude toward him and hinted that it was more than just his cross-dressing, she would cut me off with, "I don't want to hear it. I don't want to hear it."

What she doesn't understand about her father is that this sudden disappearance, without telling her, without a goodbye, is normal for him. This is what he does. He leaves abruptly, without explanation, and everyone else is left wondering why.

It's the emotional equivalent of a little boy taking his ball and going home because he doesn't like how the game is being played.

It's classic attention-seeking behavior. He wants his daughters to reach out and ask, "Why? What happened?

Are you okay?" He thrives on the drama of appearing wounded, playing the victim, and then pretending nothing was wrong.

And when confronted, he will always respond with a pitiful, "Nothing's wrong," delivered in a tone that tells you he's lying but wants you to believe he's being noble and sparing your feelings.

What a selfless human being for him to not want us to bear his emotional burden. He sacrificed his time with us and my family by leaving a day early so that he wouldn't ruin our visit with his sad mood. How very selfless of this poor soul.

Ick.

Jillian tried to explain to Claire that this was a classic move, that he always pulled this stunt when he wanted attention, but Claire wouldn't hear it. She was convinced he left early because of my "intolerance," because I supposedly couldn't handle his cross-dressing or those acrylic Christmas nails he wore in my home. In her mind, I wasn't playing "Holly Hostess" for him.

On the last night Claire and her family were with us, she finally confronted me about it.

We were standing in the kitchen when she brought it up. She said she could feel that I didn't want him there and that he must have felt it too, implying that my attitude was the reason he had left a day early. Then she asked the question she kept circling around: *Why did you let me invite him if you didn't want him here?*

I told her the truth. I wanted her and the kids to have the chance to see him. Having him come to the house was simply the least disruptive option for her family.

But she wouldn't accept that explanation. She insisted that she and Jeff would have rented a car to drive down to see him, or they could have gone to Jillian's apartment. "It would've been fine if you said no," she repeated.

And I repeated myself: "I didn't want your family to be inconvenienced. If I had it to do over again, I would still say yes for the same reason." I reminded her that he was her guest, not mine, and that I wasn't obligated to entertain him. I allowed him to participate in everything my Handsome and I planned. I was hospitable - I just didn't fawn over him the way she expected.

But she wouldn't let it go.
"Why did you let me invite him if you didn't want him here?" she asked repeatedly.

And with each repetition, I felt myself getting triggered, forced to justify what I saw as a selfless act to someone I thought would appreciate the sacrifice I had made.

It was as if she wanted me to confess that I had allowed him into my home just so I could be rude to him.

But being intentionally rude to anyone is not in my DNA. I don't manipulate situations to "get back" at people. My heart could never bend that way.

When you've been deeply scarred, when you've been made to feel "less than" for decades, you know exactly how devastating it feels to be discarded. The last thing you ever want to do is inflict that on someone else.

Healing doesn't make you colder.
It makes you more empathetic.

I may not have wanted him around, but I was never cruel. I was polite. I simply didn't insert myself into Claire's visit with her dad. I wasn't going to pretend he wasn't the source of my trauma, but I also wasn't going to treat him poorly.

I walked that tightrope the best I could.
And Claire still couldn't see it.

I felt like this was finally the moment, the opening I had been waiting for to share even a fraction of what I had endured with her dad. She wasn't letting me off the hook for allowing him into my home, so I took a deep breath and stepped through that door.

"Claire," I said gently, "if you sensed any discomfort from me, it was because of the hell I went through with your dad when we were married. Every time I've tried to explain why I feel the way I do about him, you stop me and say you don't want to hear it.

"Do you know how that feels? To know that my own daughter doesn't want to hear about the trauma I lived through, but still holds me accountable for the attitude she thinks I have toward him.

"If you knew what I endured, you would understand why I act the way I do. But you haven't wanted to know what I lived through and yet you're holding me responsible for possibly hurting his feelings."

For the first time, Claire allowed me to release some of the truth I had carried for decades. As I spoke, I watched her face change from shock, then disbelief, and finally, to confusion. I could see her struggling to reconcile the father she knew with the man who was cruel and abusive to me.

I knew it would be hard on her. It had been nearly impossible for me for all those years to reconcile the two opposing versions of him that lived inside one body. That internal war, between the man who appeared amazing to the outside world and the one who tortured me behind closed doors, is the very definition of cognitive dissonance. That tension shredded me for three decades. And now Claire was experiencing it for the first time.

It was emotional for me to speak the scars out loud. Since that terrifying dream the previous March, I had been reliving the darkness of those years over and over, trying to process it so it would stop consuming me. Aside from opening up to Barbara and, more recently, to Sophie, I had never verbalized the abuse fully. Certainly not to one of my own children.

Now the words were finally coming out.
And I could feel the weight of them, and the release.

Now I was finally speaking his abuse out loud, and as the words left my mouth, I could feel myself slipping back beneath the surface of those memories into the same darkness I had been fighting for months. Just simply recalling a few episodes for my daughter, who had just accused me of not being "hospitable enough" to her dad, threatened to pull me under again.

She had no idea, none, of the depth of her father's cruelty. I had protected her and her siblings from all of it. Jillian knew more than the others only because she bore the brunt of his moods after I escaped, but even she didn't know the full story.

I had spent my entire marriage shielding my children from the truth of who their father really was. I knew that if I exposed them to it, it would traumatize them. There would be no healing for me by placing that burden on their young shoulders. So, I held it all inside. I carried the darkness alone.

But here was Claire, cornering me into justifying why I hadn't joined in cheerful conversations with her dad, why I hadn't strolled down "memory lane" with them. How could I explain that I had no good memories with him? The only joy I ever experienced in that house came from moments with my children – moments when he wasn't there.

Everything else was trauma. Everything else was danger. I lived in constant fear, never knowing when he might snap, never knowing if one day it would end with a bullet in my head followed by one in his.

Retelling the abuse was emotionally exhausting, for both of us.

But once the floodgates opened and Claire heard even a fraction of what I had endured, her anger shifted to sympathy. We ended the painful conversation in each other's arms, hugging tightly, as if trying to hold together the shattered pieces of something that once resembled a family.

She and her family were leaving the next day to continue their holiday visit in North Carolina, and it felt like she and I had taken a significant step forward, like we'd cleared a path through the debris field that had been our family.

I needed this peace. I needed the emotional space to continue grappling with my own revelations, especially the earth-shattering realization that MKD's abuse had been intentional, purposeful, and calculated. I hadn't yet had time to fully process that truth, let alone understand what it meant for my healing.

I was relieved that Claire and I had ended well.

What I needed now was a new year with a new start. I had to find a way to lift my head out of this dark pool of memories that kept trying to pull me under.

I promised myself that next year I would prioritize "me" and put my focus on climbing out of that dark pit of torment for good.

****

An arrow can be shot only by pulling it backward.

So, when life is dragging you back with difficulties,

It means that it's going to launch you into something great.

@mypositiveoutlooks

CH. 24 — Making Changes and Finding a Breakthrough

We change our behavior, our mindset when the pain of
staying the same is greater than the
pain of changing.
Nothing changes if nothing changes.
~Henry Cloud

It was now 2024. I was heading towards one year since I had that terrorizing dream that hurled me back into the dark energies of guilt, shame, and regret. For months I had lived under a punishing internal dialogue, replaying old mistakes and keeping myself anchored to a past I desperately wanted to outgrow.

Everything shifted when I finally understood that MKD's cruelty hadn't been accidental; that it had been deliberate and calculated. That truth turned my self-loathing into anger toward him, and then it redirected some of the old, haunting questions as to "why me?" Was I being punished by God and the Universe? Why did I feel compelled to "experiment" with someone else when I already had the love of such a beautiful soul as Jack. I hoped that the new year would help me unravel those answers.

I knew it would take a lot of emotional energy to find those answers, and I knew that it would benefit me both physically and mentally to return to a real fitness routine. This time, I asked my Handsome Man to join me.

Staying active has always been important to me, but life has a way of derailing even the most committed routines.

I'd get back on track, then someone else's "emergency" would pull me off again.

I already had a modest set of dumbbells at home, and I tried squeezing in workouts whenever I could. But I needed to stop "squeezing in" and start prioritizing. So, I set new boundaries by carving out time for myself and letting everyone know that from time A to time B, I would be unavailable. No phone calls. No plans. No exceptions. To my surprise, everyone respected it and that made it easier to stay committed.

It took some time to figure out a meaningful workout routine. I was stepping back from running and focusing more on strength training. Now that I was post-menopause, it became even more important to maintain bone density with weight-bearing exercises. My hormones were shifting and so, too, my approach to wellness had to shift.

I had collected a folder of Instagram workouts and following them helped me see small changes within a few weeks. But it was still a challenge to curate all the workouts into effective routines. Then I came across Knight's Gym (knights.gym) on Instagram.

I loved Knight's energy, especially his playful line, "They don't do this at your gym." I started following his routines and then personally reached out to him to create a six-week program tailored for me. He responded quickly and sent me exactly what I had requested.

With a clear plan in hand, the mental load of figuring out each workout disappeared. Most workouts fit easily with the equipment I already had at home, but sometimes I still had to go to the gym.

That's when my Handsome Man started joining me at Planet Fitness. We made a commitment to go right after work and before dinner because we knew that once we ate, we wouldn't go.

We really enjoyed spending that time together. We each had our own workout planned and then would check in with each other between sets.

That's the heart of social intimacy – doing activities side by side because you love each other's company. It can be as simple as a walk around the neighborhood, helping with chores, tending the yard together, or playing a board game on a slow evening.

My Dearest was all in when I wanted to diversify our activities. I'd been bouncing a pickleball against the wall at home and I finally wanted to give it a real try at the community center. But the courts were limited and always full. So, we improvised by turning an unused racquetball court into our makeshift pickleball arena.

When the weather improved and the days stretched longer, we moved outside. But again, there were too many players and not enough courts. That's when Dearest suggested we buy our own net and head to the empty tennis courts near our home.

We bought the net, set it up at the tennis courts, and had fun. It felt good to share something active with my Handsome Man.

Everything seemed to be going well with my Dearest and I as we hit the gym after work and played pickleball whenever we could fit it in. But my Handsome started having trouble with his right knee and then his left hip. Little by little, he had to step back—first from pickleball, then from the gym, until the pain made both activities impossible.

Fast forward. Dearest ended up having stem-cell therapy on his right knee. Fortunately, it worked great. But his hip wasn't improving so he eventually needed a full hip replacement. I am so amazed at the advances of modern medicine. His recovery was quicker and smoother than either of us expected.

But at that time, losing that shared activity of working out and playing together was hard.

However, I did find that even that short period of physical and social connection I had with my Dearest made a huge difference in my mental state. Sharing that time with him had helped me to lift some of the dark energy that kept hovering right behind my eyes and threatening my tears to flow.

Committing myself to working out alongside my Dearest helped me to stay afloat of the darkness I was in. It reminded me that I wasn't alone and that I would eventually find my way out stronger – both physically and mentally.

Within a couple of months, I could see the commitment pay off with the visible difference in my muscle tone. But when I looked in the mirror, the only thing I saw were my droopy eyebrows left over from the lipoma surgery ten years earlier. Even as my body grew stronger, my reflection felt like a reminder of all the years I had carried my trauma in silence. The toll was written across my face.

I decided it was time to get the surgery done.

It's unfortunate, but women get judged fiercely for cosmetic procedures, so I was very cautious as to who I told. I had already heaped a huge pile of judgement on myself this last year and I didn't need any more from anyone who had no clue about the darkness that I was facing alone.

My Handsome Man was so supportive of me and even came with me to some of the consultations I had with the surgeons. Some of them wanted to do more than I was comfortable with. They tried to guide me towards "injections" and "fillers" that I wasn't interested in.

I didn't want a new face. I just didn't want to look exhausted.

When I looked in the mirror, all I saw was the years of trauma. I wanted my reflection to stop dragging me back into all those lost years. I wanted to reclaim something of myself – to look in the mirror and not immediately see the cost of the life I had escaped.

I finally found a surgeon who was empathetic; someone who kindly lifted the guilt and stigma I had been carrying. When I told him, "I know I should be happy with the way I look", he looked at me with genuine compassion and said, "You deserve to be happy. Don't talk to yourself as if you don't deserve to be happy."

Bingo. I *did* deserve to be happy.

Here was this stranger filing up my deflated balloon of self-worth by reminding me that I *deserved* it.

I had spent decades prioritizing everyone else. I had sacrificed financially over the many years, and I had sacrificed my mental health by staying with MKD long after I should have so my kids wouldn't be traumatized.

I had sacrificed my mental health to protect theirs.

The darkness that I had been fighting was trying to make me believe that I wasn't allowed to prioritize myself. But why shouldn't I be allowed to? If I wanted to look into the mirror and feel good about the person smiling back at me, then, *I was going to do it.*

Why? Because I *deserved* it.

I decided if I was going to have the surgery then I might as well do everything that I wanted to do – no regrets, AND... no concerns for anyone else's opinion.

The surgery was in early April. I took nearly ten days off from work. Dr. David Santos at Seattle Plastic Surgery was remarkably empathetic. He made me feel confident and relaxed before I went under anesthesia and at every follow-up visit. His authentic compassion and empathy confirmed I had chosen the right surgeon.

Here is a truism: *You will never regret investing in your health.*

Now, when I look in the mirror, I don't see someone who has lived years of trauma. I look rested and healthy. It was very important that I gave myself the gift of self-confidence and self-love when for so long, I had put myself last.

Because of the surgery, I had to postpone my visits to Barbara. Her daughter, Kelly, told me Barbara had been asking about me, unaware that I had already explained to her about my up-coming absence. I asked Kelly to remind her I'd be back to visit her in a couple of weeks.

Spring of 2024 had marked one year since reliving a small fractal of the abuse that I had endured in just that one terrorizing dream.

I was still searching for answers to "why me?" and why had I strayed from Jack all those years ago? I was still muttering the words "I hate him" under my breath even when I wasn't aware that my subconscious was ruminating about his intentional cruelty. And because it was two sides of the same blade, the next words were always, "I'm so sorry," for what I had done to Jack.

That March of 2024, almost exactly a year after that dark dream, my Dearest heard me say "I hate him" and he used that moment to try to ease the punishment I kept inflicting on myself.

He said, "You may not want to hear this but just listen. I know that you are hurting, but you need to understand this. You are an amazing woman, and you are who you are because of everything that has happened to you – the good and the bad. I know that there is no excuse for what your kids' dad did to you. But, because of what he did, you became the person you are now. Someone with a beautiful, kind, and compassionate heart who would never intentionally do anything to hurt anyone. For that, I want to thank him."

At first, all I heard was that my Dearest was grateful for my suffering. I bristled at the thought that anyone could be thankful for the hell I had endured. I quickly countered with, "You want to thank him? I went through a kind of hell that I would never want anyone to ever have to go through and you're grateful to him for that?"

"Just hear me," he said gently. "I would never want you or anyone to have gone through what you did. But you survived it. You could have become hateful, but you are one of the most compassionate people I know. Just look at how you go to visit Barbara. And besides… if it wasn't for your kids' dad and, for that matter, Jack, we wouldn't have met."

Jack? Why would he bring up Jack?

I hardly spoke about Jack to my Dearest. But my Dearest is not so dense. He is one of the most empathetic and intuitive people that I know. I have been so fortunate to have his soul connected to mine. I had purged my heart to him many times about how I ended up with MKD. Of course, he must have wondered to himself how much of my heart was still connected to Jack.

It was true that Jack had been both an enormous blessing in my life and part of my biggest regret. It was natural for me to wonder what my life would have been like if I hadn't made that fateful choice on Memorial Day of 1981. I know that we would have faced hard times because no one escapes this life without them. But I also know we would have still been married, and we would have built an amazing life together.

Who wouldn't choose that story over thirty-plus years of fear and trauma that I had lived?

And yet... I couldn't deny that the Universe, in its strange, nonlinear mercy, had blessed me with my Dearest. A man whose love, steadiness, and intuition surpassed anything I had ever dared to hope for. How could I hang on to the anger from the past when the same winding road had somehow led me to someone so extraordinary?

The answer to that question wasn't easy to find. I loved my Dearest with all my heart, yet I also hated that I had to walk through so much fire just to reach him. There had to be another reason for all that suffering. It couldn't be that decades of hell were required just so I could appreciate my Handsome Man. I would have appreciated him with only a fraction of the pain I endured. So why did it take over thirty years to escape the emotional and psychological prison I had been living in?

Then my Dearest revealed, yet again, the depth of his emotional maturity and the strength of the trust between us by saying, "Our hearts are big enough to hold more than one person in it. It's okay to hold Jack dear to you. I hold my daughter's mom dear to me too. Our past, and everything in it, all the people we met and all the decisions we made, brought us to this point in our lives. And I love that I am spending this last part of my life with you."

My heart just blew up ten times bigger in that moment than I thought it ever could. Tears pooled in my eyes as I looked across the family room into the gaze of this miraculous man that I was so fortunate to call mine. I got up from my chair and went to him with tears falling and my arms opened to wrap them around his beautiful soul.

He had seen right through me and understood part of the internal struggle I had been wrestling with: *How do I reconcile my emotional bond to Jack when I have this amazing man right in front of me?*

My Dearest was telling me I didn't need to feel guilty for my feelings and my past connection to Jack. I didn't have to feel ashamed of them and that I didn't have to choose. He understood that Jack had been a source of strength that helped me endure what came after the dark set in. Handsome also knew that my love for him was so complete that he had no doubt where he stood in the hierarchy of my love and commitment to him and to us.

Those words from my Dearest were profoundly healing. They loosened the grip of guilt I'd been carrying and allowed me to simply let my natural love for Jack exist. I didn't need to justify it to myself or to anyone else.

Feelings are just that … feelings. They are just a story your brain tells you about what's happening inside your body in relation to the world and your past experiences. Feelings are tied to every stimulus you have ever experienced, and, like every stimulus you have ever experienced, you can't simply just "push them aside".

With every life experience, big and small, your brain puts a label on it like fear, joy or shame. You don't have any conscious control over those feelings when they resurface. You earned each one of them through your own life's journey.

I had compassionately given *others* the right to their own feelings. Why couldn't I offer that same grace to myself?

Not long after that emotional breakthrough I resumed my visits with Barbara. It had been a couple of weeks since my surgery, and I knew she had been missing our time together. I was eager to tell her all that had happened; how my Dearest had helped soften some of the guilt I'd been dragging around, and how his words let me breathe a little bit more for the first time in months.

I also spoke to her about how I still carried the guilt of breaking up with Jack and how I felt responsible for the difficult relationships that he went through as a result.

What Barbara said next stunned me. Here is this 88-year-old woman, clearly failing in both her physical and cognitive health, uttering some of the most insightful points of view regarding my sense of guilt.

"You know, Pam... Jack had a choice too. He could have tried to get you back."

It hit me right there.

I wasn't responsible for his failed relationships. I wasn't responsible for the decisions he made *after* we broke up.

Those choices belonged to *him* and him alone. We all have free will. He could have made a bigger effort to reach out to me before it was too late.

But he didn't. Why?

I told Barbara she was right.

Jack had a part in our breakup too. I knew he loved me, and I knew how deeply I had hurt him. I can imagine that he was afraid of reaching out to me as much as I was to reach out to him. After all, what if I had rejected him a second time? It would have been too hard for his heart to take again.

In that way, Jack and I were very similar. We had fallen hard for each other, and we were both devastated by what happened between us. I didn't reach out because I was terrified he would rebuff me and he likely stayed silent for the same reason. Yes, I was the one who initiated the breakup, but he still could have pushed back. He could have made an intentional effort to understand what had happened. But he didn't.

Thank you, Barbara.

Thank you for that moment of clarity and for helping me let go of the weight I had carried all these years.

Both my Handsome Man and Barbara appeared in my life exactly when I needed them. Both were there when the long-buried emotional and psychological fallout of my past threatened to drag me back under.

Even though I had just lifted a heavy weight from my soul, I would still silently chastise my younger self for breaking up with Jack in the first place.

Enough.

It was time to treat myself like I would treat anyone else.

I decided to try something new. I decided to talk to myself as if I was talking to my best friend or one of my patients who came to me with this same heartache of guilt and shame. I had always given them my empathy and compassion to help ease their troubled mind; why couldn't I do that for myself?

So, I told myself the problem and then I waited for the empathetic, compassionate version of me to respond.

I know you are hurting, and you wish you could go back in time and change everything, but you know that you can't. What you need to realize is that you are one of the most compassionate and kind people that I have ever known. When you broke up with Jack, you did that with the best of intentions for yourself, and you were honorable enough to not just "cheat" on him. Yes, you hurt him and yes, you didn't realize that what you were doing would make it impossible for you to come back from. But you made that decision based on all the information that you had at that time. If you had known that it would have been impossible for you to come back to Jack, you wouldn't have done it. But you didn't know. You were still so young and had very little of life's experience to draw from. It's time that you finally give yourself a hug, tell yourself that you love you, and be proud that everything you have done has been done from your heart with the best of intentions. It's time that you forgive yourself.

Oh, my goodness.

How simple was that?

Why hadn't I just treated myself like I would anyone else?

Why are we so hard on ourselves? Why do we beat ourselves up and judge ourselves for something that we wouldn't do to others?

I made a commitment after that mentally altering exercise: I would stop judging myself and speak to myself only the way I would speak to my very best friend in the entire Universe. I would no longer look in the mirror and critique what I saw. Instead, I would offer myself words of encouragement because if I didn't, who would?

I thought back to last June, when I first reunited with Barbara and she asked why I had come to visit her after so many years. I remembered what she said then about my guilt over breaking up with Jack and the failed marriages that followed:

"You both were still so young."

She had nailed it from the beginning.

But I wasn't ready to receive her simple truth at that time. I had been programmed for decades to carry the weight of other people's happiness as a measurement of my own worth. Only after facing the darkness head-on and doing the internal work did I finally understand – *you cannot carry someone else's bags*. You can be there to show support, but it is up to each of us to work through our own problems.

Barbara's age granted her a clarity that only comes from a lifetime of ups and downs and the ability to honestly self-reflect. She understood that youth and inexperience, not moral failure, were at the heart of what happened between Jack and me. She had been so patient with me over the past year as I sifted through my own pain. I was deeply grateful for her friendship and the grace she offered during one of the darkest seasons of my life.

I still had unanswered questions like, "*Why me?*" But a significant weight had lifted, thanks to the insight of those two beautiful souls and the newfound ability to speak to myself with the same compassion I gave to my patients and friends.

I continued to scour the internet, still desperate to answer that lingering "why me" question. I had just let go of a couple of major emotional blockers, and I was anxious to understand what was still holding me back.

It wouldn't be much longer that I would come across something that put me on the right path. Something that would help me gather all my broken pieces and put them back together again.

****

If you are wondering who your people are,
they are the ones who make your heart feel seen and
your nervous system feel calm.

Yes, it's that simple.

@pranalign_

CH. 25 — Energy and the Law

What happened next to me was profoundly life-altering. I know some of you may be skeptical, wondering if the dark years of trauma I endured pushed me into a psychological rabbit hole so that I made this whole thing up just to cope.

Let me be very clear. I have never been more lucid in my life.

I had been knocked down to the lowest point of my mental well-being after the re-emergence of the traumatic memories that I had gone through when I was married. That terrorizing dream that came to me out of nowhere had pushed me into the darkest places that my mind had ever gone. I had been swirling in a dark soup of psychological pain for over a year, and I had been fighting to find my way out.

Slowly, piece by piece, I began to reconcile the different parts of my past with each revelation offering an explanation for my pain.

The first breakthrough was realizing that MKD's abuse had been calculated. For years I had given him the benefit of the doubt, convincing myself that his untreated depression excused his behavior. I believed he couldn't help it, that he didn't mean the things he did. Because of that belief, I stayed longer than I should have, trying to help him "get better."

But eventually I was forced to confront the truth: his cruelty was intentional. If his behavior were truly uncontrollable, he would have treated everyone the same way. But he didn't. He saved his darkest self for me.

That realization blew another hole through me, this time shifting the blame from myself and into the hands where it belonged.

Then came the understanding of his personality disorder: covert narcissism. Suddenly his manipulative "poor me" persona made sense. His need to play the victim dovetailed perfectly with my endlessly giving nature. My need to please others in order to feel worthy as a person proved to be a toxic combination with his subtle manipulations. It created the perfect storm for trauma bonding. Looking back, I see that there was almost no chance of me escaping those early years. My low self-worth and his constant emotional hold on my guilt and shame held me tightly in place.

And thanks to the loving and understanding soul of my Handsome Man, I was given the permission to let my love for Jack simply exist without guilt. That single emotional shift lifted a weight I had been carrying for decades.

And then Barbara, in her eighty-eight years of hard-won wisdom, offered a clarity I hadn't been ready to see before – that Jack had as much responsibility in our breakup as I did. He had free will. He could have reached out. He could have asked questions, pushed back, and tried to mend what had been torn. Those choices belonged to him, not me.

And finally, I offered myself the same empathy and compassion I had always given everyone else. I forgave myself for breaking up with Jack when I was too young and inexperienced to understand the permanence of that choice.

One by one, I had confronted several karmic knots that had kept me trapped in decades of self-loathing. Each realization lightened the load. But two questions still gripped me: *Why me?* And what was I missing within myself that made me look elsewhere when I already had a beautiful soul in my life who made me feel complete?

Those questions brought me to where I found myself next.

I wasn't looking for surface-level explanations anymore. I was reaching upward, outward; toward the highest source I could name: the Almighty, the Infinite, All That Is... God. I kept searching online, typing in variations of the same plea: "Why me?"
Nothing useful appeared, so I fine-tuned my queries to "meaning of life" and "why is there suffering."

Eventually, I stumbled upon a YouTube video of a woman under hypnosis, recalling events from what she claimed were past lives.

Past lives? Was that even real? I thought it was only the Hindu religion that believed in reincarnation and past lives.

I vaguely remembered stories about souls returning to learn lessons or to face consequences for past actions.

Was that what had happened to me?

Was I being punished for something from another lifetime?

I watched the entire video, unable to look away. The possibility that we could live more than one life stirred something in me. If multiple incarnations were real, then maybe the roots of my suffering were older than this lifetime. Maybe something from my past shaped the "why me" that had haunted me for decades.

I wanted answers. I needed to understand.

I found more videos of people recalling past lives under hypnosis, and soon I was obsessed with figuring this out.

A Google search led me to a couple of authors who were respected hypnotists: Dolores Cannon and Michael Newton, PhD.

Dolores had been a self-trained hypnotherapist, learning from her husband who was a Naval doctor and trained hypnotist. She never set out to explore past lives. Her goal had been to help clients with emotional struggles and eating disorders. It was by accident that she uncovered something unexpected—her clients repeatedly slipped into memories of other lifetimes while under deep hypnosis. Those experiences drew her fully into the world of past-life therapy.

She eventually developed her own hypnosis method, Quantum Healing Hypnosis Technique (QHHT), which allowed her to communicate directly with a client's subconscious.

I had been searching for my answer to "Why me?" for so long, and a part of me had already suspected that maybe something from a past life played a role in the hell I'd endured. So, when I came across this trove of information, I couldn't help but dive in and investigate as much as I could on the subject.

As I was exploring Dolores Cannon's work, I was also led to the work of Dr. Michael Newton and his extensive case studies of people recalling prior lives under hypnosis. What caught my attention even more was that his hypnosis method didn't just take people back into their past lives, it took them *between* lives. He documented clients describing what it was like in the spirit world, the place they returned to before incarnating again.

If I was truly going to understand why my life unfolded the way it did, then learning about what part the spirit realm plays before we incarnate was essential. I immediately ordered his first book, *Journey of Souls,* and two days later, I ordered the next two: *Destiny of Souls and Memories of the Afterlife.*

While I waited for the books to arrive, I went deeper into online research about past lives and reincarnation. Soon, I came across scientific information that made something "click" inside of me and supported the idea that there is life after physical death.

Before I go on, I need to make something clear: I have a very scientific brain. I look for empirical evidence; evidence that is backed by direct observation, experimentation, and collecting observable and measurable data that can prove or disprove a hypothesis.

I don't latch onto an idea simply because it fits my narrative. I can explore new concepts and challenge my own beliefs, but in the end, I need to see how they align with scientific theories, postulates, and the natural laws of physics before I accept them.

But what I came across next in my search struck me at how much I "knew" about science, but how "little" I had allowed myself to apply it beyond the high school curriculum I taught.

Please allow me to take you back to basic high school science so you can understand the magnitude of what I eventually understood as the basis for realizing that the spirit realm is real and that life after death is only the end or our physical life – not our spiritual life.

Let's start with what we know about the atom.

Around 400 BC, Democritus first proposed the idea that the material world had to be made up of the smallest possible unit, he called the atom. It wasn't until the early twentieth century, when technology finally caught up to curiosity, that scientists started to realize that the atom wasn't solid but rather made up of even smaller particles.

In a relatively short time, from 1904 to 1926, the atomic theory changed drastically. What was once thought to be a tiny solid sphere evolved into something far more complex: a structure made of particles with an enormous amount of empty space between them.

Think about that:
Every atom is mostly empty space.

So why can't we pass our hands through a table or through a wall?
Excellent question. I'll come back to that later. For now, just hold onto the idea that everything you see, including your own body, is built from atoms that are mostly empty space.

At the center of each atom is the nucleus, where nearly all the mass is concentrated. This is where the protons (positively charged) and neutrons (no charge) reside. Spinning around outside the nucleus are the electrons, tiny negatively charged particles, that don't seem to occupy any fixed area – they are just actively spinning around the nucleus in a cloud-like area.

So, what makes up the protons and neutrons themselves?

Again, only when technology caught up to our scientific inquiries were researchers able to break open the neutron and proton and see what was inside. With this ability, they discovered that the proton and neutrons are composed of even smaller particles called quarks. There are six different types of quarks with the final quark being identified as recently as 1995.

And what makes up the quark?

Current theories suggest that quarks may be made of even smaller, more fundamental components of tiny vibrating one-dimensional "strings." This is where String Theory comes from.

So, let's take a step back and start from the beginning.

1. All matter is made up of atoms that are mostly empty space.

2. Atoms are made up of swirling electrons around a positively charged nucleus of protons and neutrons.

3. The protons and neutrons are made up of quarks, and...

4. The working theory right now is that quarks are made up of tiny vibrating strings of energy.

Understand this: **everything** is made up of these fundamental particles. ***EVERYTHING!*** That means all forms of life and all forms of non-life like rocks, grass, coffee cups, spark plugs for your car, the book that you are holding, are all made up of tiny vibrating strings of energy. Or, if you want to just grasp onto what is scientifically proven, then everything is made up of these six different types of quarks.

If everything is fundamentally made from just these six tiny quarks/tiny vibrating strings of energy, then what do we attribute as to why there are so many different types of matter?

What makes the different types of matter is the number of protons each atom has.

When you look at the periodic table of elements, each different known element is organized by the number of protons. What separates Beryllium (Be), a metal, from Boron (B), a nonmetal, is only one proton. When you change the number of protons, you change the element.

Imagine, the only difference between being a metal and a nonmetal is just one proton.

It follows, then, that when you change the number of protons in an atom, you also change the number of quarks and those tiny vibrating strings of energy inside it.

Which means this:
The fundamental difference between any type of matter is simply the number and behavior of its vibrating strings of energy.

Yes, at the atomic level there are other considerations like how atoms form molecules and molecules form compounds, and so on. But at the most basic level, everything that exists is built from these tiny strings of vibrating energy. The difference among all forms of matter—air, rocks, water, the human body—lies in how those vibrating strings interact and combine.

I knew all of this. I had taught all of this.
But what I hadn't done was apply this basic scientific foundation to anything spiritual.

So let me connect the dots.

First, we need to understand what energy actually is.
Energy is simply the ability to do work and "work" means causing change. Energy is always being transferred or transformed as systems shift or interact.

Energy can show up in many forms:

- light (electromagnetic waves combined of alternating electric and magnetic fields)
- electricity
- magnetism
- sound
- nuclear energy
- thermal energy
- mechanical energy
- chemical energy
- kinetic energy
- or stored as potential energy

Every form of energy has the same capability: it can cause a system to change. When that happens, work has been done, which is the definition of energy.

Now, here is the key:
The First Law of Thermodynamics states that energy cannot be created **or** destroyed.

All the energy that exists in the Universe already exists. It always has.
It is infinitely fixed in quantity.

Energy never disappears.
It can only be transferred from one place to another or transformed into a different form of energy.

That's it.

I knew all of this. I taught all of this. I was able to prove it by calculating the transfer and transformation of energy using any physics equation you put in front of me.

What I didn't do was apply it to the human level or the spiritual level.

So, I began to ask myself a question I had somehow never asked as a teacher:

What happens to our energy when we die?

Could we mathematically calculate all the energy transferred out of the body at the moment of death? *I mean all of it.* Every measurable form of heat, electrical activity, and every potential energy stored in the cells? To do that, we would first need to know exactly how much energy a human body contains just before death so we could accurately know if the transfer of energy at death was the same.

It hasn't been done.

Which leaves the question standing... What happens to our energy when we die?

Since energy can't be destroyed, what happens to it?

I hope you see where I'm heading. Let me keep going.

If we go back to the most fundamental property of anything that exists, we know that everything is made of quarks – tiny vibrating strings of energy.

Anything that vibrates has a frequency. Frequency is simply the number of waves passing a given point in one second. Faster vibrations mean more waves past that point each second. And more waves mean they have a higher frequency.

Since all matter is in a constant state of motion vibrating at the quantum level, then everything has a frequency. And, interestingly, if everything vibrates, then everything has their own "signature frequency" which is a unique energetic fingerprint known as the "fundamental frequency".

And a frequency isn't fixed; it changes when energy is added or taken away.

Consider a simple example: water waves.
A still surface has no visible waves. Throw in a small rock, and some of the energy from the rock is transferred to the water and waves are generated. Now, throw a larger rock into the water and you will see larger waves generated.

Now, zoom in to water at the molecular level.

When water is frozen, its molecules vibrate slowly. They still vibrate, just at a very low frequency. Now transfer heat energy to the solid water (ice) and the molecules move faster. Raise their frequency enough, and the ice melts into liquid.

If you continue to add more heat energy to the liquid form of water, then the molecules vibrate even faster. The water molecules vibrate so rapidly that the liquid changes into the vapor; a state of water that is so fast-moving you can't see it.

Once you take energy away from the water vapor, and its frequency drops again. It condenses back into the liquid form.

The pattern is simple and universal:

Adding Heat Energy increases frequency – solid to liquid to gas

Removing Heat Energy decreases frequency – gas to liquid to solid

The only difference between these three states of matter is the amount of energy they have which, in turn, affects the frequency. Each state is still water. That hasn't changed. What has changed is their physical state due to the differing frequency.

If everything is made of tiny vibrating strings of energy, then everything is always in motion. Everything is vibrating. And because everything is vibrating, everything has its own frequency. And if everything has its own frequency, then everything carries its own unique frequency fingerprint what physicists call its **natural frequency**.

Here's where it gets interesting.

When you match an object's natural frequency, you can make that object vibrate without ever touching it. All you need is a different source producing waves at the same frequency as the natural frequency of an object. Once those waves reach the object, every tiny particle inside it begins vibrating in sync at the same frequency – without ever having to come in contact with it. That is called resonance.

You've seen this happen.

A singer hits the perfect high note and produces the natural frequency of glass and causes the glass to break. Or when you weed-whack your lawn and your whole body feels like it's still humming afterward. That humming sensation in your body is an example of resonance.

So, all matter is giving off frequency waves all the time just because the tiniest particles are constantly in a state of vibration. And because of that, each object has its own "frequency".

This is a scientific law, which means, under *all* conditions in *all* parts of the Universe you will *always* get the same results.

And if that is true, then it must also apply to the *essence* that makes us human—not the physical body, but the *energy* that animates us. The part we often call the spirit or the soul. The pure, non-physical energy, light energy, at the core of who we are. This essence of energy behaves the same way as any other vibrating form of energy/matter because it is a fundamental law of thermodynamics.

So, when we die, what happens to it?

The energy that makes us uniquely us, is released from our bodies when we die where it is free from our dense human bodies to vibrate at a higher frequency. This is a frequency that we cannot perceive.

Just like water vapor:
It is still water, just simply vibrating so fast that our eyes can no longer see it.

Because the Law of Thermodynamics is universal, then it follows that the energy that makes up our essence also continues, just vibrating at a higher frequency when our physical bodies cease to function. That energy that makes us uniquely us, our essence, is still here.

We just can't physically detect it.

The problem with being human is that our bodies are limited in what we can perceive.

The electromagnetic spectrum (EMS) contains all possible frequencies in the universe. We've learned to use the lowest frequencies like radio waves, television signals, microwaves for communication. And we've learned to use the highest frequencies, X-rays and gamma rays for medical imaging and cancer treatment.

But the only reason we even know these frequencies exist is because technology detects them for us. Otherwise, our bodies aren't capable of detecting them directly.

Our physical senses operate within a very narrow band. The only part of the EMS we can actually *see* is the tiny sliver called the "visible light spectrum", and it is made up of the familiar colors of the rainbow: red, orange, yellow, green, blue, indigo, and violet (ROYGBIV). Everything outside that range is invisible to us, not because it doesn't exist, but because our eyes and our brain can't detect it.

However, there are plenty of other animals that have no such limitations.

Some animals can detect earthquakes before they happen, and others detect frequencies that are only visible to them. The same goes for the human limitation of sound. Dogs can hear high frequencies that are generated from a dog whistle when humans can't.

Here's the important point:

Just because humans can't **perceive something** doesn't mean **it doesn't exist.** It simply vibrates outside our sensory range and what our brain is capable of processing.

Water may seem to "disappear" in the form of vapor, but it is still there, just vibrating at a higher frequency than our eyes can detect – outside our sensory limits.

So why wouldn't the same be true of the human essence, the energy that is unique to each of us? Why, then, can't our human essence, once it is free of our dense bodies, still exist – just vibrating at a higher frequency than our human senses can detect?

Of course it can. The First Law of Thermodynamics proves it. And when you go down to the atomic levels and even smaller, you are now operating in the realm of quantum physics.

I knew all of this. I just didn't apply it beyond the state-mandated curriculum I was teaching. But the Laws of Thermodynamics and how energy works are fixed and universal. This is why they became laws and not just theories.

And it was exactly at this point, while I was searching the internet and waiting for my books by Michael Newton to arrive that everything started to click.

This was **HUGE** for me. I didn't need to be convinced.

The science was always there. I just had to connect the dots.

I think back to my years teaching science at Havelock High School in Havelock, NC. I remember the constant controversy over the part of evolution in the biology books between the religious conservatives and the scientific community.

The conservatives were offended that biological evidence contradicted their interpretation of the Bible's timeline. They insisted the Earth was only a few thousand years old, not the 4.5 billion years supported by radiological dating.

It seemed you had to choose a side.
If you were a scientist, you were assumed to be anti-religion.
If you were religious, you were expected to distrust science.

I never understood the "war" between the two.
I had always believed that the two went together.

The more I learned about science and the physical world, the more convinced I became that a higher intelligence had to be involved in its creation. Life and the cosmos are too exquisitely organized for it all to be dismissed as a random accident. I always believed that there was room for both science and religion in the same conversation.

And here I was, years later, seeing scientific principles support what spiritual traditions had been saying all along.

Why *can't man*, who is said to be made in the image of God, be capable of deciphering the mysteries of creation? Why wouldn't we be able to use the intellect and intuition granted by our Creator to understand how astonishingly perfect the Universe is? Why can't man be allowed to connect the dots and empirically show evidence pointing toward a higher being, the source of All That Is?

I believe that's exactly what our Creator intended: that we recognize our connection to His source and to understand that all of existence is woven from the same fabric – quarks and vibrating strings of energy.

Doesn't the Bible say that man was made in His image?

This scientific understanding should feel like vindication for anyone who has carried a lifelong belief that there is life after death. It transforms faith from believing into knowing. Death is not the end of us, only the end of our physical bodies. Our essence continues, vibrating at a frequency beyond human perception.

And if that's true, then doesn't it make sense that our loved ones could still be near us even if we can't see them?

Why not? Water vapor doesn't vanish simply because our eyes can't perceive it.

How many of you have experienced something you couldn't explain, an odd sensation, a sudden knowing, a moment of protection or comfort that arrived out of nowhere? Almost everyone has at least once. Why couldn't that be the presence of a loved one's essence, still connected to us?

We are limited only by our senses, by the narrow band of frequencies we can see, hear, and feel. The rest is still there. Always has been.

Imagine if we were able to see colors beyond the rainbow spectrum. What would they look like?

It's almost impossible to picture. We struggle even to describe our *existing* colors to someone who has never seen them, so how could we imagine colors our eyes and brains have never processed?

But I believe those colors exist. They're simply vibrating at frequencies our human bodies cannot perceive. And when we become pure essence, pure energy at the moment our bodies fall away, I believe we will be able to see them all.

Isn't that incredible?

I look around now and marvel at how connected we all are to one another and to SOURCE. I marvel at how only six different tiny quarks, each made of tiny vibrating strings of energy, can combine to create everything in existence.

It reminds me of *The Matrix,* when Neo finally "sees" the true nature of reality – how everything is simply made of vibrating strings of energy.

Does this suggest that energy creates matter?

Yes, it does.

Pure energy is the source of all matter since the smallest building block of matter is simply vibrating strings of energy.

Everything is energy. Energy is everything.

So, why can't we put our hand through a solid object? Because that object's frequency is too low. Once that object's frequency increases high enough, it will also become invisible to us, just like the water vapor, and then we can put our hand effortlessly through its energy.

So very cool. So very quantum.

If I've lost some of you here, I'm sorry but this is exactly where science and spirituality finally meet. This is where the foundations of religion can be reconciled with scientific facts.

And honestly?

This is exactly what I believe our Creator intended us to discover.

After all, we're said to be created in *His* image. We were given curiosity and intellect for the reason to explore, to question, to observe, and to uncover the deeper truths that connect us to everything in existence; to realize that we are all connected to the ONE SOURCE, God, the Divine, All That Is.

It's so flipping cool.

If you trust that the Creator has a greater plan for each of us and for everything that has been created, along with the unlimited energy all around us, then you should take a step back and look at the wonder of it all.

How *do* we connect?
What is my *purpose* in this vast plan?
How do my choices, my emotions, and my actions impact and ripple outward into that plan every single day?

This merging of science and spirituality was exactly what I'd been searching for in my quest to find out, "Why me?"

I hadn't found the full answer yet but for the first time, I knew I was on the right path. I couldn't wait for my books to arrive so I could piece together the scientific principles I had just rediscovered. And, hopefully, with decades of evidence from Dr. Michael Newton's hypnosis case studies that suggest that the soul continues long after the body dies, I'll get my answers.

I could feel the goosebumps emerging on my arms as I allowed the excitement of how science and spiritual convergence was starting to take hold in my being.

And at that moment, I knew one thing with absolute certainty: I would never go back to the dark again.

****

Goosebumps is your body's way of translating high frequency energy into a physical sensation.

It means you're resonating with truth or alignment in that moment.

~Bashar

CH. 26 — Making the Spiritual Connection

I was riding a high wave of internal excitement after re-acquainting myself with the laws of thermodynamics and the quantum realm. For the first time, I didn't just "believe" there was a bridge between the physical and the spiritual, it was a "knowing". The evidence was too strong to ignore.

Knowing that energy cannot be created or destroyed, only transferred or transformed to another form of energy, I realized that the possibility that our essence, the purest energy that makes each of us who we are, can also be transferred back into another physical body to experience life once again.

Reincarnation was no longer an abstract concept. It was now very real to me. I became almost obsessed with finding out as much as I could about reincarnation and living a past life along with understanding more about our connection to the spiritual world.

I was still trying to figure out my place in all of this. The big question, *"Why me?" was still unanswered.* It was the last and most significant torment that I was carrying. But for the first time, I could feel I was on the right path to figure it out.

Let me be clear on what I was trying to discover. I couldn't understand why I had gone through all the hell that I went through for all those years when I tried so hard to be a good person. I felt like I had exhausted every other route so now I was reaching much higher for spiritual answers. The thought was if we all lived multiple lives then maybe I could find the answers to my struggles in this life from one of the past lives that I had lived.

You may believe that I was just grappling for anything to help me find meaning and relief in the hell that I had lived. And you are partly right. I knew that the darkness that had come over me with such force would be with me forever if I didn't find some answers that would help me understand the meaning behind all the years of abuse.

I had already discovered a meaningful scientific connection to the knowing that our essence still exists after our physical body is gone. Now, I was hoping that Dr. Newton's case studies of lives between lives would give me more insight into why I lived this tormented life.

So, when the books I'd ordered from Dr. Michael Newton finally arrived, I eagerly started reading them. Their pages shifted something in me, and I had to learn more.

I ended up ordering books from other authors like Dr. Joe Dispenza and Suzanne Giesemann. I listened to recorded seminars from Dolores Cannon and Darryl Anka and then I tuned into contemporary podcasts like *Next Level Soul*. They were different voices with different approaches, yet they all told the same essential story: that there is a larger spiritual architecture, and a meaningful role for each of us within it.

I won't attempt any book reviews for you. There are so many layers and so much to dissect. The information that I discovered was so profoundly life-changing that I will leave it to you to investigate if you are inspired to learn more. Instead, I'll share what rose to the surface for me and what ultimately helped me begin to answer the question I had been carrying for so long: *Why me?*

*   *   *   *   *   *   *   *   *   *   *   *   *   *

To begin with, we are all made from the same source: those tiny vibrating strings of energy that make up a quark – scientist call this infinite source the Quantum Field, but it is also referred to as the One Source, the Universe, The Almighty, or All That is. You can call the most divine source that we come from whatever you want. The name doesn't matter. What matters is this source we all come from is made of pure, unconditional love.

In that ultimate state of pure energy, there is no judgment and there is no hell. There are no individual denominations of religion. There is only unity.

We are all just fractals, pieces of the whole, parts of the divine that broke off from the "All That Is", from God. We are *all* made up of His image, and we are *all* His children because we are literally made from the One Source. Those fractals of energy are our souls, our spirits.

Imagine an endless sea of vibrating strings of energy. That "sea", that Quantum Field, is God, the One Source, All That Is. That "source" is our true home. That is our beginning. It is where everything begins and everything is made of.

There is also evidence to suggest that this sea of endless pure energy is conscious of itself. The One Source, the All That Is, somehow is aware of its own existence.

How can that be? I don't know. That lack of knowing how consciousness can exist in pure energy is just an example of how our human brain is limited in what it can process. We can't fully understand how consciousness can ebb from pure energy when we only experience consciousness through the heart and brain of our human bodies.

This is where I take a leap of faith and choose to believe because science has not caught up with proving that pure energy has a consciousness. But science is getting close.

Currently there are theories and postulates in Quantum Physics that show that energy arranges itself to create matter only when it is observed. The Observer Effect, as illustrated with the double slit experiment, shows how the smallest observable particle changes its behavior depending on whether it is being observed or not. It strongly suggests that our consciousness influences energy – and, in turn, consciousness creates matter.

So, if pure energy is pure consciousness, then why did God, All That Is, the One Source – create the Universe and each individual living thing in it? What is the point? If we are all a part of the One Divine Consciousness, if we ourselves are inherently divine, then what is the point of going through this human experience?

The reason? So that God, The One Source, could experience and discover itself through our individual experiences and our human limitations.

With every human being and their individual experiences in each life, God can better know itself. The religious and spiritual teachings all include how the One Source created us all in Its image. If so, then we are *all* from divine origin. We *are* all God. We are just small fragments of Its whole playing out a part in each lifetime to experience all that we can of this wonderful creation.

When this life experience comes to an end, our essence is returned to the endless sea of pure consciousness – back to where we are originally from – our real home; back to our creator where there is never any judgement and only unconditional love so that we can step back and fully assess all that our essence had learned.

According to those who were under hypnosis, we have all agreed to come to Earth in this human form so we can fully experience the limitations through our human bodies. This is how our souls get to experience the full range of emotions that can only be experienced in human form. With those experiences come lessons and those lessons are how our soul grows and learns. And, in turn, our Creator grows and learns from our experiences.

Our souls get to choose what kind of life we want to experience. We chose where we wanted to live, our sex, our parents and family. We choose what profession and what experiences – good and bad – that we wanted to go through so we could tailor our experience to achieve our "soul plan" that we agreed to before we incarnated.

We chose it all so that our own particular part of God's whole – that fractal of the endless sea of consciousness that is us – could experience the most out of this life and learn what it means to be divine and human at the same time.

But there was a condition: when we came into this life, we understood that we would not remember our divine origin. We would lose that awareness and have to start over with a blank slate with each new life. And due to the limitations that this human body has, we knew it would not be easy.

That may not seem fair, but if we were born knowing our divine origins and we already knew all the answers to everything in the universe, then we wouldn't have any reason to learn. It would be like someone giving you the answers to the crossword puzzle before you even had an opportunity to try to figure it out for yourself. Where is the fun in that? Where is the growth? Nothing was learned.

Growth only comes through challenges. Every obstacle, every emotional bruise, every moment that forces us to navigate uncertainty becomes the ground where wisdom is built. Nothing meaningful is simply handed to us; it's earned through the stumbling and the rising.

It's through these series of heartaches and hardships that we learn and grow. And once a lesson is learned, we use it as a foundation for the next step in our growth. With each challenge we face and overcome, we expand our emotional strength, sharpen our understanding, deepen our compassion, and move a little closer to remembering the Divine Source we came from.

But it isn't all heartaches and hardships. There is also joy and all the other feel-good emotions that we get to experience as well. But, as I mentioned in an earlier chapter, how can we really appreciate the good times and good experiences unless we have the contrast of the challenges and frustrations in our lives?

How do we feel the exhilaration of our accomplishments if it weren't for the experience of overcoming tremendous odds? Where is the joy in winning a game when you already knew what the outcome was going to be? What about the immense pride that you get for finally getting that degree that you worked and sacrificed for years to earn?

If you knew all the answers from the beginning, knew all the right decisions to make, then you would deprive yourself of experiencing that delicious sense of accomplishment. And you would also deprive the entire Universe – your brothers and sisters – of sharing in that experience.

Whether we like it or not, the good comes with the bad – it has to.

Ultimately, our goal *is* to reach a point where we *remember* our own divinity; to recognize where we came from and know, fully, that we are part of the One. That remembering is what we often call an "awakening."

Every person in this Universe came here with their own mission to accomplish; their own lessons to learn. Within those plans that we make, we create soul contracts with other souls. We agree to cross each other's paths in meaningful ways, sometimes to teach, sometimes to be taught. Some connections are painful, some uplifting, but all contribute to the lessons we signed up for.

At the core of both our divine existence and our human experience is unconditional love. Love for ourselves, for others, and for all that exists, because we are all made from the same Source.

So, why would anyone choose a life of extreme hardship? Maybe because we had a very important lesson to learn that only years of pain and suffering could produce. Maybe the hard times were to get you ready for something that would demand the honed skills that you developed during that trying time. Maybe you agreed to go through the hardships and suffering in this life so you could be the "contrast" or the "lesson" for other souls as they make their way on their own path towards their own growth.

As much as we plan out our experience in each lifetime, nothing is set in stone. Our loving creator made sure that we had free will so that we could alter our experience at any time.

Think of our life plan as taking a cross-country road trip. You know where you are going to end up and you know the fastest, smoothest route to get there, but there are countless side roads and scenic detours you might decide to explore. You take one exit, one moment of curiosity, and suddenly you're off the original path.

These detours often come with potholes and rough patches, little nudges to guide you back to the route you intended. But sometimes there's unexpected beauty along the way, enough to make you believe this new direction is worth pursuing.

Eventually, though, the potholes become more prevalent and the little exit you took catches up with you. Your body and spirit grow tired, and you find yourself longing for the easier stretch of road that you mapped out for yourself before you ever began this journey. So, you look for the on-ramp back to your chosen path.

We tend to call those exit ramps mistakes or poor decisions that led to pain instead of the adventure we imagined. But every wrong turn offers something valuable. Each one teaches us, strengthens us, and helps us become a stronger version of ourselves than when we first set out.

We should look at these "mistakes" as just lessons. And, once a lesson is learned, you never have to face that lesson again unless, of course, the Universe gives us a gentle "pop quiz" to make sure you truly learned it.

As we continue to follow our path towards our ultimate destination, we will still reach the key milestones our soul agreed upon before incarnation. You may marry around the same time you planned, you may still have the same number and sex of children you chose, buy your home at roughly the same point in life, and eventually leave this earthly experience in the way your soul selected. What changes is everything in between.

And it's in that "in-between," shaped by our free will, that we experience the richest opportunities for growth. It's where we learn who we truly are, and where our spiritual selves expand through the full texture of human life.

And when we incarnate on this planet, we may forget where we come from, but we are never alone. Each of us has at least one spirit guide who stays with us throughout our entire human experience and remains with us when we return to our true spiritual home.

Our guides won't interfere with our path in this chosen life. They may offer downloads of insight and encouragement but they are usually in subtle ways. It could come in the form of a solution that appears out of nowhere, an intuition nudging you to turn left instead of right, a vivid dream that feels more real than a memory. These can all be their gentle ways of reaching us.

Because everything is energy, everything can be influenced by frequency. Our guides and angels, unbound by the dense physical form we inhabit, vibrate at a much higher frequency. They move easily through the spaces we can't perceive and can manipulate energy by sending us messages. Their signs are everywhere. The challenge is simply slowing down enough to notice them.

We often miss these signs because we're tangled up in worries about tomorrow or replaying what happened yesterday. Presence, living fully in each moment, is what allows us to recognize the help that's already around us.

It's also important to know that your guides and angels want to help you. They won't interfere with your chosen path, but the moment you seek support or guidance, they respond. You only need to ask and then wait.

Here is the part that matters most: your guides, your angels, the Universe, God – they all see the bigger picture. They know what you need long before you do. When you ask for help, try not to cling to a specific outcome. Your spiritual partners may have something far better planned. Holding too tightly to how things *must* look can blind you to the blessings placed right in front of you.

Ask for what you desire but leave the *how* to your spiritual partners. Be clear in your intention. Be grateful for every small blessing along the way and trust the process. Being grateful is so important. When you acknowledge the smallest blessings, it activates the energetic doorway to the larger ones waiting to come through.

You can *see* what you want. You can *feel* what you want, then just *know* that it will be yours. Your patience is simply the space the Universe needs to deliver it at the moment that you're energetically aligned to receive it. In the meantime, your responsibility is to take the preparatory steps needed in the direction which shows the Universe that you are ready to receive the very thing that you have asked for.

The Universe is always watching for that alignment. When your actions and your intentions match your dreams, when you've done the inner work and shown you're ready, the Universe responds. It moves pieces you can't see. It brings opportunities you didn't expect. It places your desires directly on your path.

And through all of this, remember, you are never alone. Spiritual guidance surrounds you and they all want to help. Your role is simply to get ready for the blessings you've requested.

When I finally was able to make the scientific connection to the spiritual existence of God and All That Is, a huge weight lifted off my shoulders. I began seeing my life from an entirely new point of view. The pain I had carried for years found context. I understood for the first time why bad things happen to good people. And beneath it all is a never-ending steady stream of unconditional love from our Creator, who is urging us to find our own divinity by discovering our own self-love.

I look back at my life, and I can no longer be sure if Jack and I were meant to be together. Maybe his purpose early in my life was to provide me with a strong foundation of love before I set out on the painful thirty plus years with MKD.

Maybe having me ending up with MKD was always meant to be because I was supposed to learn that hard lesson of self-love, self-worth and to know that making personal boundaries of how you expect to be treated by others is not an act of selfishness.

But this is where I get very confused.

My connection to Jack has been so strong all these years that his energy has come to me many times in the form of dreams to remind me that I am loved and that I deserve to be loved. His loud voice that came to me in that fateful dream in 2014 that told me I didn't have to live like this anymore propelled me to make my escape plan. A large part of his essence has always been connected to mine as it cloaked me in unconditional love and support through so many hard times.

Plus, there are so many parallels between our lives, many major milestones that we set at nearly the same time that makes me wonder how it could be that we weren't meant to be together. I used to call these milestones coincidences, but now I have learned that there are no coincidences, only synchronicities.

Synchronicities are messages from the Universe that this person, this moment, this event carries deeper meaning for you. For instance, you wake up with a song in your head then turn on the radio and that very song is playing. Or your thoughts center on an old friend and then they call you.

For Jack and me, the synchronicities were undeniable and I have already included many of them in earlier chapters. But there were many more synchronistic events that aligned between the two of us that I will keep private.

So why didn't I end up with Jack?

Was it because of free will? Once I took that exit ramp to explore my sexuality and I got caught up with MKD and his manipulations, there was no way for me to find my way back.

Or maybe it was always designed that I ended up with MKD. Maybe my soul planned this hard life so I could learn the hardest lessons while I was here in this body during this lifetime and then turn around and share my lessons with you.

I won't really know the truth about that fateful decision I made back in May of 1981 until I leave this human body and return to my spirit form.

Until then, I can say that it was only after I turned to face this darkness that was destroying me did I realize that I was offered many opportunities to get away from the torment and the trauma that MKD had laid out for me. Unfortunately, this physical body and my human brain were too poisoned with imbalanced hormones from the relentless stress and trauma I endured that I was incapable of recognizing those options.

Our souls, as powerful as they are, are restricted to this dense human body of ours. And when your brain is under attack from a real perceived threat, it makes it difficult to hear or see any messages from your spirit guides, angels, or higher self.

Your brain does its best to evaluate its surroundings for danger and then try to protect you from it. Unfortunately, this protection mechanism also mutes the messages that your spirit guides are trying to send to you. This includes all those opportunities to escape that any other sound-minded person could have seen.

Now looking at what happened to me from a higher perspective, I can see that every emotional blow and every mental collapse that I went through was just MKD's soul trying to show me that I deserved more.

That I deserved to be loved by someone who could love me back.

His intentional cruelty, his emotional and mental manipulations were designed to have me snap out of the illusion that it was my responsibility to make him happy.

I can imagine the conversation his soul would have with mine:

Pam, don't you get it? I'm never going to change, and it doesn't matter how hard you try. My job is to get you to realize that you are not responsible for anyone's happiness. You are only responsible for your own.

So, I am going to keep treating you with no respect and making you feel less-than until you finally realize that you don't deserve to be treated like this and understand that you setting boundaries and putting yourself first is not being selfish or self-centered. It means that you recognize that you deserve the same love, compassion, and empathy from yourself that you give everyone else.

And for every major blow that doesn't get your attention, I will increase the abuse even more until you can't ignore it anymore.

How about that for perspective?

Why did it take me so long to see that I deserved more?

As a pure soul in the spirit form, we are pure energy – pure consciousness. We see and know everything. But put that essence into our dense human bodies and now our soul has to compete with the body's ego.

The ego is our body's sense of self. It's the *I*, the *me*, the *my*, and the *mine* that our human consciousness frames. Our ego is very strong within us when we are younger. As we get older, many of us will let go of some of our ego. We will eventually not care what other people think about us, how we look, what we say, and what we do.

But the ego is sly and can slip into our mindset during seemingly altruistic intentions:

If I leave him now, the children will be traumatized.

I can't take the day off from work, my patients need me.

It's important that I make sure everyone has a good time.

I know my personal experiences can help them feel better about themselves.

These simple statements that we say quietly or out loud seem innocuous, but this is our ego's way of making us believe that our actions alone will determine everyone else's experience.

It was my ego that convinced me that it was my responsibility to make him happy. My ego was so strongly programmed from an early age to prioritize everyone else that it took a long time and a lot of trauma before that part of my ego stepped aside and allowed me to hear the messages from my angels, guides and higher self.

It was because of this ego from my human brain that I didn't recognize my own self-worth. I believed that I was worthy only if I made others around me happy by sacrificing my own desires.

For years I blamed MKD for everything. And yes, at the human level, he knew what he was doing. His cruelty was deliberate. But what I now understand is that, at the human level, I also played a role in all of it. My own wounded belief system—my conviction that love had to be earned by keeping everyone else happy, kept me in that toxic marriage far longer than I should have stayed.

I gave and gave, pouring everything I had into trying to fix his broken being. What I didn't see, what my ego hid from me, was that my own being was just as broken.

It took his dark, self-loathing, manipulative and cruel behaviors over thirty years of constantly beating me down before I finally realized that I was *not* responsible for anyone else's happiness *or* their misery. That I *was* worthy of love just for *being*.

I didn't need to contort myself into something more "acceptable" to gain approval. I didn't need to shrink so my light wouldn't threaten him. For years, I believed his discomfort was my fault. I thought it was my job to dim myself so he could feel bigger. Now I know I should have stood tall and proud of myself and kept my inner lantern burning bright.

I could have left him many times, but I convinced myself that doing so would traumatize the children. In truth, I sacrificed my authentic self for what I believed were their needs. I told myself I didn't have the right to disrupt their world. Once again, I believed I wasn't worthy of the same compassion I gave everyone else.

So, I stayed. And I carried more pain than anyone should because I refused to see that I wasn't responsible for everyone else's happiness, including to some degree, my children's. My ego led me to believe that prioritizing my emotional needs would come at the expense of my children's.

But what I didn't understand then is that each of my children has their own soul journey to follow; one that they agreed to before they incarnated. They have their own path to follow, their own free will to shape their experiences. If one of them was meant to face a darker milestone as part of their growth, it would have happened regardless of what I chose in my marriage.

At the time, I made the decisions I made with the information I had at that time and with a brain and body poisoned by years of stress and manipulation. Knowing what my cognitive limitations were at that time, I have forgiven myself for not leaving sooner.

So why me? Why did I go through so much pain?

If I was meant to be with MKD, then I believe I took the harder path because I had a huge lesson in self-love to learn.

If I was supposed to be with Jack, then I took the hard road due to free will. And because of my low self-worth, my ego wouldn't let me humble myself to Jack and ask for forgiveness.

I had convinced myself, along with my human ego, that I was responsible for carrying everyone else's bags. No wonder my life felt so heavy. I had been taught to adopt other people's beliefs and then haul the beliefs around as if they were my own responsibility.

Here's the truth: **your** own beliefs weigh nothing.

If you feel weighed down by old beliefs, then it's probably someone else's belief system that you picked up along the way. Let it go.

Regardless of which path was the intended path for me, I know that there were going to be lessons that my soul had to learn. I may not have been able to solve that deep question I had for myself as to why I left Jack, but I was content to know that I did my best in those thirty plus years to be the best version of myself that I could be. For that, I am very proud of myself for surviving that long journey and knowing that I will never have to face that kind of emotional and psychological prison again.

I was still visiting Barbara every other Wednesday. I was so excited to share my discoveries about past lives and how we choose our families and experiences to deepen our understanding of what it means to be fully divine.

Barbara was absolutely captivated. She loved the idea that we had multiple lives and that we chose the lessons we wanted to learn. She told me she would have loved to be a Samurai warrior, and we talked about what living multiple lives might mean and what our true mission was in this lifetime.

She was clearly getting closer to the end of this life, and now she was contemplating what the possibility of living multiple lives would mean to her. Did she cross the prairie in a covered wagon? Did she live in a palace as royalty or was she just a servant?

We talked about what we accomplished in this life and what we might have done if we had more time.

Though she had dementia, she spoke with striking clarity about this subject. We both benefited from our shared willingness to explore these questions. We felt safe in each other's presence to contemplate that there was far more to us than this single body in this single lifetime.

Quietly, I began to wonder why she was still alive. Supposedly we leave this world when our soul's work is finished. Was one of her remaining missions to help guide me through my darkness and toward my spiritual center? Was she holding on because I was one of her last missions to fulfill?

Once I understood that we all come from the same Source and we are all connected beyond this world, I began to see the arc of my life differently. The darkness of my past was held on both ends by this luminous woman, a soul who had been placed in my story with purpose.

She had always been so compassionate toward my pain. She encouraged me to go deep into the darkness to find my answers, and she held space for every emotional purge without a hint of judgment. She was pivotal in freeing me from the guilt I carried; this belief that if I hadn't broken up with Jack, then both our lives wouldn't have been so hard. She helped me release that burden.

As she neared the end of her life, I began wondering what my part in her story was now. Maybe I was meant to help her spiritual transition with my latest discovery before she passed. Her clarity amazed me; even as her brain declined, she spoke with such insightful and contemplative lucidity.

What I did know was this: she valued my company, and I valued hers. I wanted to be with her as much as possible if for nothing else, to give her someone to laugh with and to sit beside her as she approached the end of her journey.

I was emerging from my own tunnel of darkness into a light of new self-awareness. I was beginning to understand how deeply we are all connected to everyone and to everything. And with that understanding came a desire to connect even deeper; to reach across the veil of higher frequencies and connect to the spirit side.

With this new awareness, I found my inner self becoming calmer. I became more purposeful in my thoughts and actions, aligning them to my true self.

But what and who was my true self?

That would be my next step. And I would start to find it through meditation.

****

The man who sat with his own demons long enough
found they were only teachers in disguise.

When we stop running from our demons and sit with
them, we can discover they are our greatest teachers.

They aren't here to destroy us, they are lessons, guides,
and teachers in disguise.

@einsofvision

CH. 27 — Meditation and Mindfulness

A spiritual awakening is not usually pleasant.
Often it feels like confusion, frustration, anger,
sadness, grief, or being out of place.
This can be uncomfortable because it's an intense time
of personal growth.
But despite how difficult it may feel,
you're not going crazy.
You're evolving, awakening.
@lawoflight

I used to think meditating was silly. The only people I'd ever seen do it looked like they'd stepped straight out of the drug-filled, psychedelic sixties. You know the type: long hair, headbands, beads, incense, sitting on beanbag pillows, chanting "OMMM" into the air.

But when I finally looked more closely at the practice, I realized I had been doing something like it long before I even knew the word.

I was the fourth of six kids, which should have meant constant company. Yet I felt alone much of the time surrounded by noise but without a space of my own. So, I created one. I'd go outside and claim tiny corners of the world where no one would look for me.

In third grade, I discovered a little bush on the empty lot next to our house in Granger. I climbed inside that little bush and pushed down the interior branches to hollow out a center for myself. No one ever went into that little bush except for me.

I would use that quiet place as my escape. It was a place where I could sit still and let my thoughts drift without interruption.

When we moved the next year to the outskirts of Outlook, I found another refuge. We lived there only five months, from March to July, but during that short time, I found myself roaming the open farm fields that were nearby and hollowing out the tall grass so that I could create another secret space for myself. It was there, for the first time, that I learned I could clear my mind completely.

It was like a game. I would lie in this hollowed out space with the tall grass all around me, hidden from anyone's view and protected from the wind. I would just lie there, looking up at the sky, marveling as the clouds changed shape and moved across the sky.

I wanted to see if I could create a blank space in my mind. I lay there quietly with my eyes closed, with the ambient sounds buffered by the tall grass standing around me, and I would try to erase any thoughts in my head. Whenever a thought crept in, I'd nudge it away with a quiet "Stop," or "Don't think," or "Clear." Eventually, for a few precious seconds, everything inside me went still.

What a celebration on my part. I thought it was so cool to be able to eliminate all images and thoughts to just be in that hidden space with only myself.

When I completed my game, I remember opening my eyes and looking up at the sky with the clouds drifting past. I felt a beautiful sense of calm settling over me like a soft blanket. It felt so lovely that I promised myself I would do it again.

And I did do it a few more times that summer before we moved again. After that summer, it would be a long time before I recreated that same experience.

By then, I was already babysitting to earn extra money for the things I wanted. As I grew older, those extra responsibilities only increased, pulling me closer to all the expectations that come with adulthood. There were more chores and less time to explore. And even less space to simply be a kid. With the chores came the worries about tomorrow; about doing everything right and about meeting my parents' expectations.

That's just the way it is.

If you look back at your own childhood, you can usually pinpoint the moment you started worrying about the future and fretting about the past. It often lines up with the arrival of extra responsibilities put upon you. These responsibilities only get bigger and multiply as we get older and then they follow us into our adulthood.

All those responsibilities create noise of perceived responsibilities and accountabilities. These noises muffle the quiet voice inside us that knows our true self and what it is trying to show us. When I was young and had so little to worry about, it was easy to just "be" in the moment. It was easy to find time to just sit and listen to the wispy thoughts in my head.

That is basically what meditation is. It doesn't require incense or chanting. It's simply choosing a quiet space where you won't be interrupted and letting the noise from the world and your head settle so you can hear your true self again.

It's interesting how our brain waves change depending on what we are focused on. When our minds are busy planning, solving problems, going about the plans of the day, the brain produces Beta waves. Meditation shifts the brain away from the stressful Beta waves and towards the slower, more calming Alpha and Theta wave patterns. This shift in the brain waves calm the brain, creating less stress and producing a sense of calm.

When a brain is in deep meditation, the Alpha waves give way to the more prominent Theta waves. These brain wave activities promote creativity and will increase your intuition abilities by promoting deep relaxation. No wonder I felt such peace after playing my "little game" in the tall grass that summer.

When you meditate, you allow yourself to connect to the real you. When you sit still long enough, without distractions trying to pull you back into Beta activity, you make space for clarity in a busy world. You begin to hear the truth buried beneath the noise. With consistent practice, you may even slip into an even deeper state marked by higher frequency Gamma waves, a frequency linked to heightened awareness.

I began meditating at the end of July 2024, right after discovering the scientific–spiritual connection at the quantum level. I wanted to see if I could reach my spirit guides or any spirit presence because the idea fascinated me. I had questions I wanted to ask, and I craved some kind of verification that consciousness continues beyond this physical life.

To start, I tried some of the guided meditations on YouTube. I would lay down in a dark, quiet bedroom and put on my headphones. I followed the voice leading me through each step. Almost instantly my body softened with the meditative music and the guide's slow, hypnotic voice. By the end, I felt deeply relaxed.

I was impressed by how different I felt. But what I really wanted was to connect with my spirits and higher self just as others that I had read about had done. I quickly realized that achieving that is easier said than done – it takes a lot of practice.

As adults, we carry so much noise in our lives. With every new technology we were promised that it would "save time" and give us more room to rest. But what we discovered was that the time we gained was simply filled with more obligations, more expectations, and more mental clutter.

No wonder it takes practice to quiet the mind. Most of us aren't used to silence anymore. Our brains stay in motion from the moment we wake up.

Think about the first hours of a typical day. The alarm goes off. Maybe music comes on while you get ready. If you have a family, then there's the shuffle for bathroom space, the rush to pack lunches, the background hum of worrying about being late. Some people turn on the morning news, listening to traffic reports as they get dressed. Then comes the car ride with the radio on, or in the morning bus commute with headphones and a phone screen filling every spare moment.

We don't realize how loud our lives have become until we try to sit in stillness.

That's just the morning. Now stretch that over an entire day. When do we ever give ourselves real quiet other than when we sleep?

We've become so accustomed to constant stimulation that we no longer notice how much the noise pollutes our minds. It fuels stress, anxiety, and nonstop mental chatter. Beta waves—the brain's stressed problem-solving state, dominates so much of our day that cortisol becomes a steady drip, contributing not only to tension but also to weight gain.

Exercise helps, of course. But even then, many of us stay plugged in, streaming music or podcasts as we workout. We don't know what it feels like to simply be in silence.

As I began climbing out my mental darkness created by years of trauma, I became acutely sensitive to the energy around me. The news felt abrasive. Commercials hit with an almost frantic intensity. Even the soft, impersonal voices floating out of the television seemed to drain what little strength I had rebuilt.

So, I cut out the excess noise that was stripping the little positive energy that I was trying to cultivate for myself. I had fought too hard to overcome the dark energy to let something as small as radio and tv chatter pull me back down. Now I drive with the radio off, and when I'm alone, I don't turn on the TV. I've given myself the gift of silence, and I love it.

As my meditation practice grew, I began eliminating the guided sessions and background music on YouTube. I didn't want external voices or energy interfering with my attempts to connect with my higher self and my spirit guide. That approach worked for me. Others may prefer meditative music. If you choose to use meditative music, then look for those that produce Theta waves, which align with your subconscious mind and are linked to deep relaxation.

Above all, meditation requires practice and patience. You won't help yourself by expecting breakthroughs every time you sit down. Even if you don't reach the state you hoped for, you still benefit from the act of quieting your mind. Each session helps your brain shift into Alpha and Theta rhythms, creating calm and clarity. And the more you practice, without forcing an outcome, the better you become at clearing the mental clutter. Eventually, you will create the inner stillness that allows you to connect beyond it.

It took time before I finally heard a voice reach back to me during meditation. The message was simple: "Don't be afraid of the answers."

How prophetic. Even though I wanted so badly to connect with my spirit guide and my higher self, a part of me was still anxious about what I might hear. That quiet message reminded me that I'd been holding onto expectations; trying to shape the outcome instead of simply receiving whatever was meant for me. I realized I still had work to do.

Let me pause here to explain something important. Our spiritual family vibrates at a frequency much higher than ours. That difference is why we can't see or hear them in our everyday state. For communication to happen, there has to be cooperation between us and the spirits in order to merge our frequencies. It's like trying to communicate via a walkie talkie – we won't be able to unless we are on the same channel or "frequency".

So how do we do our part, when our dense human bodies operate at such a low frequency compared to the spirit world?

Cooperation.

We *raise* our vibration during meditation, and the spirit side lowers theirs so we can meet in the middle.

Raising our frequency happens through our settled mind and the *feelings we manifest during meditation. The easiest way is* to be grateful for the blessings we already have. When we meditate with a sincere sense of appreciation, engaging both the heart and the mind we naturally lift into a higher emotional and energetic state. Pairing your intention with a feeling of gratitude, and even visualizing your energy expanding outward, amplifies that shift. Something as simple as smiling can help the heart and brain synchronize, creating an even higher combined frequency.

So, when you meditate, pay attention to how you feel. Settle into gratitude. That feeling becomes the bridge.

There are many wonderful books that can help you learn techniques for meditating with the intention of connecting to the spirit world. One that I found especially helpful was written by Suzanne Giesemann. In *The Awakened Way: Making the Shift to a Divinely Guided Life*, she teaches a simple, practical method for connecting with the spirit side. I followed her steps, and they genuinely helped me become more focused and productive in my meditations.

It is possible to make that connection. I've experienced it myself.

But how do I know I'm not just talking to my own mind? It's a fair question. What I've learned is this: when you're truly still, when your mind is as blank as you can make it, and when you've released any insistence on what the message should be, then you simply listen.

The messages that come through arrive gently. They are never harsh or condemning. The spirit realm does not judge us. Judgment is something that our human egos do to ourselves and to each other, here in this earthly life.

Sometimes the voice I hear in meditation sounds like my own, but I know it isn't mine because the phrasing isn't how I would naturally speak. Other times the voice carries an accent I don't recognize. I've held long "thought conversations" this way, and problems that felt complicated in my everyday life were suddenly resolved with surprising simplicity. I would come out of meditation thinking, Why did I make that so hard? The *answer* was *right there.*

There are also many times when I'm unable to connect at all. But even then, I always end with gratitude for the quiet, for the healing, and for the moment I gave back to myself.

This is where I want to emphasize something important: staying in a consistent state of gratitude matters. Negative thoughts lower your frequency and make connection harder.

Remember: *everything* is energy, and *energy* is everything.

It is no secret that our brain produces electrical impulses that can be detected with technology. It should be no surprise then that our thoughts generate a frequency, and that frequency travels outward into the Universe, interacting with other energies. The important emphasis is this: If you want to attract positive outcomes, you need to emit positive energy. What you send out *is* what returns to you.

There are excellent books that explore this relationship between mindset and reality. *The Power of Positive Thinking* by Norman Vincent Peale, published in 1952, is a classic.

A more contemporary exploration is Dr. Joe Dispenza's *Becoming Supernatural.* Both explain how what we think and feel shapes the world around us.

My dad was the first to introduce me to positive thinking. He was a big proponent of Norman Vincent Peale's work, and he showed me firsthand how powerful the mind can be with a simple demonstration. It was 1972 when he taught me this little "trick," and I still use it to remind myself that our thoughts truly affect the world around us.

Let me walk you through this exercise.
You will need a button and a long piece of thread.

- Tie the thread to the button by putting the thread through one of the holes.

- Now, place the end of the thread between your thumb and your forefinger and hold it tight.

- Sitting down, place your elbow on a table or solid surface. The button should be hanging freely by the thread without touching the table or solid surface. When you are holding the thread with your elbow on the table, the button should be ¾ down the length of your arm.

- Now, make sure the button is still. Keep your hand and elbow very still.

- In your mind, give a direction that you want the button to move in. For instance, you may say to yourself while you are focused on the button, "back and forth – back and forth". Just keep repeating this to yourself and visualizing the button moving in response to your commands.

You will soon see the button start to move back and forth in the direction that you commanded it to go.

This is so cool.

This simple exercise shows how the energy of your brain is influenced by your thoughts and how these newly generated frequencies are transferred to the button to cause it to swing back and forth in the direction that you commanded.

You can have more fun with this exercise by telling the button to "stop". Just repeat the word "stop" and visualize it stopping. The button will slow down and stop.

I like to command the button to swing in a circle. "Swing clockwise. Swing clockwise" and visualize the movement as you speak it. Within moments the button will begin tracing a slow, deliberate circle. You can make the circle wider, reverse its direction, slow it down, and stop it again all with your thoughts and visualization.

If our thoughts can influence something as simple as a button on a string, imagine how powerful they can be with the right mindset. Because our thoughts create frequencies that affect the world around us, we need to be conscious that we are only putting out the thoughts that promote a positive outcome.

Every moment gives us a choice. We can fill our minds with positive thoughts, or we can slip into negativity. No one else controls that inner space. It belongs to us. So, if we have a choice, why not choose thoughts that support the life we want?

Living in a positive state, day after day, noticing the blessings around you and staying grateful for them, naturally lifts your frequency. And the higher your frequency, the easier it becomes to connect with your spirit family in meditation.

Of course, staying positive isn't always easy. We're souls having a human experience, navigating real challenges. But we can always shift our perspective.

Here's a simple example of how to shift your point of view: You end up behind a slow driver. You miss the green light that they manage to squeeze through. Instead of slipping into irritation or frustration, pause. Breathe. Look for a different possibility.

Maybe being stopped at that light kept you from having an accident up the road.
Maybe arriving a few minutes later allows you to cross paths with someone you haven't seen in years.
Maybe those extra minutes at the intersection are exactly what you needed in order to unwind from a stressful day.

There is always a positive angle if you choose to look for it.

There are so many positive thoughts you can choose to replace the negative ones, if you practice. When you consistently train your mind toward positivity, especially in moments of stress or challenge, your life naturally becomes calmer and less chaotic. You begin to notice how your angels and spirit guides are already guiding you toward the best outcomes. All you have to do is trust… and relax.

This is what sitting quietly with your own mind can do. This is meditation.

One of the greatest anxieties I carried through life was the fear of death, especially the fear of leaving this world before I had "finished" everything I believed I was meant to do.

But if you accept the idea that your soul chose the moment and manner of your passing before you ever incarnated, that fear begins to loosen its hold. You can exhale. You can focus on living while you are here.

When you understand that life is always unfolding in your best interest even when it doesn't look or feel that way, you can soften your grip on fear. You can turn toward your anxieties, examine them, understand them, and finally let them go.

The peace that comes from trusting the Universe is profound. The old saying "Let go and let God" is simple, but it holds immense truth. It doesn't mean you should act recklessly. It means you can live fully, knowing you are supported by the Universe, by God, by All That Is, by Allah, by Yahweh, by Elohim, by Waheguru, by Ahura Mazda... whatever name you use for the divine. We are all expressions of the ONE.

This also means you are free to change courses in your life. You can try new directions, explore new desires, and follow your curiosity. If the experience isn't what you hoped for, you simply adjust. You redirect yourself toward what feels right.

Remember, there are no mistakes, only lessons.

No one purposely makes a decision that they know will not benefit them. We always do what we think is the best for us at that moment, given all the information that we have at that time. New information may eventually present itself to us that, if we knew about it from the beginning, we would have made a different decision. But we didn't know, so we made the best choice for ourselves that we could.

So, does it truly matter that things didn't unfold according to our original plan? What we often call a "mistake" is simply a lesson learned. Nothing more.

When we change our point of view, we change our mindset, and then we change our frequency. We glow from the inside out. We become more of who we were always meant to be. And we make it easier for others in the world who are like us to find us.

Like attracts like. Same frequency attracts the same frequency.

If you truly believe that we are all made in God's image, then you must believe that each of us has our own inherent gifts from our Creator. You must also believe that we were always meant to live our lives as authentically as we can. We just have to figure out what we were meant to be and do, then get busy being and doing it.

So, how do we figure out who we were meant to be?

There is an easy formula to follow that will help us find out and to help us find our joy in this life. This formula comes from Bashar, an Anunnaki deity, who channels himself through Darryl Anka who, himself, is a writer, director and producer at Zia Films LLC.

Here is the formula:

1. Act on your excitement, your passion, whatever is most exciting to you, in the moment. Do this every moment that you can. (When you have a choice, always choose the option that is the more exciting option, even if just by a little bit.)

2. Do this to the best of your ability. Take this passion and excitement as far as you can go until you cannot take it any further.

3. Act on your excitement or passion with absolutely no insistence, assumption, or expectation of what the outcome should be.

4. Choose to remain in a positive state regardless of what happens.

5. Constantly investigate your belief systems. Release and replace the un-preferred beliefs: fear-based beliefs, and the beliefs not in alignment with what you prefer to be.

That's it. This is how you figure out who you are supposed to be.

How nice is that? It is so simple.

How wonderful is it that we just have to follow our passion and excitement at any given moment. We tend to carry so much negative weight in this world when we buy into someone else's belief system on how we should live our lives. This formula makes it simple.

I grew up believing that I had to please others in order for me to be worthy of love in return. How'd that work out?

I believed that I had to put myself last in needs, wants, and desires or I would be viewed as selfish, self-centered, and conceited. How'd that work out?

Using this formula with the right mindset will help you to find more joy in your life. Taking time out to meditate will help you to calm your stressful mind, clarify your priorities, and help you to move towards a more peaceful and satisfying life. Who doesn't want that?

There is one more channeled insight from Bashar that I want to share with you. It has helped me, and I know it will help you. It is simply this:

"Our mission is to be yourself as fully as you can, the best way you know how. How you express yourself is up to you. But your expression is not your mission. Your mission is to be yourself as fully as you can, the best way you know how."

Understand this: when we fully embrace our authenticity, when we step into who we were truly meant to be we offer the world the gift of our whole self. That is what our Creator intended all along. When we hide who we are, we deny the world our unique contribution, and everyone's human experience becomes a little less rich.

With this understanding, I've gained a deeper appreciation for the courage it takes to live authentically. I used to judge people who dressed against the norm. I would sneer at rainbow-colored hair, elaborate tattoos, or multiple piercings and think they were ridiculous. Now I see something entirely different.

I see courage.

These individuals are expressing themselves freely, living in alignment with who they are, and finding joy through their own creative choices. They are living more authentically than those of us who stay small out of fear of judgment.

I don't personally have a desire to get tattoos or purple hair, but now I look at people who do, and I have a greater appreciation for their courage to be themselves. I challenge myself to be more like them, to live with courage, to stop shrinking, and to show up as myself without apology.

When you realize that each of us has our own path, our own lessons to master, you begin to see your place in the larger mission. Every single person you meet is part of that. Maybe they're here to help you learn something. Maybe you are here to help them.

When you look at life that way, judgment becomes unnecessary. Instead, you can step back and simply ask, "Isn't that interesting? What is it that I am meant to learn here or what might I be helping someone else to learn?" Then you move on and live *your* life as authentically as you can while you allow others to live *their* lives in their own way.

Shifting my perspective on the meaning of my life and the meaning of everyone else's has been pivotal for me. It has helped me to release the burdens that kept me from living an authentic and rich life.

While I was going through my own personal transformations, my dear Barbara was slipping further into decline. I had now committed to visiting her several times a week. I knew her time was close, and I couldn't bear the thought of her passing alone.

I could see she was preparing for the end. She spoke often of her old neighbors and friends as if they were just in the next room. She asked me to check on her "garage door" because she thought it was going up and down. She wanted me to talk to her neighbor about the garbage cans and make sure her dog had been fed.

I pretended to do everything she asked. What would be the point of correcting her? Being "right" would only make her feel wrong, and what purpose would that serve at this stage of her life?

It was now September 2024.

I talked to Barbara about Yakima, one of our favorite subjects. When I told her that the apple season had begun, she lit up with excitement. She spoke of the smell of harvest in the air. I mentioned I'd be heading over the mountains that coming weekend, and I promised to bring her back an apple on a twig, with leaves still attached, so she could hold a little piece of the memories she cherished so dearly.

She loved that.

I knew, from Barbara's weakened state, that she would never get to hold that apple.

I sat beside her while she slept, something she did increasingly more lately. I marveled at how gracefully she accepted her failing body. She never complained about her limitations or voiced fear about the end approaching. I would watch her, this beautiful soul, and silently thank her for the grace she had given me over the past two years while I navigated the darkest parts of my mind.

If we truly plan when and how we will die, I wondered if I had been Barbara's final task. Had she been meant to help guide me back into the light? And in return, was I meant to help her understand that death is not an ending at all?

Maybe I played some small part in her transition from her physical body to her spirit body. I won't know until it's my time to pass. But I do know this: I absolutely loved and cherished that woman.

She connected me to a time in my life that was beautiful, long before I slipped into the darkness. And when I emerged on the other side of it, she became that same connection again, a reminder that beauty had always been part of my story.

In my heart, I knew Barbara wouldn't make it through the weekend. I was leaving for Yakima to attend a memorial service for my beloved Uncle Harold, who had passed in January. He was the uncle I had run into at the farmer's market the very first weekend I returned to Yakima ten years earlier, and he was the one who taught me how to play golf. This was another beautiful soul I was blessed to know.

I saw Barbara for the last time on Wednesday, September 18. She was sleeping and never woke up while I sat beside her. When her daughter Kelly arrived, I quietly left, knowing Barbara was in loving hands. Early the morning of Friday the 20th, Kelly texted to tell me that her mother had passed.

My first question was, "Was she alone?"
Kelly wrote back that she wasn't. Jack and Celina had come from Yakima and were with her at the end.

Relief washed over me. Knowing that Jack was there so she did not pass alone felt like a blessing. Our presence is the final gift any of us can offer someone at the end of their life.

As I write this, it is almost one year to the day of Barbara's passing. How synchronistic is that?

She is in my thoughts quite often and I make a point to talk to her, both out loud and in my meditations. Her physical body is gone, but her spiritual essence is still here, just vibrating at a higher frequency than any of us limited humans can perceive.

It also happens to be almost one year ago that I decided that I had to write my first book, **The Big Dark**. I know that Barbara and my dad, who are now both in spirit form, are so proud of how I have emotionally conquered my darkness.

My dad lived the last half of his human life as an example when he would say, "Life is too short not to be happy.

Figure out what makes you happy and get busy doing it". And then he would go about and only do things that made him happy. I now realize that my dad was living his life like the formula that Bashar has given us to find our joy and passion.

Just follow your passion and your joy to the best that you can and as far as you can without any insistence of any outcome and always stay positive.

How simple is that? Why do we make life so difficult?

I know why.

Because that was the plan all along.

We were always meant to fight our way through the hard times and all the challenges that come with living in a limited vessel like our human bodies.

Facing our challenges, facing the dark, is where we learn and grow and become more fully connected to our spiritual roots.

This is where we rise up and become who we were meant to be all along.

This is how we remember who we really are; that we are all divine and made from the One in our Creator's image.

For that, I thank MKD for helping me see that I deserved better than what he was capable of giving. And I thank him for helping me to see that my biggest love affair has always been with myself and that I have always been the creator of my own happiness.

It is said that those who have experienced the darkest side of life, are the ones who have the biggest questions as to "why" it happened. And it is this clawing back out of the darkness to answer these questions that these wounded souls tend to be the ones who find the spiritual connection.

If you haven't experienced this deep, dark implosion of your inner being, then it may be difficult for you to understand how those who have experienced it ended up gaining this spiritual point of view.

That's ok. You don't have to understand it. Not everyone chose this experience for their life's journey.

In the meanwhile, maybe part of my purpose was to go through these experiences and then put them in a book so that others can see themselves and see that they are not alone in their darkness; to see that there is purpose and reason behind the suffering.

Either way, like a rubber band pulled back, the hard times that hold us down will eventually propel us towards the best times that we have yet to experience.

Keep the faith.

****

First you suffer, then you awaken, and only then do you begin to ascend. Strange, isn't it. That pain is not a punishment but a summons, a knock on the inner door that says, "Wake up".

Not to the world but to yourself.

You see, suffering shakes the foundation of who you think you are, so you may discover who you truly are. And when that veil lifts, something extraordinary happens. You stop identifying with the wound and begin identifying with the witness.

This is awakening. From here, ascension isn't about floating off into the clouds. It's about returning fully to the present. Unburdened by the past. Undistracted by illusion. Unmoved by the ego's hunger for control.

You begin to live as the soul, not the story. And you realize, the pain didn't break you. It built the staircase. And now, you're rising.

Alan Watts

CH. 28 – Reconciliation

In true healing, there comes a moment when the pieces of your life finally fit together, and you can release the anger, guilt, shame, regret, and blame. You reach a peaceful reconciliation of all the fractured parts that attempted to destroy you.

True healing doesn't take prisoners. You can't escape the oppressive darkness by intentionally hurting others along the way. All you do is to add to the shadows that you are trying to leave behind.

I believed my life was moving forward. I had put distance between myself and my abuser. I had built a new career, a new home, and a new love. What I didn't understand was that my subconscious, the part of the mind that stores every buried memory, had reached its limit.

It could no longer hold on to the traumatic images and emotions I had hidden away for all those years. What followed was a psychological vomit of the toxic memories and events that I had locked away for all those years. And when my mind finally rejected all the poisons that I had been holding onto, it blasted out in a massive flood of fury and grief. It was so profound that I had no choice but to turn into the darkness, face it and claw my way out. It was the only way that I could reclaim the life I was always supposed to live.

As Alan Watts, the philosopher said, *"You must face the shadows within yourself. You must let go of the old, rebuild yourself from the ground up."*

And that is what I did.

I proved my strength by refusing to back down. I was willing to look directly at the truth—no matter how painful, no matter how frightening, and no matter what role I had played in it. That is the essence of doing the "shadow work".

The shadow work is simply the process of facing the parts of yourselves that you shut away so you didn't have to face the pain in the moment that it happened. It's not just for those who've endured major trauma. It's for anyone who wants to release the negative emotions, limiting beliefs, and hidden fears that keep them from living a joyful, authentic life.

Doing shadow work is learning how to shed the toxic "bags" we've carried for years; the emotional weight that holds us down. It's about releasing the negative self-talk, the old stories, the resentments, and the inherited beliefs that poison the subconscious but still dictates our conscious decision and behaviors.

To do this inner work, you have to be willing to accept all the parts of yourself that surface. You can't pick and choose what counts as truth. If you do, you leave pieces of that psychological "cancer" behind, and those fragments will eventually demand attention again, often through another painful purge.

When I was forced to face the darkness that was drowning me, I had no idea where it was going to take me. All I wanted was for the heaviness to be gone and for me to be able to live the rest of my life in a peaceful, joyful balance with everything else.

As difficult as that journey was, I am so grateful that I turned and faced the demons. Now I can say that those dark days are behind me.

What I didn't expect when I came out of this abyss was that I would not only reconcile all that happened between MKD and me, but I was also able to reconcile all my angsts that I had with anyone else. I was able to look at those events, the betrayals by family and friends, all the hard feelings brought on by the little slights over the years through a different lens and see the lessons that were in it for me. I could see how the other souls in their human form were playing their part to help my soul grow and I to help them.

We all carry baggage from childhood that we assume is ours, but it isn't. These beliefs were handed to us, often with good intentions, by people who thought they were preparing us for life. But when those beliefs don't align with who we truly are, they become heavy. We start fighting against them inside ourselves, and that inner struggle shows up as sadness, depression, and the kind of self-talk that slowly destroys our confidence.

Every negative thought, every moment of criticism or judgment, is rooted in beliefs that don't serve our growth. We subconsciously battle them while trying to force them to "fit" into our lives, maybe even trying to justify keeping them around.

We cannot become who we're meant to be in our authentic, whole selves until we face these fears, anxieties, and inherited burdens. We must trace them back to their origins and allow ourselves to say, "This isn't mine. And it's okay to let it go."

Releasing these beliefs doesn't make us ungrateful or unloving to the people who passed them on. It simply means those beliefs no longer align with the truth of who we are. Letting them go frees us from the guilt and shame attached to them. Holding onto them only leads to regret, which is heavier than any lesson.

When you finally turn toward your pain, the dark part you've been avoiding, you must be honest with yourself. You must allow yourself space to feel everything: the hurt, the anger, the guilt. Let the emotions rise. Then write them down at the height of their intensity, so you can identify them.

And then own them. They are yours. You survived them. You earned the wisdom they bring. Know exactly what the pain is and what it looks like.

You must do this first so that you know what you are facing. If you hide your feelings, you will never know what it is that you need to conquer. But when you turn toward them and say, "Bring it on—*I can* take whatever *comes,*" something shifts. You stop bracing. You put on your cape, lean into the storm, and discover the strength that was always waiting in you.

I promise, it won't kill you. But depending on the depth of your scars, it may bring you to your knees through the darkest, most crushing pain.

But remember, once you're on your knees, there is only one way to go and that is up.

And when you pull yourself up, not on the backs of others, but by taking care of you…when you pull yourself up with honest, loving, compassionate and empathetic means, you will come back stronger. You will begin to understand that you *can* conquer.

You may even find yourself welcoming new challenges just to prove how strong you are and that you are not going to be pulled back into the darkness.

It will become a triumph.

It may even become a kind of game you get to play, one where you get to show how strong you are and how resolved you are in who you've become.

When you finally turn toward your shadow with courage – when you face it without flinching, you see something you couldn't see before: that you only had the most positive intentions for yourself. You were doing the best you could with what you had. And once you can understand that, then the negative actions of your past start to transform. These "negative" events simply become lessons that offer you the opportunity for growth.

You *will* find forgiveness. For yourself and for others.

This is where you find personal growth. This is where you become more aware and conscious. This is where you find peace.

I faced the darkest part of my life. What I discovered about myself, this world, and our Universe was profound. It changed my life. It changed my point of view. It allowed me to find forgiveness, not only for myself, but also for MKD.

Anyone whose life is relatively free from this depth of pain has little motivation to look farther for answers. It is those of us who have survived the profound pain who will look for the deepest for answers.

And when you finally climb out of the darkness that once consumed you, you start to see how judgment of yourself or others holds you back from healing. You begin to make a conscious effort to let people be who they need to be. You shift into the role of a neutral observer, watching life unfold with curiosity instead of criticism.

And when you step back even farther, you see that we are all here to learn. Every event, every struggle, every moment carries a lesson. And you will recognize how every one of us is here to help others learn their lessons.

That also means that even though we are all part of the ONE, each of us still has our own path to walk. When you can pause and take that in, you start allowing people to make their own mistakes, to find their own way without judgment. That is when compassion replaces control. That is when growth becomes possible for them and for you.

As I look back on my life, I can see that I was always spiritual. I've always marveled at the magnificence of creation and wondered about the meaning behind it all. But during the darkest years of my marriage, when the emotional and psychological abuse was relentless, that spiritual connection became almost impossible to reach. My brain, flooded for so long with stress hormones, simply couldn't access that higher part of my consciousness.

I stayed active in my Episcopal church and tried to connect through scripture, but then the next wave of abuse would hit, and my mind would snap back into pure survival. My entire awareness narrowed to hypervigilance, protecting myself and my children from whatever eruption MKD might unleash. There was no bandwidth left for anything else.

This is why we must be cautious with our virtuous intentions when we question why someone hasn't turn to God or why they don't show more faith. These questions are really disguised as criticism and judgment; that's the ego talking. It should be our compassionate mission to hold space for those who are in their darkest times so their nervous system can reset, and they can find their own way back. We cannot do it for them, and we don't help when we judge or criticize their journey.

You may think of my first book, **The Big Dark,** as a story of healing after years of abuse. But it wasn't healing. What I was doing in those pages was reclaiming pieces of my power that I had ceded away long ago. In that sense, I was finally moving in the direction of healing. But true healing didn't begin until more than nine years after I escaped; not until that horrific dream pushed me to find the answers.

There is a profound shock to the psyche when you discover that the one person who was supposed to love and protect you has become the person you fear most. Something inside of you fractures. The mind shifts into survival mode and starts creating explanations and excuses to make sense of the trauma. It's not a personal flaw but a psychological coping mechanism.

I had to make excuses for the abusive events, and I had to invent rational explanations so my brain and body could survive the intimate betrayal. I was on an emotional overload and drowning. So, I pushed those excuses to the back of my mind so I could function each day. But eventually, the dam broke.

For some people, the emotional and psychological weight of trauma rises to the surface in months. For others, in a year or two. For me, it took nine years. And when it came, it shattered me.

That was the moment the real healing began.

When I finally faced every slight, every cut, and every humiliation. I had to confront something I had never *allowed* myself to see: my own complicity. I had accepted the abuse because, deep down, I didn't believe I deserved better.

That truth was devastating. And it was liberating.

Growing up, I was taught that my role in any relationship was to be the one who compromised. The one who surrendered her needs so others could have theirs. My worth came from self-sacrifice. I didn't fight for myself; I betrayed myself, over and over again.

I convinced myself that the crumbs I received in return for my "virtuous" acts of selflessness were enough. I even justified it with my religious upbringing, telling myself this was how Christ wanted us to be. And when someone had a problem I couldn't fix, I saw myself as a failure.

I endured thirty-three years of degradation, humiliation, discard, and disregard, because the programming to please others was woven so deeply into me that I believed it was my responsibility to make MKD happy – everyone happy – at the expense of my own well-being.

And so, the abuse continued because I couldn't see a way out of it.

What I now understand is that I was never meant to save him.

His soul's message to me was, *"It's not your job to try to change me or anyone. It's not your job to try to make me or anyone happy. Your self-identity of worth and love is not contingent on whether or not you please the people around you. You are already worthy just for being you."*

That was his soul's lesson for me. A painful one, yes, but ultimately a clear and loving lesson.

At the soul level, he was showing me over and over again that he wasn't going to change and that my time, my energy, and my heart weren't going to make a difference. He kept revealing, in every way that his soul knew how, that I deserved better.

The more I resisted learning that truth, the harder my life became. The abuse intensified. The suicide threats. The loaded guns. The emotional chaos. From the soul's vantage point, all of it was designed to jolt me awake; to make me realize I wasn't meant to live like this.

At the human level, my brain was so chemically battered by chronic stress that I couldn't think clearly. Even if some spiritual awareness had tried to break through, my body simply couldn't access it.

I had developed enormous resilience to trauma. That resilience inside a physical, egoic mind, kept me clinging to the belief that I could "fix him." It convinced me that his happiness was my responsibility, and that belief is what kept me in the marriage. It kept me convinced that this was all I deserved.

And my ego, operating inside a hormonally toxic body, wouldn't allow me to see that my children would ultimately have been okay. I believed I was responsible for their happiness too. I believed that sacrificing myself was the only way to protect them.

My ego took pride in that sacrifice. It told me I was strong for staying. It told me I was virtuous for enduring. But that same ego blinded me to the deeper truth: I deserved more. I was betraying myself, my heart, my intuition, and my soul every time I refused to demand better for my own life.

Eventually, my ego couldn't withstand my physical body breaking down. It couldn't overcome the subconscious me that said, **"Enough** and **You deserve better."**

I know that I did the best I could with what I had and with what I knew to do. I only did what I felt in my heart was right, and what you might call, the Christian thing to do; to forgive, and to give people the benefit of the doubt. And I did this over and over again. And I did this at the expense of my own being.

Jesus said, *"Love thy neighbor as thyself."* But I was only loving my neighbor. I didn't love myself.

How twisted is that? You try to be virtuous with virtuous intentions, and you end up destroying yourself.

That is not what our Creator wanted. He wants us to know that we are all deserving of love for just *being*. Lessons are put in our way so that we can re-learn what our spiritual selves have always known – that we *are* love and to help us find our way back to our divine self. And these lessons also remind us that *everyone* has their *own* path.

We have to stop judging ourselves and others. When you take judgment out of the equation and approach life from a neutral place, you create room to see what each experience is really offering you. Even when something painful happens, neutrality allows you to look for the lesson underneath it; the lesson that ultimately teaches us how to love ourselves and others more deeply.

When we incarnate into these bodies, we forget our divine origin. The lessons we encounter here are placed on our path so we can experience the full spectrum of human emotion and find our way back to the truth: that we are all part of the ONE, and that every single one of us is loved and deserving.

So, we must release the blame and the judgment we think comes from others and the judgment we place on ourselves. Hardships are not punishments; they are lessons.

When we set the ego aside, we realize that it isn't what *happens* to us that matters most, it's how we *respond*.

The contrasts of life, the good and the bad, give us clarity. They help us understand what we prefer; what aligns with our soul, and what doesn't. And we don't need to experience every difficult lesson firsthand. If we pay attention, we can learn by observing the experiences of others. We can witness someone else's struggle and decide: *Is that a lesson I want to live through, or is the witnessing enough?*

My hope is that many of you can look at the lessons in my life and see your own worth reflected there. I hope my experiences help you recognize that you, too, deserve better than years spent trying to change someone who was never going to change.

The truth is that MKD's selfishness, entitlement, and self-centeredness were a profound contrast to my own selflessness, forgiveness, and willingness to sacrifice. But extremes on either end can be toxic. My intentions may have been virtuous, but they came at the cost of betraying myself, my integrity, my intuition, and my heart. What I lacked were boundaries that could say, "You've gone too far. I deserve more."

Selflessness and forgiveness are beautiful qualities, but when you use them to abandon yourself, they become weapons turned inward. Instead of offering light, they create sadness, depression, self-loathing, and resentment.

It's human nature, when you're still in the thick of pain and not yet healed, to blame, to point fingers, to judge. That's the ego reacting from inside a wounded body. You can't yet see how the trauma fits into your transformation, from human survival into spiritual awareness.

A real part of healing is recognizing your pain, feeling it fully, and letting it hit you. Go ahead and turn toward the person you believe hurt you.

Be angry.
Feel the hate.
Blame, judge, criticize do all of it.

Because eventually you will discover something essential: you cannot sustain that low form of emotional energy without being consumed by it. You will reach a point where you no longer want to walk the path of pain. You will want more.

You will start to sense the difference between the heavy vibrations of shame, guilt, and regret contrasted against the higher vibrations of joy, acceptance, and forgiveness.

And you will realize that the painful experiences weren't meant to punish you, they were meant to redirect you toward a greater purpose: living your life with passion, freedom, and joy.

For me, turning directly toward my pain is what finally broke me free from it. Every dark thought, every shame and every guilt, had a question behind it. And when I faced them one by one, the answers finally came.

And I can say now, with clarity, that the biggest question of all, *"Why me?"* has given me the most profound lessons of my life.

I learned that:

- I am not responsible for anyone else's happiness.

- My worth is not conditioned on my ability to please others.

- Someone else's beliefs of me and how they think of me don't impact what I believe and know of myself.

- I can't change anyone. I can only change myself.

- I deserve more than just "crumbs" of affirmation and affection.

Healing from trauma isn't the same for everyone. The stages and the phases of healing are a good guide of what to expect, but it will look different for each person.

Remember, victims of long-term traumatic abuse will experience extreme exhaustion due to the prolonged imbalance of Cortisol and Adrenaline running through your body once they have reached a place of safety. And the victim's cognitive functions are also impaired due to parts of the brain shrinking and having restructured many of the connections.

Be patient with yourself and others as you heal. Take it one moment at a time.

One thing you can begin immediately is choosing what thoughts you allow into your mind. The only person we truly control is ourselves, and that includes our thoughts. We can choose negativity, or we can choose thoughts that lift us.

When you understand that the human brain emits energy and that those frequencies attract similar frequencies, you see why it's essential to feed your mind with positivity. If you want more positive experiences and if you want a life filled with joy, start by placing positive thoughts into your head.

Does that mean bad things will stop happening? Of course not. But it does mean you don't have to let those moments drag you back into a darkness where your soul can't breathe.

We cannot control the world outside of us. We can only control our thoughts and our reactions. How we respond is always our choice. So, when something painful happens, don't fixate on the event itself, you can't change it anyway. Instead, look for the lesson tucked beside the hardship. Choosing to respond with a positive, open-hearted mindset is a powerful skill that builds resilience.

Learn to recognize what you cannot control and let those unwelcome events drift past you like a dandelion carried by the wind. In doing so, you protect your emotional and mental health while growing stronger.

If our mission in life is to live as authentically as possible and to seek joy, then how do we know we're on the right path? The answer is simpler than we think:

You know you're on the right path when it feels easy; when it aligns with your heart and your integrity – when you no longer negotiate with who you are to make others comfortable. Then you will know that you are exactly where you're meant to be.

Our paths won't always be smooth. There will be bumps in the road, and those bumps are the lessons we meet along the way. They help us understand what we truly want to experience in this life. They guide us toward our passion and our joy.

And remember, we always have free will. We can take detours anytime we choose. If you wander off your path, pay attention to how it feels. If that detour is filled with pain, resistance, and hardship, that's the Universe whispering, *"This isn't aligned with who you are."*

Even so, those detours are valuable. Learn from them. They help you get clear on the direction you were meant to go. And once you're headed back toward your true path, life begins to flow again. Things feel easier. You feel more like yourself.

I often think of it like a mouse navigating a maze for the first time. There is one true path that leads to the cheese. Every wrong turn is simply information. The mouse learns, adjusts, and keeps moving until it finds the right path.

That's us. We all take wrong turns. Instead of complaining, blaming, or judging, we can simply turn around and choose differently. The roadblocks are there to keep us aligned if we pay attention to them.

If I hadn't been so filled with shame and so determined to please everyone around me, I could have put myself back on the right path early in my relationship with MKD and returned to Jack. The red flags were all there. The roadblocks were unmistakable. But my conditioning to put others first, to blame myself, to forgive endlessly, to self-sacrifice, kept me from seeing how deeply I was betraying the most important person in my world: **me**.

During the darker stage of my healing, when joy felt unreachable, I went back to the simple pleasures of my childhood. I remembered how I loved to swing, ride my bike, draw, and color. So, I started with the simplest of those activities and bought the biggest Disney coloring book I could find at Target along with a giant box of crayons. And in sitting down with that book, letting my mind soften and drift, I rediscovered a quiet, uncomplicated joy.

What about you? What did you love doing when you were a kid? Can you still do those things now? If so, begin removing whatever stands in the way. Start small, like I did.

And whatever you choose, make sure it puts a smile on your face.

You know why?

Because you deserve it.

I have come a long way from the naïve twenty-year-old who made the "temporary" decision to break up with Jack on Memorial Day weekend in 1981. That moment led me into more than thirty years of darkness. And now, I have forgiven myself for not understanding what I was stepping into.

I've released the burden of carrying Jack's pain and MKD's abuse on my back for decades, trying to redeem myself for that one decision. I see now that it took me more than thirty years to learn the lesson that my ego refused to see: it was okay to let go. It was okay to choose myself. It was okay to walk toward my own happiness.

It was the biggest lesson our Creator had for me. And through it, I learned not only that I **am** loved, but that **I am love**.

I now try to look at others through the soul's perspective and wonder: what lessons are they learning? What has their soul chosen to experience and grow through? We each walk our own path, carrying our own story, and when we share those stories truthfully and vulnerably, we strengthen the collective and move closer to the lives we long for.

It was only by telling my story, as honestly as I could, that I finally healed and found my peaceful center.

To those of you who feel trapped or burdened by your life right now I understand. Don't judge yourself. Find even the smallest speck of joy each day. And whatever you do, don't let the darkness define you.

Face it.
Feel it.
Own it.
Then learn from it.

When you release the fear, guilt, shame, and regret you've been carrying, you create space for all the goodness waiting to enter your life. Only then can you discover the power that has always lived within you. Only then can you move forward in peace.

And with all of that said, whatever you do, do it for love.

****

If you pay attention to the patterns of your life,

You'll realize everything always works out.

Everything always leads you to a greater destination.

You are always growing, and despite all the challenges
you think you can't survive, you somehow divinely make
it through.

That's life.

Always remember that
consciousreminder.com

EPILOGUE

I used to believe there would be a moment when the past loosened its grip completely. When the memories softened into something distant and manageable, when my body no longer remembered before my mind did. I thought healing would feel like arrival.

It didn't.

What came instead was a slow, unremarkable shift. A growing ability to stay present. A widening space between what had happened and who I was becoming. The past did not disappear, but it stopped insisting on being the loudest thing in the room.

There are still days when it surfaces without warning. A sound. A look. A sudden tightening in my chest. But those moments no longer define the shape of my life. They pass. I remain.

I have learned that healing is not the absence of pain, but the restoration of choice. The ability to move toward what feels true instead of what feels familiar. The courage to trust my own perceptions again, even when they challenge what I was taught to endure.

I am not who I was before, and I no longer wish to be. That woman did what she had to do with the tools she had. I carry her with me, not as a wound, but as a witness.

This life is quieter now. Not empty, but steady. Built with intention instead of fear. I pay attention to what my body tells me. I leave when something feels wrong. I stay when something feels right. These choices would have once seemed small. Now I understand how much they matter.

The story does not end here. It never really does. But I am no longer living in reaction to what was done to me. I am living forward, with an honesty that does not require explanation.

If there is anything I know for certain, it is this: survival was only the beginning. What followed, what continues, is the work of becoming.

And that work, at last, is mine.